REFERENCE

REFERENCE

The Hutchinson Dictionary of World Myth

REFERENCE

The Hutchinson
Dictionary of
World Myth

General Editor: Peter Bently

Helicon
in association with
Duncan Baird Publishers

First published 1995
Paperback edition first published 1996

Helicon Publishing Ltd
42 Hythe Bridge Street
Oxford OX1 2EP

A DBP book,
conceived, created and designed by
Duncan Baird Publishers
Sixth Floor
Castle House
75-76 Wells Street
London W1P 3RE

Editor: Judy Dean
Designer: John Laing
Commissioned artwork: Ron Hayward Studios
Indexer: Lucy Curtin

British Library Cataloguing-in-Publication Data

A CIP catalogue record for this book is available from the British Library

ISBN 1–85986–058–3 (hardback)
ISBN 1–85986–168–7 (paperback)

Typeset in Times NR MT
Colour reproduction by Colourscan, Singapore
Printed in Singapore

2 4 6 8 10 9 7 5 3

Contents

How To Use This Book

This dictionary has entries on gods, goddesses, heroes, heroines, supernatural creatures, mythical episodes and major sources of myth, all arranged in A to Z order. Interspersed with these entries, at the appropriate point alphabetically, are highlighted feature panels on the treatment in myth of general themes (Animals, Culture Heroes and so on).

Cross-references in the margin relate to entries elsewhere that expand upon other names in the text.

The illustrations are mostly based on contemporaneous artefacts. In all cases the artist has simplified these for the sake of clarity.

The Index of Themes (p.235) refers to subjects that occur across a wide range of cultures (Creation, the Flood Myths and so on).

The Index of Supplementary Names (p.238) covers minor characters, episodes, places and so on which are not themselves the main subjects of an entry.

Foreword

What is a myth? This question has exercised some of the world's greatest thinkers over the past 2,500 years, but still without any finally definitive conclusion. The term "myth" was first coined by the Greek historian Herodotus in the fourth century BC, to distinguish what he saw as essentially fictional accounts of the past from factual description. Probably, in thus labelling certain traditional narratives as mere "stories", even as "lies", Herodotus hoped or assumed that they would disappear from human consciousness, displaced by the unvarnished "truth". But as the appearance in the late 20th century of this *Dictionary of Mythology* shows, these seemingly fantastic tales about the world and its imagined origins still retain their mysterious power to engross the human mind.

One of the greatest theorists of myth of the modern era, the French anthropologist Claude Lévi-Strauss, put his finger at once on the power of myth and its puzzling essence when he remarked that, even in a mediocre translation from the language of its original narration, the present-day reader spontaneously recognizes a myth for what it is. Yet in his life-long labour to unveil the secret of myth, Lévi-Strauss has done no more than demonstrate that myths universally make use of a structure of contraposed ideas and successive resolutions of what he calls "binary oppositions" – a structure shared by all story-forms, from detective novels to orally transmitted "dirty jokes". The specifically "mythic" nature of "myth" continues to elude explanation. One school of modern scientific thought, which might appear to have come closer than any to resolving the enigma of myth, is psychoanalysis. In interpreting the famous Oedipus cycle of ancient Greek mythology in terms of supposedly universal but unconscious drives directed by the male human offspring toward its parents, Sigmund Freud thought he had found a kind of explanation which might eventually unlock the secrets of all myth. Freud's colleague and rival Carl Jung made even grander claims in seeking to identify major figures such as the "Mother" and the "Wise Old Man" in various European mythological traditions with what he believed were "archetypal" inhabitants of a posited Collective Unconscious. Unfortunately, all these ventures have been undermined by evidence from anthropological field research among non-European cultures around the world. This work has shown that the supposedly "universal" explanations of mythical themes emanating from the various schools of psychoanalysis are valid only for certain sections of European societies at particular historical epochs. As Lévi-Strauss has suggested, these seemingly final explanations of myth are really no more than the latest versions of the myths they seek to dissolve. So once again the tantalizing essence of myth escapes the scientific and scholarly grasp.

In the end, we are left with the less ambitious conclusions of the great American expositor and interpreter of myth, Joseph Campbell, who devoted his life to understanding the myth-making faculty in human beings. In his final statement on the subject, *The Inner Reaches of Outer Space* (1986), Campbell begins by reminding us of a crucial distinction in mythical analysis first made by the nineteenth-century German anthropologist Adolf Bastian. This theorist distinguished between the particular local expression of a mythical theme, what we would now call its cultural and ethnic content, and what Bastian saw as "elemental" or "fundamental" ideas (*Elementargedanken*), which he believed were part of the biological inheritance of all human beings. Seen in this light, all "scientific" attempts at accounting for the perceived beauty and strangeness of mythical narratives are no more than our culturally specific endeavour, as members of a socially and historically defined group called the Western scientific community, to express what is ultimately inexpressible except perhaps in the language of art. The mystery remains.

There are nonetheless, as Campbell maintains, intriguing clues to the nature of this hidden mystery to be gleaned from comparative study of world mythology, a vast and still continuing project of scholarly research which this *Dictionary* uniquely distils – clues such as the widely distributed image of the primordial Cosmic Egg; the peculiar significance of certain animals, notably birds and serpents, in creation myths; and the common perception of the universe as divided into a three-layered structure and united by a central axis, sometimes called the "Tree of Life", which in turn has a mysterious symbolic resonance, as Campbell observes, with the human spinal column.

Dr. Roy Willis

Abnoba *Celtic regions*
A Romano-Celtic goddess of the hunt. Abnoba's cult was centred around the Black Forest.

Abuk *Africa*
The first woman, who, according to the Dinka people of the southern Sudan, was responsible for the arrival of death and illness on earth. In the beginning, the High God allowed Garang, the first man, and Abuk, his wife, to plant one grain of millet a day, which satisfied all their needs. But one day Abuk greedily decided to plant more. In doing so she struck the High God on the toe, making him so angry that he withdrew to a great distance from humanity and severed the rope which linked heaven and earth. Since then humans have had to work hard to procure food and have suffered sickness and death.

Acheron *Greece*
The "River of Woe" in northern Greece, which, because it flows partly underground, was believed to be one of five rivers linking this world to the underworld realm of the dead. The name

Acheron was sometimes used to refer to the underworld itself.

Achilles *Greece*
A celebrated hero of Greek mythology and the central character of the *Iliad*, Homer's great epic of the Trojan War. The son of a mortal king, Peleus, and the Nereid (sea nymph) Thetis, Achilles was born in Thessaly. Thetis dipped him in the Styx, a river of the underworld, to render his body both immortal and invulnerable – except for the heel by which she held him. Achilles was educated by Chiron, a wise Centaur.

The Fates offered the young Achilles the choice between a long life of ease or early death and immortal glory in the Trojan War: he chose the latter. (In one account Achilles was reluctant to join the campaign and disguised himself as a woman. He was unmasked by his comrades when a war trumpet sounded and he alone reached for a weapon.)

During the siege of Troy, Achilles angrily withdrew from the fighting after the Greek commander, Agamemnon, claimed Achilles' war booty, the Trojan Briseis, for himself. With Achilles, the

Abuk: *see*
DEATH, THE ORIGIN OF

Acheron: *see*
Charon; Cocytus; Hades; Styx; UNDERWORLDS

Achilles: *see*
Agamemnon; Amazon (1); Centaur; Fates, The; Hector; *Iliad*, The; Nereid; Odysseus; Paris; Peleus; Styx; TROJAN WAR, THE HEROES OF THE

Achilles, the central character of the Iliad, *and a celebrated Greek warrior.*

most feared Greek warrior, no longer fighting, the Trojans under Hector pushed the Greeks back to their ships. Patroclus, Achilles' best friend, persuaded the hero to lend him his armour so that the Trojans would think Achilles had returned to the fray. Patroclus was killed by Hector and Achilles returned to the battle to avenge his death. He pursued Hector three times around the walls of Troy before killing him in single combat. Achilles refused to give up the corpse for burial until the gods forced him to accept a ransom from Hector's father, King Priam. During the final battle for Troy, Achilles fought and killed the Amazon queen, Penthesilea, falling in love with her as she died. Achilles himself was killed by Hector's brother, Paris, who shot him in the heel, his vulnerable spot, with an arrow. The Greeks awarded Achilles' armour to Odysseus.

Actaeon *Greece*

A hunter. One day, while hunting in a forest, Actaeon happened upon the goddess Artemis bathing. Artemis, outraged at being seen naked, turned Actaeon into a stag, whereupon he was torn to pieces by his own hounds.

Adapa *Middle East*

In Babylonian (Akkadian) myth, a priest of the god Ea (known as Enki to the Sumerians) and one of the Seven Sages of prehistory.

Aditi *India*

"The Limitless", a primordial goddess who is seen as an all-embracing divine spirit, the personification of infinity and sustainer of all things. In the early Vedic hymns she is referred to as the mother of the major gods, who were called the Adityas after her. There are various lists of their names. Among the more important are Varuna, Indra and Daksha.

Admetus *Greece*

A king of Pherae in Thessaly. After the god Apollo had killed the Cyclopes, Zeus ordered him to serve Admetus for one year as a shepherd in penance. Apollo later helped him to win the hand of Alcestis.

Adonis *Greece*

A young hunter, the lover of the goddess Aphrodite. He is possibly of near eastern origin and is sometimes identified with the god Dumuzi or Tammuz. The goddess Aphrodite caused an Assyrian princess, Myrrha, to fall in love with her own father, King Theias. Myrrha duped him into having intercourse with her, as a result of which she became pregnant. When Theias discovered the deception he would have killed his daughter, but the gods transformed her into the myrrh tree, from which Adonis was born.

Aphrodite handed the beautiful child over to the fertility goddess Persephone, queen of the underworld, for safekeeping. However, Persephone later refused to give him back. The god Zeus decided that Adonis would spend a third of the year with Aphrodite, a third of it with

Persephone in the underworld, and a third as he wished.

In one account, Adonis chose to spend his free months with Aphrodite. During one of his spells with the goddess he was killed by a boar, said to be Aphrodite's jealous lover Ares in transformed guise. Adonis became an anemone.

Adrasteia *Greece*

"Necessity", one of two primal deities (the other being Chronos, "Time") present at the beginning of creation, according to the Orphics.

Aeëtes *Greece*

A king of Colchis on the eastern shore of the Black Sea. Aeëtes, a son of Helios, possessed the Golden Fleece sought by the hero Jason.

Aegisthus *Greece*

A scion of the feuding house of Pelops, the son of Thyestes by Thyestes' own daughter, Pelopia. Aegisthus seduced Clytemnestra, the wife of his cousin Agamemnon. With her connivance, Aegisthus assassinated Agamemnon on his return from the Trojan War and became king of Argos. Aegisthus and Clytemnestra were later killed by Agamemnon's son Orestes.

Aeneas *Greece and Rome*

A Trojan prince, a minor character in Greek mythology but a central figure in Roman myth as the founder of the dynasty which established the city of Rome. Aeneas, the son of King Anchises and the goddess Aphrodite (the Roman Venus), is portrayed in Homer's *Iliad* as a valiant warrior. According to Roman mythology (as related in Virgil's *Aeneid*), he escaped the destruction of Troy, and carried his father Anchises and his son Ascanius to

Aeneas hunting, from a mosaic.

safety. His wife Creusa perished, but her shade told him to travel to the land of the Tiber. Aeneas embarked on a long voyage during which Anchises died and he had a famous doomed love affair with Dido, the queen of Carthage.

When Aeneas reached Cumae in Italy he consulted the Sibyl, a priestess of Apollo. The Sibyl led him to the underworld, where Anchises told of the future glories of the Roman race. From Cumae, Aeneas then sailed on to Latium, where he founded the town of Lavinium. Ascanius established the town of Alba Longa and its ruling dynasty, from which sprang Romulus and Remus, the founders of Rome. According to one tradition, Aeneas founded Rome itself.

Aeneid, The *Rome*

A Latin epic poem, the unfinished masterpiece of Virgil (Publius Vergilius Maro, 70BC–19BC). Begun *c.*30BC, its twelve books recount the wanderings of Aeneas from Troy to Latium in Italy.

Aeolus *Greece*

The keeper of the winds, whose abode, the Aeolian Islands off northern Sicily, were named after him. A son of the god Poseidon, Aeolus gave the epic hero Odysseus a sack in which all the winds, unfavourable to his voyage, were confined. When curious crewmen opened the bag, the winds escaped and blew Odysseus' ship off course.

Aesir, The *Germanic regions*
The Scandinavian sky deities, one of two divine races – the other being the Vanir – said to reside in Asgard, the realm of the gods. The Aesir include Odin (ruler of Asgard), Balder, Frigg, Tyr and Thor.

Aeson *Greece*
A king of Iolcus in Thessaly and the father of the hero Jason.

AFTERLIFE
See panel on opposite page

Agamemnon *Greece*
A king of Argos (or Mycenae) and leader of the Greeks in the Trojan War. As well as being the most famous of the feuding Pelopids, Agamemnon was the son of Atreus, king of Argos, and his wife Aerope. Aegisthus, Atreus' nephew, murdered Atreus and enabled his father Thyestes to seize the throne. Agamemnon and his brother Menelaus fled to safety in Sparta. The Spartan king Tyndareos later helped Agamemnon to recover his father's throne, forcing Thyestes into exile.

Then, with the blessing of Tyndareos, Agamemnon married Clytemnestra, daughter of Tyndareos and his queen, Leda, and was appointed commander of Menelaus' campaign against the Trojans. He assembled his forces at Aulis in Boeotia, but the goddess Artemis caused adverse sailing conditions and, in order to secure good winds, Agamemnon had to sacrifice his daughter, Iphigeneia. The Greeks finally left Aulis, and Agamemnon established camp outside Troy. After ten years the city fell and the victorious Agamemnon headed for home with Cassandra, the prophetess daughter of King Priam, as his prize.

However, Clytemnestra, who grieved bitterly for Iphigeneia, had become the lover of Aegisthus and connived in his plot to murder Agamemnon. When her husband arrived with his entourage, Clytemnestra greeted him and invited him to take a bath. As Agamemnon stepped out of the water she threw a fine mesh over his head. Aegisthus appeared and cut down Agamemnon as he struggled in the net. He fell into the bath and Clytemnestra beheaded him. Cassandra was also murdered, but Agamemnon's children, Orestes and Elektra, lived to avenge their father.

Aglaia *Greece*
"Splendour", one of the three Graces.

Agung, Mount *Southeast Asia*
A sacred volcano on the island of Bali, locally called Gunung Agung ("Great Mountain"). In Balinese Hindu myth, when neighbouring Java converted to Islam (*c*.1600), the gods moved to Bali and built high mountains to reflect their exalted rank. In the middle was Gunung Agung, the highest of them all and the centre of the world. Shrines to Mount Agung exist in all Balinese temples, the holiest of which, Pura Besakih, stands on the volcano itself.

Ah Mun *Central America*
A Maya god of corn (maize), who is typically depicted with a maize cob sprouting from his head.

Ahalya *India*
The wife of Gautama, a powerful sage and ascetic. She was seduced by the god Indra, but when Indra left her he met

AFTERLIFE

A belief in continued existence after death is found in the mythology of most peoples. The dead are commonly said to inhabit underworlds, overworlds or regions which may be on the same plane as the earth but are otherwise imprecisely located (for example, the Aztec paradise Tlalocan and the Slavic land of the dead). The abode of the dead may be very close to this world: the mythical Greek underworld was accessible to any mortal prepared to venture into its deep caverns and rivers that flowed underground (such as Orpheus and the hero Herakles). In ancient Celtic belief, the worlds of the dead and the living were thought to be particularly close at night.

A detail from an Attic vase depicting the afterlife in the Greek underworld. The hero Herakles is seen dragging Cerberus from the gateway to Hades (one of his twelve labours).

Often in myth, the afterworld resembles this world. For example, the Chinese heaven and hell were administered in a manner that mirrored the imperial government on earth, each with its sovereign overseeing a vast bureaucracy. The Native American peoples of the Great Plains conceived of the "Happy Hunting Ground", an afterworld very similar to the present but with more game.

The destination of the dead is frequently thought to depend on their conduct while alive, with sinners typically being dispatched to regions of judgement as well as punishment: for example, regions such as the Christian hell or the Japanese Jigoku.

The great and the good may have their own special place in death, which is separated from those who transgressed during life: such as, the Elysian Fields or Islands of the Blessed, paradisal regions of the ancient Greek underworld.

The spirits of the dead may also roam among mortals, or they may be invoked by prayer and ritual to intervene in the destiny of the living. Reincarnation is a belief found in religions of Indian origin among other cultures. The nature of the reincarnate form may depend on how one has acted in the previous existence. In the Chinese heaven, the imperial bureaucrats keep a careful record of an individual's balance of merit and demerit in past lives, in order to determine the nature of his or her next incarnation.

Another category of afterlife is that of the revenant undead, most famously the vampires of central and eastern European folklore. In Slavic myth, "undesirables" such as murderers, whores, heretics and witches leave their coffins at midnight to feed on the blood of the living.

AFTERLIFE: *see* DEATH, THE ORIGIN OF; Elysium; Hades; HERAKLES, THE LABOURS OF; Orpheus; Otherworld, The; Tlaloc; UNDERWORLDS; Vampire

Gautama, who knew at once what had happened. In punishment, the sage cursed Indra to lose his testicles, while Ahalya was cursed to lie, invisible, on a bed of ashes for thousands of years with only air to live on. Her plight would be lifted only when the god Rama visited her. On hearing this story, Rama went to the hermitage and finally freed Ahalya from the curse.

Ahat *Middle East*

The son of Daniel, a patriarch, according to Ugaritic (Canaanite) myth. Daniel was childless until, at the instigation of the storm god Baal, the supreme god El granted him a son, Ahat.

When Ahat grew up, a divine craftsman gave him a bow and arrows, but the goddess Anath coveted them. Anath sent her attendant, Yatpan, to kill Ahat and take his bow, but the weapon was broken in the assault and the goddess's plan came to nothing. Baal, furious at the murder of Ahat, withheld the rains from the land as punishment for the craftsman's murder.

The end of the myth is lost, but it probably tells of the resurrection of Ahat and the end of the drought. The story may account for the summer drought and its eventual breaking, which is symbolized by the death and subsequent resurrection of Ahat.

Ahau Kin *Central America*

The Maya sun god. Ahau Kin ("Lord of the Sun Face") possessed both daytime and nocturnal aspects. In his daytime manifestation the sun god was often depicted with some jaguar features. However, between sunset and sunrise he actually became the Jaguar God, the lord of the underworld, as he travelled from west to east through the lower regions of the world.

Ahriman *Middle East*

A later form of Angra Mainyu, the name of the Persian god of dark forces.

Ahura Mazdah *Middle East*

"Wise Lord", the supreme god of the ancient Persians, also known by the later form of his name, Ohrmazd. Ahura Mazdah represented the sky. He was the embodiment of wisdom, fruitfulness and benevolence. His opponent (and also his creation) was Angra Mainyu, the god of darkness and sterility. These were not the only deities, but life was essentially a struggle between the two gods of good and evil.

In the 7th or 6th century BC the prophet Zoroaster, who was the founder of Zoroastrianism, made Ahura Mazdah alone worthy of absolute worship. Ahura Mazdah was the essence of beneficent nature, the creator of heaven and earth, the fount of law and morality and the supreme judge of the universe. His offspring includes Gayomart, the archetypal man.

Air Spirit, The *Arctic regions*

One of the three great spirit forces in Inuit belief, together with the Sea Spirit and the Moon Spirit. Known in far northern regions as Sila ("Weather", "Intelligence"), the Air Spirit lives far above the earth, controlling rain, snow, wind and sea. It is inherently benevolent but is perceived as threatening because of its sensitivity to human misdeeds, to which it responds by sending sickness, bad weather, and failure in hunting.

Aither *Greece*

"Ether", the bright upper air, one of the elemental deities which, according to Hesiod's *Theogony*, came into being in the first stages of creation. The deity features little in myth.

Ajax (1) *Greece*

A Greek hero, son of the Argonaut Telamon, king of Salmacis, and known as the Greater Ajax to distinguish him from Ajax (2). Described in Homer's *Iliad* as a stubborn and taciturn man of huge physical stature, Ajax was, after the hero Achilles, the most distinguished

Ajax and Achilles playing checkers, from a black-figure amphora of the 6th century BC.

Greek warrior in the Trojan War.

After the death of Achilles, Ajax rescued the hero's corpse and armour while Odysseus, fought off the enemy. Both men claimed the dead hero's armour as a prize, and when it was awarded to Odysseus, Ajax was so furious that he planned to kill his own commanders. To thwart the assault, the goddess Athene drove Ajax mad, so that instead he slaughtered a flock of sheep. After the madness had passed Ajax, who was deeply humiliated, killed himself.

Ajax (2) *Greece*

A Greek hero, son of the Argonaut Oileus and known as the Lesser Ajax to distinguish him from Ajax (1). During the sack of Troy he raped King Priam's daughter Cassandra on the altar of Athene, a desecration for which the gods caused the victorious Greek fleet to be shipwrecked on its way home. Ajax swam to a rock but drowned after it was struck by a thunderbolt hurled by the god Poseidon.

Alalu *Middle East*

The first supreme deity, according to Hittite mythology. In the beginning Alalu was king in heaven for nine years before he was deposed by his servant, the god Anu, and descended to the underworld.

Alcestis *Greece*

A Greek princess, the daughter of King Pelias of Iolcus and his wife Anaxibia. Alcestis was renowned for her beauty and had many princely suitors, but Pelias insisted that any man wanting to marry her must first yoke a lion and a boar to a chariot. King Admetus of Pherae achieved this feat assisted by the god Apollo.

According to one account, Apollo got the Fates drunk one day and extracted a promise that when the time came for Admetus' death he would live on if someone volunteered to die in his place. The Fates came for Admetus soon afterwards, but no one was prepared to die instead of him, so Alcestis offered herself. The Fates accepted her sacrifice but she was later rescued from the underworld by the hero Herakles and restored to Admetus.

Alkmene *Greece*

A queen of Tiryns, the mother of the hero Herakles. Alkmene married her uncle, King Amphitryon of Tiryns. Amphitryon set off to fight some cattle raiders and the god Zeus took advantage of his absence to assume his form and visit Alkmene. She was delighted to see what she thought was her husband and that evening the couple made passionate love – the disguised Zeus lengthening the night to three times its normal duration in order to extend his pleasure.

Amphitryon returned home victorious the following day and was surprised at his wife's lack of sexual ardour, while Alkmene in turn was surprised that her husband had forgotten the previous night's pleasures. The couple eventually learned the truth from the blind prophet Teiresias. Alkmene subsequently had twins, Iphikles, son of Amphitryon, and Herakles, son of Zeus.

Ama-no-uzume *Japan*
A beautiful young goddess, possibly a deity of the dawn, who is important for her role in resolving the "Divine Crisis".

Amalthea *Greece*
A she-goat or a nymph with goat-like features which suckled the infant Zeus on Crete. According to one account, the grateful god broke off one of Amalthea's horns, promising that it would produce a never-ending abundance of fruit, nectar and ambrosia. This horn was known as the Cornucopia ("Horn of Plenty").

Amanominakanushi-no-kami *Japan*
"Lord of the Centre of Heaven", the oldest of the gods. He was the first of three invisible deities who came into existence when the earth was not yet fully formed, and was one of the five primordial "Separate Heavenly Deities".

Amaterasu *Japan*
The sun goddess, in full Amaterasu-no-mikoto ("August Person Who Makes The Heavens Shine"). Perhaps the greatest deity in the Shinto pantheon, Amaterasu is revered as an ancestor of the emperors of Japan. Her shrine at Ise on Honshu island is the most important of all Shinto shrines.

The goddess was born from the left

Amaterasu emerging from her cave, from a 19th-century print triptych.

eye of the primal creator Izanagi as he bathed in a stream on the island of Kyushu. Izanagi assigned her the realm of the heavens. Her brother, the moon god Tsuki-yomi, was entrusted with the realms of the night and another brother, Susano, was made ruler of the ocean.

Susano declared himself unhappy with his lot and Izanagi banished him for ingratitude. Before leaving, Susano went to bid farewell to Amaterasu in heaven. The goddess suspected, rightly, that her unruly brother wanted to usurp her domains. When he arrived, the storm god suggested that they prove which of them was the mightier by having a reproduction contest: whoever bore male deities would win. Amaterasu agreed and broke Susano's sword in three, chewing the pieces and spitting them out as three goddesses. Next, Susano chewed Amaterasu's beads and spat them out as five male gods. He declared himself the winner, but Amaterasu pointed out that the five gods had sprung from her possessions. Her brother refused to concede and began to celebrate his victory by causing havoc in Amaterasu's realm.

Terrified, Amaterasu withdrew into a cave, depriving the world of the sun and causing various calamities during what is known as the "Divine Crisis". None of the deities succeeded in drawing her out until the goddess Ama-no-uzume performed an erotic dance, causing the gods to laugh so loudly that Amaterasu was overcome with curiosity and came out. The sunlight returned. The deities fined Susano and expelled him from heaven.

Amaunet *Egypt*
One of the eight primal deities or divine forces known as the Ogdoad.

Amazon (1) *Greece*
One of a race of mounted women warriors of Scythia (southern Russia) or the north of Asia Minor (modern Turkey). Amazons, expert riders and archers, displayed their fighting abilities in raiding expeditions. They kept men as slaves for procreation. Any male off-

The Amazons fighting the Athenians, based on a frieze on the Parthenon, 5th century BC.

spring of these unions was abandoned to die, while the girls were brought up to be warriors like their mothers.

The Amazons were eventually defeated in a famous battle, known as the Amazonomachy (which means "Battle of the Amazons"), fought against the Athenians under Theseus. The conflict was depicted on the Parthenon, Athens.

Amazon (2) *Slav regions*
The name given to a woman warrior of Slavic mythology. An 11th-century Bohemian legend tells of a group of Amazons who fought like men and took the initiative sexually. Led by their bravest warrior, Vlasta, they lived in a castle on the banks of the river Vltava (Moldau). In Russian folk epic the Amazons (*polenitsa*) are lone riders. In one story a hero, Dobrynia, encountered an Amazon and attempted to overcome her. However, she wrenched him from his horse and dropped him in her pocket. She eventually agreed to release him on condition that he married her.

Amida *Japan*
One of the three major deities (the others are Kannon and Jizo) in the popular tradition of Japanese Buddhism. Amida (the name is derived from the Sanskrit Amitabha) is the central figure in the Buddhist sects Jodo-shu and Jodo-shin-su (the "Pure Lands" sects), which are grounded on the belief that the faithful, by invoking Amida at the hour of death, are able to be reborn into a paradisial "Pure Land", where they will be ready for the final Enlightenment.

Amitabha *India*
"Unending light", the name that was given to a Bodhisattva who was said to rule a paradise in the west. Amitabha offered rebirth in a state of bliss before

Amaunet: *see*
Ogdoad, The

Amazon (1): *see*
Antiope (2); HERAKLES, THE LABOURS OF; Penthesilea; Theseus

Amazon (2): *see*
Amazon (1)

Amida: *see*
Amitabha; Bodhisattva; Buddha; Jizo; Kannon

Amitabha: *see*
Bodhisattva

final salvation, to anyone who invoked his name and showed true repentance for their sins. When Buddhism reached China, Amitabha (rendered as Emituofo in Chinese) became one of the most popular of Bodhisattvas. He was also of great importance in Japan, where he is known as Amida or Amida-butsu.

Amma *Africa*
An egg which, to the Dogon people of Mali, existed at the beginning of creation and was the seed of the cosmos.

Amon *Egypt*
One of the eight divine forces of chaos known as the Ogdoad. Amon was worshipped as a fertility god at Thebes in Upper Egypt and became a national deity in the 2nd millennium BC. His name was fused with that of the supreme solar deity, Ra, to give Amon-Ra, one of the four great creator deities (the others being Atum, Khnum and Ptah) Amon-Ra was the hidden power who made the gods. According to one account, the snake form of Amon was the earliest being to exist in the primeval waters.

Amphitrite *Greece*
A sea nymph, and the wife of the god Poseidon. When Poseidon made advances to the nymph Scylla, the jealous Amphitrite dropped magic plants into the water where Scylla bathed, transforming her into a hideous monster.

Amphitrite and Poseidon had two daughters, Rhode ("Rose"), from whom the island of Rhodes was said to take its name, and Benthesicyme. Their only son, Triton, had the body of a man above the waist and that of a fish below.

Amphitryon *Greece*
A king of Tiryns. He was the husband of Alkmene and a consort of the god Zeus.

Amphitrite (left) with the god Poseidon, from a vase fragment.

Anahita *Middle East*
"The Immaculate", a Persian fertility goddess of Assyrian and Babylonian origin. She was believed to be the source of the cosmic sea and all the waters on earth, as well as that of human reproduction. Sometimes identified with the goddess Aphrodite/Venus and the planet Venus, Anahita later became a popular goddess in many parts of the Near East and even farther west.

Ananta *India*
"The Infinite", a giant serpent on whose coils the god Vishnu rests in the cosmic waters during the intervals between the emanations of the cosmos. He is also referred to as Shesha ("Remainder"). Ananta is said to be the son of Kadru, a daughter of the god Daksha and the ancestor of all snakes.

Anat *Egypt*
A female warrior deity of Syrian (Canaanite) origin: she is derived from the goddess Anath. In Egyptian mythology Anat is the daughter of the solar deity Ra. She was usually depicted carrying a shield, spear and axe. Anat was also a cow goddess.

ANCESTORS

Many peoples believe that the invisible spirits of ancestors remain active in this world. For example, the Slavs used to leave food by graves for their ancestors to consume, and the Chinese honour their ancestors to this day in the annual festival of Qingming.

In many cultures, myths about ancestors often reinforce social distinctions, such as those between hereditary rulers and their subjects or between social classes or castes. Kingship tends to be validated by claims to divine ancestry: the pharaohs of Egypt claimed descent from the deities Isis and Osiris, and until 1945 Japanese emperors traced their lineage back to the sun goddess Amaterasu. The social hierarchy is frequently reflected in the order in which the ancestors first appeared on earth. For example, the Carabaulo people of Timor in Indonesia relate how their first ancestors came out of a huge vagina in the ground: the first to emerge were the landowning aristocrats, followed by commoners and tenants.

A representation of ancestral spirits, based on a ceremonial Yoruba mask from Nigeria.

ANCESTORS: *see* Aeneas; AFTERLIFE; Amaterasu; Dreamtime; HUMANITY, THE ORIGIN OF; Isis; Osiris

Anath *Middle East*

An Ugaritic (Canaanite) fertility goddess, warlike sister and chief helper of the storm god Baal. Anath descended to the underworld to try to persuade Mot, the god of death, to release Baal from his power. She also played an important role in the legend of Ahat.

ANCESTORS

See panel above

Anchises *Greece and Rome*

A king of Dardanus near Troy and father of the hero Aeneas. Anchises was a shepherd when Aphrodite (the Roman Venus), the goddess of love, seduced him in the form of a mortal young woman. Having become pregnant, Aphrodite prophesied that Anchises' child would be the ancestor of an everlasting dynasty. The child was Aeneas, the ancestor of the Romans.

Andromeda *Greece*

A princess of "Ethiopia" (now Joppa in Palestine). Andromeda was the daughter of King Cepheus and Queen Cassiopeia. Cassiopeia made the sea god Poseidon angry by declaring herself to be lovelier than the Nereids, a race of beautiful sea nymphs. Poseidon flooded the kingdom

Anath: *see* Ahat; Anat; Baal; Mot

Anchises: *see* Aeneas; *Aeneid*, The; Aphrodite; Zeus

Andromeda: *see* Nereid; Perseus; Poseidon

Angra Mainyu: *see*
Ahura Mazdah

Antaboga: *see*
Bedawang; CREATION

Antaeus: *see*
Gaia; Herakles; Poseidon

Antigone: *see*
Oedipus; Seven Against
Thebes, The; Teiresias

Antiope (1): *see*
ZEUS, THE CONSORTS OF

Antiope (2): *see*
Amazon (1); Hippolyte;
Theseus

Anu (1): *see*
Alalu; Apsu; Ea; Enlil; Ki;
Kumarbi; Marduk; Nammu;
Teshub; Tiamat

and sent a hideous sea dragon to ravage the land. An oracle told Cepheus that he would save the kingdom if Andromeda was sacrificed to the dragon. At the insistence of his subjects, Cepheus had Andromeda chained to a rock and left to be eaten by the creature. As Andromeda lay naked on the rock, the hero Perseus flew past and fell in love with her at once. He offered to kill the monster in return for her hand.

Cepheus accepted the offer and Perseus, who was wearing his cloak of invisibility and winged sandals (and, in some accounts, riding the winged horse Pegasus), cut off the beast's head with his curved sword. He freed Andromeda and married her. After death Andromeda became a constellation.

Angra Mainyu *Middle East*
Persian god of dark forces, the opponent of the supreme deity, Ahura Mazdah. He is also known as Ahriman.

ANIMALS
See panel on opposite page

Antaboga *Southeast Asia*
A great primordial serpent which, according to the Balinese account of creation, existed when there was neither heaven nor earth. Antaboga initiated the process of creation by bringing into being, through meditation, Bedawang, the cosmic turtle which was the foundation of the earth.

Antaeus *Greece*
A giant, the offspring of the god Poseidon and the goddess Gaia. Antaeus lived in Libya and challenged travellers who came his way to wrestle to the death. The giant always won because he could renew his strength by touching the earth with his feet. He was killed by

Herakles, who lifted him off the ground long enough to throttle him.

Antigone *Greece*
A princess of Thebes, the elder daughter of King Oedipus and his mother Queen Jocasta. After Oedipus had discovered his unwitting acts of parricide and incest, he blinded himself and eventually went into exile, accompanied only by his daughters Antigone and Ismene.

Antigone died tragically having been shut up in a cave by Creon (Jocasta's brother) for burying the body of her brother, Polyneices, against Creon's orders. The prophet Teiresias insisted that Creon set her free, but when the cave was opened they discovered that Antigone had already hanged herself.

Antiope (1) *Greece*
A princess of Thebes, who became pregnant after the god Zeus took the form of a satyr to have intercourse with her. She subsequently gave birth to twin brothers, Amphion and Zetheus, who became joint rulers of Thebes.

Antiope (2) *Greece*
An Amazon warrior, the sister of the Amazon queen Hippolyte and the wife of Theseus.

Anu (1) *Middle East*
One of the senior deities of ancient Mesopotamia, Anu (who was known as An to the Sumerians) was revered as lord of the heavens and father of the gods. In the Sumerian account of creation, the goddess Nammu, the primeval sea, was the mother of An and Ki, the goddess of the earth, who coupled to produce the great gods, such as Enlil. In the Akkadian creation epic, the union of Apsu (the sweet-water ocean) and Tiamat (the salt-water ocean) produced

ANIMALS

Animals often take on cosmic dimensions, with fabulous birds symbolizing the upper world of spirits and immense serpents representing either the entire cosmos or the chaotic energy of the underworld. In North America the huge Thunderbird engages in a continual battle with the water-dwelling serpents or dragons. A very similar idea is found in southern Africa, where the Lightning Bird rules the sky and the cosmic serpent governs the watery underworld. An image which is often found in North America, China and southern Asia is the turtle or tortoise which carries the earth or the heavens on its back.

A bear redrawn from a box drum of the Haida Indians.

In some mythologies animals are seen as precursors or even creators of humanity. An Egyptian myth describes how the world was brought into being by the cry of a heron, the manifestation of the creator sun god. Additionally, according to the Khoisan peoples of southwest Africa, the first living thing on earth was the tiny mantis, which created the earliest races, including the human race.

Myths have often been seen to affirm a kinship between humans and animals. In Central America, for example, it is said that every human being enjoys a physical and spiritual coexistence with an animal double (an idea also found in parts of west Africa). Many Native American myths refer to an ancient time when people and beasts were indistinguishable and would readily assume each other's shape and form. Native Americans and the Inuit believe that no animals are closer to humans than bears, which are often said to harbour the form of a human beneath the bear coats that they are seen wearing in public.

The idea of metamorphosis occurs in most cultures. The werewolf figures in the mythology of many peoples of Europe and elsewhere, and has parallels in African traditions whereby some men and women have the extraordinary power to transform into predatory beasts such as lions and hyenas. The tribal shamans of Central and South America are said to be able to transform themselves into jaguars.

Another common motif found in mythology is the animal consort. A myth that is widespread in southern Africa tells of the python-god who marries a human wife, sometimes dragging her down with him to his watery underworld home. The Gaelic folklore of Scotland abounds in stories of seals which assume female form and marry men.

ANIMALS: *see*
CULTURE HERO;
DRAGON; HARES AND
RABBITS; JAGUAR; LION;
Mantis; SNAKES AND
SERPENTS; TRICKSTER

a succession of deities culminating in the great gods Anu and Ea.

In Hittite mythology, Anu deposed Alalu, the first king in heaven. The god Kumarbi (who may be equated with the Sumerian Enlil) then waged war on Anu and bit off his penis in the struggle. Anu's sperm impregnated Kumarbi with the weather god Teshub, who eventually triumphed over Kumarbi.

One Akkadian myth tells of Adapa, a priest of the god Ea in the city of Eridu and one of the Seven Sages (powerful beings who were evoked during magical rites). One day, Adapa angrily stopped the south wind after it had overturned his fishing boat. In doing so he deprived the land of the moisture brought by the wind, so Anu summoned him to heaven to justify himself. Ea warned him not to accept Anu's food or drink, because it would cause his death. In fact, Anu offered Adapa the food and water of immortality. When Adapa refused the offering, Anu realized the mistaken advice Adapa had been given and, laughing, sent him back to earth. At this point the narrative breaks off, but it appears that Anu granted special privileges to Eridu and its priesthood.

Anu (2) *Celtic regions*
An Irish earth and fertility goddess, described as the mother of the gods. She may be related to (or even identical with) the goddess Danu or Dana, the ancestor of the heroic race called the Tuatha Dé Danann ("People of Danu"). Anu has strong links with the province of Munster: in County Kerry there are twin hills known as "The Paps of Anu".

Anubis *Egypt*
The jackal-headed god of embalming, also known as Anpu. He is sometimes said to be the son of the god Osiris, the

Anubis forcing Bata, the bull, to carry the mummy of Osiris. From an early Greco-Roman papyrus.

first king on earth, and his sister Nephthys. After Osiris was killed by his brother Seth, Anubis embalmed the body and wrapped it in linen bandages, making Osiris the first mummy. Anubis later defended the corpse against the attacks of Seth. After death Osiris became the ruler of the underworld. Anubis, as one of his most important officials, guided the deceased through the underworld into the presence of Osiris and oversaw their judgment.

Apaosha *Middle East*
In Persian myth, the demon of drought. Apaosha was overcome by Tishtrya, the rain god.

Apep *Egypt*
A great serpent or dragon of the underworld, also known as Apophis. Apep, lord of darkness, was the arch-enemy of the sun god and attacked his barque every night as it travelled through the underworld. The barque was successfully defended by the hosts of the dead, led by Seth, the strongest of the gods.

Aphrodite *Greece*
The goddess of love and sexuality. Aphrodite ("Born of Foam") sprang fully grown from the white foam which arose from the severed genitals of the

castrated god Uranos, at the point where they fell into the sea. After her birth the goddess came ashore either on the island of Cythera or on Cyprus, where she was attended by the Graces and the Seasons.

Aphrodite married Hephaistos, the craftsman god, but also took several lovers, most notably the war god Ares. The lovers were spotted in flagrante by Helios, the sun, who told Hephaistos. The god trapped the couple in a wonderful net and then summoned the other gods and goddesses to witness the outrage. To his annoyance they simply laughed. In the end Ares was freed when he agreed to pay Hephaistos a fine.

Another famous lover of Aphrodite was the young hunter Adonis, who was killed by a wild boar. In some accounts the boar was in fact the jealous Ares.

Aphrodite bore numerous sons, some of whom were Aeneas (by Anchises), Hermaphroditus (a son by Hermes) and Priapus (by Dionysos, Hermes, Pan or Zeus). Eros ("Desire"), the winged god who often accompanies images of the goddess, is sometimes said to be the child of Aphrodite and Ares.

Apollo *Greece and Rome*
The god of light, music and medicine, the son of the Titan Leto and the god Zeus (Latona and Jupiter to the Romans) and the twin brother of the goddess Artemis (the Roman Diana).

Apollo was said to have been born on the island of Delos, the site of his most important festival. His other principal place of worship was Delphi. According to myth, Delphi was the centre of the world, sacred to the goddess Gaia, and was guarded by the dragon Python. Apollo established a sanctuary at Delphi and killed Python, an act for which he was exiled by Zeus for many years. When Apollo returned to Delphi, he founded the famous Delphic oracle and the Pythian Games, a great athletic festival in his honour.

Apollo had a wide range of attributes. He came to be associated with the sun and was often referred to as Phoebus ("Brilliant"). As the patron of music and the arts, Apollo was often depicted with a lyre and among his retinue were the nine Muses, the goddesses of artistic inspiration. Apollo was also the patron of medicine, and the father of Asklepios, the demi-god of healing. Zeus killed Asklepios for resurrecting a dead man and Apollo avenged his son's death by killing Zeus's servants, the Cyclopes. As penance for this act Zeus sent Apollo to Thessaly for one year as the humble herdsman of Admetus, king of Pherae.

Apollo hated to see his prowess contested. The satyr Marsyas found a flute (abandoned by the goddess Athene) which played wonderful music of its own accord. Everyone said that Apollo himself could not play more beautifully on his lyre, and Marsyas agreed. Apollo challenged him to a musical competition and won. He then had Marsyas flayed alive for presumption.

Most of Apollo's many love affairs ended in tragedy. He granted Cassandra, the daughter of King Priam of Troy, the gift of prophecy in return for her love, but she rejected his affection and he cursed her never to be believed.

Apsu *Middle East*
A Babylonian (Sumerian-Akkadian) deity embodying the primordial sweet-water ocean. In Sumerian myth, Apsu is described as the home of Enki, the god of wisdom. According to the Akkadian creation epic, in the beginning Apsu and his female counterpart, Tiamat, the salt-water ocean, united to produce a succession of divinities culminating in the gods

Apollo: *see*
Admetus; Agamemnon; Artemis; Asklepios; Athene; Cyclops;

Aphrodite, from a terracotta figurine of the 11th century BC.

Apollo, from a Parthenon frieze, 5th century BC.

Apsu: *see*
Anu (1); Ea; Enki; Marduk;
Tiamat

Ara and Irik: *see*
HUMANITY, THE ORIGIN
OF

Areop-Enap: *see*
CREATION

Ares: *see*
Adonis; Aphrodite; Hera;
TROJAN WAR, THE
HEROES OF THE

Argonauts, The: *see*
ARGONAUTS, THE
VOYAGE OF THE; Jason;
and individual names

**ARGONAUTS, THE
VOYAGE OF THE:** *see*
Argonauts, The; Herakles;
Jason; Medea

Argula: *see*
TRICKSTER

Anu, Ea (the Sumerian Enki) and Marduk. Ea killed Apsu in a struggle for supremacy that eventually saw the emergence of Marduk as the greatest of all the gods.

Ara and Irik *Southeast Asia*
The two primordial creator spirits which, according to the Iban people of Borneo, were the first beings to exist. The Iban creation myth recounts how Ara and Irik floated above a vast expanse of water in the form of birds. They gathered from the water two great eggs, from one of which Ara formed the sky while Irik formed the earth from the other. Ara and Irik moulded the first humans from earth and brought them to life with their bird-spirit cries.

Areop-Enap *Oceania*
The primordial spider, which, according to the mythology of Nauru in Micronesia, initiated the creation of the sea and sky. Areop-Enap found a clamshell and asked a shellfish to prise it open. The shellfish was only partly successful, so Areop-Enap turned to a caterpillar for assistance. The caterpillar opened the shell fully, but died of exhaustion. The top part of the shell became the sky and the sweat of the caterpillar became the salt sea. The caterpillar became the sun and the shellfish the moon.

Ares *Greece*
The god of war, son of Hera and Zeus, generally depicted as a strong, even brutal warrior who relished the violence and carnage of battle.

Apart from his appearances on the battlefield (for example during the Trojan War), Ares figures in myth primarily as the lover of Aphrodite. The pair were trapped in bed by a net made by the god

Hephaistos, Aphrodite's husband, and humiliated before the other Olympians.

Ares is sometimes said to be the father of Aphrodite's son Eros. There is also a tradition that the boar which killed Adonis was the jealous Ares in transformed guise.

Argonaut *Greece*
One of the fifty members of the crew of the ship *Argo*, in which the hero Jason voyaged on his quest for the Golden Fleece. Eminent Greeks often claimed that they had an ancestor among the Argonauts, who included the following mythical figures:

ARGUS, builder of the *Argo*.

ATALANTA, huntress and the only woman Argonaut.

CASTOR and POLYDEUCES, heroic twin sons of Zeus and Leda.

HERAKLES, the greatest of all heroes.

IDMON and MOPSUS, legendary seers.

LYNCEUS, so sharp-sighted he could see beneath the earth.

MELEAGER, brother-in-law of Herakles.

NAUPLIUS, father of Palamedes, a noted trickster.

OILEUS, father of the hero Ajax (2).

ORPHEUS, great singer and player of the lyre.

PELEUS, father of the great hero Achilles.

PERICLYMENUS, son of the god Poseidon.

TELAMON, father of the hero Ajax (1).

TIPHYS, the *Argo*'s helmsman.

ZETES and CALAIS, winged sons of Boreas, the north wind.

ARGONAUTS, THE VOYAGE OF THE
See panel on pages 26–27

Argula *Australia*
A trickster figure associated with sorcery in the Aboriginal mythology of the western Kimberley region. In this area,

anti-social behaviour may be punished by painting a distorted human figure in a rock shelter and singing insulting songs at it which are believed to inflict disability or death upon the transgressor. The paintings are sometimes said to be the work of Argula.

Argos *Greece*

An unsleeping giant with eyes all over his body, only one pair of which were ever closed. Argus was set by the goddess Hera to guard Io, the lover of her husband Zeus. Io was freed by the god Hermes, who lulled Argus to sleep with stories and then cut off his head. Hera scattered his eyes on the peacock's tail.

Ariadne *Greece*

The daughter of King Minos of Crete and lover of Theseus. Before Theseus entered the Labyrinth, the lair of the monstrous Minotaur, Ariadne gave him a ball of twine, by means of which he was able to retrace his steps to find his way out after killing the monster.

Ariadne went with Theseus when he set off on the return voyage to Athens, but he deserted her on the island of Naxos, leaving her asleep on the shore. The god Dionysos found the princess weeping on the beach and fell in love with her, and they were married amid great celebrations attended by the gods and goddesses. Dionysos later turned Ariadne's wedding garland into the Corona Borealis (Northern Crown).

Artemis *Greece*

Goddess of hunting and childbirth, the daughter of the Titan Leto and Zeus and twin sister of the god Apollo. Like her brother, Artemis possessed a wide range of divine attributes. She was a virgin and fiercely protective of her chastity and that of her companions. Her wrath was notorious, especially if she was seen by mortals or crossed in her desire to remain chaste. Myths which illustrate her anger include those of Actaeon, Callisto, Iphigeneia, Niobe and Orion.

Artemis was usually depicted as a young woman archer in hunting garb, sometimes accompanied by young animals. Although she hunted and killed animals, Artemis was also the divine protector of young creatures.

As the goddess of childbirth, Artemis protected women when they were in labour, but she also brought them death and sickness. Many of her numerous cults were connected with important female times of transition, such as birth, puberty, motherhood and death.

Arthur *Celtic regions*

A king or military leader of the ancient Britons, a figure of myth, legend, folklore, literature and (most tenuously) history. Hard facts about any real Arthur are lacking. Most of the familiar Arthurian characters and exploits – such as the knights of the Round Table and the quest for the Holy Grail – are part of a European literary tradition which began with the *History of the Kings of Britain* by the Norman-Welsh scholar Geoffrey of Monmouth (*c*.1150).

In one of the earliest known references to him, in the *History of the Britons* (*c*.830) by the Welshman Nennius, Arthur is a British military chieftain fighting against the Saxon invaders of post-Roman Britain. His name is derived from Artorius, a well-known Latin name recorded in Britain in the 2nd century. According to Nennius and later writers, Arthur fought at the battle of Mount Badon (*c*.500), the undiscovered site of a great British victory over the Saxons.

Most Arthurian tales place Arthur in a

Argos: *see*
Hera; Hermes; Io; ZEUS, THE CONSORTS OF

Ariadne: *see*
Dionysos; Minotaur; Theseus

Artemis: *see*
Actaeon; Alcestis; Apollo; Callisto; Iphigeneia; Leto; Niobe; Orion; ZEUS, THE CONSORTS OF

The goddess Artemis.

Arthur: *see*
Finn; Merlin

King Arthur, from a medieval illustration.

ARGONAUTS, THE VOYAGE OF THE *Greece*

The greatest exploits of the hero Jason, a prince of Iolcus in Thessaly, took place during his journey to the easternmost shore of the Black Sea to obtain the Golden Fleece of Colchis at the behest of his uncle, the usurper, King Pelias.

The fleece came from a magic flying ram. This ram had been sent by the god Hermes to help the children of King Athamas of Boeotia (another of Jason's uncles) when their stepmother had threatened their lives. One child, Helles, fell off the ram during their escape and drowned in the sea (which has since been known as Hellespont, meaning literally "Helle's Sea"). However, the other, Phrixus, managed to reach the shores of Colchis. Once there he sacrificed the ram to Zeus and donated its fleece to the Colchis king, Aeëtes. The king kept the fleece under the watchful eye of an unsleeping dragon.

In order to attempt his voyage Jason ordered the construction of a ship, the *Argo*. Sometimes said to be the first ship ever built, the *Argo* was fashioned by the shipwright Argus with the help of either the goddess Hera or the goddess Athene. Its construction incorporated a bough from Zeus' prophetic oak tree at Dodona and it was fitted with fifty oars for each member of Jason's fifty crew.

Eventually, the *Argo* set sail and its first port of call was the island of Lemnos. Here the women had killed all their menfolk because they had taken concubines, claiming that their own women stank. The Argonauts were told that the Lemnian women had merely forced their men to flee and they stayed for several months in order to repopulate the island. Jason was taken by the island's queen, Hypsipyle, who bore him twins.

The Argonauts then sailed on to an island called Cyzicus. Here they were well received by the king

The Argonauts, with their protector in some accounts, the goddess Athene (on the left), redrawn from a crater.

and Herakles cleared the land of marauding giants.

However, the visit ended in tragedy because when the *Argo* put to sea again it was driven back to shore at night by a storm. The Cyzicans, believing they were under attack from pirates, assailed the ship and were unintentionally massacred by the Argonauts, who were also unaware of the identity of their attackers. When the truth was discovered Jason ordered funeral games in honour of his former hosts.

The land of the Bebryces was next on the Argonauts' itinerary. It was ruled by a son of Poseidon, Amycus, who challenged strangers to box to the death, hurling those who refused over a cliff. In Herakles' absence, Polydeuces accepted the challenge, and succeeded in killing Amycus.

The Argonauts sailed on. Near the Bosphorus they encountered Phineus, an old and blind king who was eternally plagued by Harpies, bird-like monsters with the faces of hags, which snatched his food and defecated on it. Calais and Zetes saw off the monstrous creatures and, in gratitude, Phineus gave Jason valuable guidance for the onward journey.

However, the route to Colchis was barred by the Symplegades, two huge moving rocks which crashed together like cymbals, allowing no vessel to pass safely. Phineus advised the Argonauts to send a dove on ahead: if it succeeded in passing through the rocks, so would they. The dove negotiated the Symplegades safely except for the loss of a tail feather. The *Argo* proceeded and, with the help of Athene and Hera, sailed through the rocks without danger, but lost its helmsman, Tiphys. Thereafter, the rocks became stationary for ever.

Eventually, the expedition reached Colchis, the land of the Golden Fleece. King Aeëtes said that he

Map of the Argonauts' Voyage

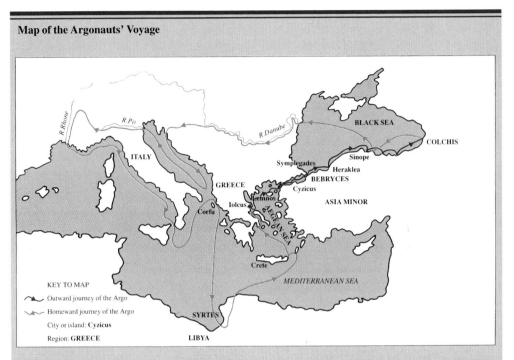

KEY TO MAP
- Outward journey of the Argo
- Homeward journey of the Argo
- City or island: **Cyzicus**
- Region: **GREECE**

would hand the fleece over if Jason would fulfil certain tasks: yoke the king's bronze-footed, fire-breathing bulls; use them to plough a field; sow the teeth of a dragon; and kill the giants who would spring from the planted teeth. The gods caused Medea, the sorceress daughter of Aeëtes, to fall in love with Jason. She gave him a magic potion so that he was able to succeed in the tasks.

However, Aeëtes refused to hand over the fleece, so Medea bewitched the dragon that guarded it and Jason seized his prize. The Argonauts and Medea fled from Colchis with Aeëtes and his entourage in pursuit. In order to delay their pursuers, Medea murdered her brother, Apsyrtus, and dismembered his corpse, hurling the pieces from the *Argo*. Aeëtes had to stop to retrieve the remains so that he could afford his son a proper funeral. The Argonauts escaped.

In one of the many accounts of the *Argo*'s long journey home to Iolcus, a bronze giant, Talos, barred the Argonauts from landing on Crete. So Medea charmed him to sleep and then killed him by pulling

The map illustrates the voyage of the Argo *and her crew (labelling the most important stopping points) according to the most famous account of the journey, the* Argonautica, *which was written c.3rd century BC by the poet Apollonius of Rhodes.*

out a plug in his ankle, unstopping the only vein in his entire body.

The *Argo* was also said to have sailed up the Danube and to have become stranded on the sandbanks of Libya, forcing the crew to carry the vessel overland on their backs for twelve days. Before they finally returned to Iolcus, Jason and Medea visited the witch Circe (who was featured in the *Odyssey* and was also Medea's aunt), in order for her to ritually purify them for the murder of Apsyrtus.

The *Argo* itself ended up in Corinth and it is said that Jason was killed sitting underneath its rotting hulk, when a piece of the ship fell off and hit him. In some accounts the gods lifted the ship to the sky where it became a constellation.

context of myth and folklore. In general he fights monstrous adversaries, giants or magic animals. Some 12th-century texts describe him as the ruler of a subterranean kingdom and later traditions present Arthur himself as a giant.

Ascanius *Rome*
A son of the Trojan hero Aeneas and his first wife Creusa, and grandson of Anchises and the goddess Venus (the Greek Aphrodite). Ascanius established the town and ruling dynasty of Alba Longa in Latium, and was the ancestor of Romulus and Remus, who were the founders of Rome.

Asgard *Germanic regions*
The realm of the gods, according to ancient Scandinavian cosmology. Two races of deities, the Aesir (sky gods) and Vanir (earth gods, who also had their own realm, Vanaheim, beneath the earth) were said to dwell in Asgard, which was ruled by the god Odin.

Asgard was apparently located in the heavens. A bridge, Bifrost – said to be a rainbow or the Milky Way – connected it with the earth. Bifrost was guarded by the god Heimdall against the giants who were the gods' enemies. Their realm, Jotunheim, was beneath Asgard but could be reached from it by a long and dangerous route overland. A similar route linked Asgard with the realm of the dead ruled by Hel, the daughter of the trickster Loki.

Within the walls of Asgard the gods built fine halls, including Valhalla, the Hall of the Slain, to which Odin summoned kings and heroes who had fallen in battle. They spent their time feasting and fighting, always ready to defend Asgard against attack. However, the realm was destroyed at the apocalyptic battle of Ragnarok.

Ashera *Middle East*
A Ugaritic (Canaanite) fertility goddess, the consort of the supreme god El and mother of the Canaanite pantheon. Also called Astarte, she is said to be related to the Mesopotamian Ishtar or Inanna. She was also supposed to be the mother of seventy gods.

Asklepios *Greece and Rome*
The demi-god of medicine, son of the god Apollo and the princess Coronis. The wise Centaur Chiron, taught Asklepios the arts of medicine. He was so skilled at healing that he was able to resurrect the dead. However, Hades, who was ruler of the underworld, feared losing his subjects and complained to Zeus about the demi-god. Zeus killed Asklepios with a thunderbolt. Then, in revenge, Apollo slew the Cyclopes, makers of Zeus's thunderbolts.

In 293BC, during a plague in Rome, Asklepios was adopted into the Roman pantheon (as Aesculapius) on the instructions of an oracle.

Astarte *Egypt*
A warrior goddess of Middle Eastern origin (her Mesopotamian counterpart was Inanna/Ishtar), said by the Egyptians to be the daughter of the sun god or of the creator god Ptah. Astarte was a wife of the god Seth.

Asura *India*
An opponent of the great gods or Devas. In earlier (Vedic) mythology "Asura" appears to mean "mighty" or "lord" and could be applied interchangeably with Deva in referring to the same figure, such as the god Varuna. In later Hinduism "Asura" acquired the sense of anti-god or demon, as in the myth of the churning of the ocean, when the Devas and Asuras are clearly differentiated.

Ataentsic *North America*

The first woman and the ancestor of the human race, according to Iroquois and Huron mythology. Ataentsic was born in the sky world. When she was older, she married a great chief. Ataentsic became pregnant and the chief convinced himself, wrongly, that the father was a dragon. When Ataentsic gave birth to a baby girl, "Breath of Wind", her husband hurled mother and daughter through a hole in the sky.

Ataentsic fell towards the landless waters which then covered this world. The animals who lived in the waters tried to form earth for her to land on. The muskrat succeeded in bringing up some mud from the depths. He placed it on the back of the turtle and it grew at once into the dry land. Supported by the water birds, Ataentsic came safely to earth.

Atalanta *Greece*

A huntress, the daughter of Iasus or Schoenus and Clymene. When Atalanta was born her father was disappointed at not having a son and abandoned her to die. However, she was discovered by a band of hunters who raised her as their own child. Atalanta became renowned for her ability to hunt and run faster than any other mortal.

An Aetolian prince, Meleager, recruited her to join the hunt for a monstrous boar which plagued his town, Calydon. After the boar was killed, Meleager (who had fallen in love with Atalanta) awarded the huntress its pelt because she had drawn first blood.

Atalanta's fame spread and she was reunited with her father, who decided that she should find a husband. Atalanta swore that she would marry only the man who could beat her in a race – and would kill anyone she defeated. A man named Milanion took up the challenge.

The goddess Aphrodite gave him three golden apples, which he dropped during the race. Atalanta stopped to pick up the apples, with the result that she lost the race and duly married Milanion.

Atalanta is usually said to have been the only woman Argonaut.

Athene *Greece*

The goddess of intellect, kings and heroes. Athene was the daughter of the god Zeus and the Titan Metis ("Cunning Intelligence"). A prophecy had claimed that Metis would bear a goddess equal to Zeus in wisdom, so the god devoured his wife in an attempt to prevent the birth. However, one day Zeus had a raging headache and asked the craftsman god Hephaistos to split his head open with an axe. Hephaistos did so and Athene emerged, fully formed and armed, from her father's head.

True to the prophecy, Athene rivalled Zeus in wisdom and was symbolized by the owl, once believed to be the wisest of all birds. She was a patron of crafts and was credited with the invention of the potter's wheel, the first vases, the olive tree and the flute.

Athene was a military figure as well as a great counsellor who was revered by kings. In myth, she was the protector of heroes, such as Odysseus, Herakles, Jason and Perseus. Perseus presented the goddess with the head of the Gorgon Medusa, which she wore on her *aegis* (breastplate).

Athene contended with the sea god Poseidon for the patronage of Athens, the city which bears her name and which was the centre of her cult. The Athenians offered the protectorship of the city as the prize for the best invention either deity could come up with. Poseidon produced only a salt-water spring, while Athene produced the first olive tree, a

Ataentsic: *see*
Earth Diver

Atalanta: *see*
Argonauts, The; Meleager

Atalanta hunting with a bow and arrow, taken from a mosaic.

Athene: *see*
ARGONAUTS, THE
VOYAGE OF THE; Artemis;
Hephaistos; Herakles; Jason;
Odysseus; Panathenaia,
Perseus; Poseidon; ZEUS,
THE CONSORTS OF

The goddess Athene, based on a marble statue of the 4th century BC.

source of oil for lighting, cooking and perfume. So the Athenians decided to have Athene as their patron.

Like Artemis, Athene was an unmarried virgin goddess. Among her titles were Parthenos ("Virgin"), hence the name of her most famous temple, the Parthenon at Athens.

Atlantis *Greece*

A mythical island said to have existed in the western ocean beyond the Pillars of Herakles (Straits of Gibraltar). Atlantis apparently flourished until it was suddenly and catastrophically submerged.

Atlas *Greece*

A Titan, the son of Iapetus and the sea nymph Clymene, and the brother of Prometheus. Following the defeat of the Titans by the Olympians, Atlas was banished by Zeus to the western edge of the world and condemned to hold up the heavens (or, in some accounts, the whole world) on his shoulders.

Later on in life, Atlas refused hospitality to the hero Perseus. In punishment for this rudeness, Perseus produced the Gorgon Medusa's head from his bag and turned the Titan to stone. He is said to have become the Atlas mountains in

A detail, from a bowl, showing Atlas (left) watching the torment inflicted by Zeus on his brother, Prometheus.

northwest Africa (modern Morocco), and the Atlantic Ocean is also supposed to have been named after him.

Atrahasis *Middle East*

A king of Shurupak, a town on the river Euphrates (he has been identified with Utnapishtim from the Akkadian version of the epic of Gilgamesh). According to the epic of Atrahasis, the human race was created to serve the gods and relieve them of the necessity of labour. But within twelve hundred years the noise that the people made disturbed the gods. The god Enlil decided to reduce their numbers. To do so he sent first a plague and then a series of droughts. But the wise god Enki always warned King Atrahasis beforehand and told him what precautions to take. Finally, Enlil told the gods to send a great flood to wipe out humanity, binding the other deities to an oath of secrecy. Enki got around the oath by warning not the king directly but the reed hut in which he lived. Atrahasis built a boat in which he, his family and several animals took refuge when the flood struck.

Every other human being perished in the inundation and the gods soon began to miss the benefits of their labour. After seven days the flood subsided and Atrahasis reappeared to offer a sacrifice to the gods. Enlil was furious that he had once again survived but finally accepted that the human race should continue. Atrahasis was granted eternal life and a place among the gods.

Atreus *Greece*

A king of Argos or Mycenae and a son of Pelops and Hippodamia. Atreus seized the throne of Argos from his brother, Thyestes. He was the father of Agamemnon and Menelaus and the uncle of Aegisthus, who murdered him.

Atum *Egypt*

One of the four principal creator deities (the others being Amon, Khnum and Ptah). Atum, whose cult centre was at Heliopolis, first emerged from the primeval chaos in the form of a serpent, but was usually represented in human form. Like other creator deities, the god represented a totality which contained both male and female. He caused the first division into male and female when he put his semen in his mouth and sneezed or spat it out, creating the first divine couple, Shu and Tefenet. As Ra-Atum, he represented the evening sun.

Avalokiteshvara *India*

"The Lord Who Looks Down", the Bodhisattva of compassion, who is also known as Padmapani. Avalokiteshvara achieved supreme enlightenment but postponed his own release from the cycle of birth and death so that he was able to assist in the salvation of humanity. He is especially revered by Buddhists in Tibet, where he is known as sPyan-ras-gzigs (or Chen-re-zi) and is believed

A redrawing of a 16th-century Aztec flint showing the departure from Aztlan.

to be incarnate in the Dalai Lama. Avalokiteshvara is sometimes said to have one thousand arms, symbolizing his endless capacity to dispense mercy.

Aztlan *Central America*

The place of origin of the Aztec people, from which the god Huitzilopochtli was said to have led them to their eventual homeland in central Mexico. Aztec means "people of Aztlan".

Atum: *see*
Amon; Knum; Ptah; SNAKES AND SERPENTS; Shu; Tefenet

Avalokiteshvara: *see*
Bodhisattva; Buddha; Guanyin; Kannon

Aztlan: *see*
Huitzilopochtli

B

The Middle Eastern storm god, Baal.

Baal *Middle East*

The Ugaritic (Canaanite) storm and fertility god, identified with the Babylonian weather god Hadad. The young Baal ("Lord") is the central figure of the most important cycle of myths, probably intended to mark the end of the agricultural year and the coming of the autumn rains.

The primeval monster Yam ("Sea"), claimed royal power on earth. Baal killed Yam in battle and proclaimed himself king. In defeating Yam, who represented the forces of chaos, Baal showed that it was he who controlled the flow of water from the heavens.

A great banquet was held in honour of Baal's victory. There then followed a great massacre of the god's worshippers by the warlike goddess Anath, Baal's sister. Baal sought to placate Anath by revealing to her the secret of the lightning which heralded life-giving storms and the end of drought.

Baal built a palace and challenged the primeval earth monster, Mot, the lord of death, to resist his power. Their struggle was inconclusive, as death can never be vanquished, not even by a god.

Baba Iaga *Slav regions*

A witch or ogress, the best known figure in Slav folk mythology. The Baba Iaga is described as a scrawny aged crone who travels in a mortar, propelling herself along with a pestle and erasing her tracks with a broomstick. However, she is more often encountered in her hut, which stands on chicken legs in a dense

Baba Iaga waving a pestle and riding a pig, from an 18th-century woodcut.

forest often said to lie beyond a fiery river. The witch fills the entire hut, her legs straddling its single room from corner to corner and her long nose touching the ceiling. Around the hut is a fence of bones.

The Baba Iaga was said to possess power over birds and beasts. As well as creatures, Day and Night are purported obey her commands. It has been suggested that she may originally have been a powerful (but not necessarily malign) goddess of the Slav Other World, the land of the dead, which was reached after a journey across a fiery river and through a thick forest.

Bacab *Central America*
One of four wind gods who, according to Maya cosmology, supported the heavenly upper world, believed to exist above this one.

Bacchus *Greece and Rome*
One of the names of Dionysos, the god of wine and ecstasy, and the name by which he became known to the Romans.

Baladeva *India*
See Balarama

Bacchus, from a mosaic dating from the 1st–2nd centuries AD.

Balar *Celtic regions*
A leader of the Fomorians, a monstrous race of brigands who, in Irish myth, were the descendants of Ham, the cursed son of Noah. Known as Balar of the Evil Eye, he possessed a single huge eye with a venomous glance that meant instant death. Balar was killed by his grandson Lugh at the Second Battle of Magh Tuiredh (Moytirra). Lugh cast a slingshot at the eye, killing Balar. The eye was propelled through Balar's head and into the view of his own troops, who perished at the sight of it.

Balarama *India*
The elder brother of the god Krishna. In Hindu myth, Balarama grew up with his brother among the cowherds, and helped in his adventures, such as killing Kaliya, the snake, and evil King Kamsa.

In Jainism, Baladeva was known as the hero Balarma. He was one of the Shalakapurushas, a series of spiritual and temporal leaders who play a prominent role in the Jain account of the history of the universe. The universe passes forever through alternate periods of ascent or decline (the present epoch is said to be one of decline). Sixty-three Shalakapurushas appear in each period. Among them are nine triads of heroes, each triad consisting of a Baladeva, a Vasudeva and a Prativasudeva. The Baladeva is always described as the elder brother of the Vasudeva and the Prativasudeva is their evil opponent.

Balder *Celtic regions*
The favourite son of the god Odin and his wife Frigg. Frigg tried to protect him by asking every living thing and all objects made of metal, wood or stone to swear an oath never to harm her son. All the gods amused themselves by hurling weapons at Balder, because they were

Barong: *see*
Rangda

Bastet: *see*
Sekhmet

Basuki: *see*
SNAKES AND SERPENTS;
UNDERWORLDS

Batara Guru: *see*
Manuk Manuk

Batara Kala: *see*
Antaboga; Basuki; Bedawang,
The

Bedawang: *see*
Antaboga; Basuki; Batara
Kala

Beli the Great: *see*
Bran the Blessed;
Mabinogion, The;
Manawydan

The goddess Bastet,
based on a bronze

certain that he would come to no harm.

However, Loki the trickster discovered that the mistletoe had not sworn the oath to Frigg. He made it into a dart and gave it to the blind god Hother, who threw it at the young god and killed him. The deities mourned deeply for Balder, whose wife, Nanna, died of grief. At Frigg's request Balder's brother Hermod rode to the land of the dead to free Balder. Hel, the queen of the dead, said that only the weeping of every person and thing in the world would secure his release.

Hermod returned to the gods and messengers were at once dispatched all over the world asking everything to show its love for Balder by weeping. However, a female giant – believed to be Loki in disguise – refused to weep and Balder was therefore unable to return from Hel.

Bannik *Slav regions*
The "Being of the Bath", a malign spirit said to inhabit bathhouses, which in Slav folk mythology are traditionally places of divination and magic. Belief in the *bannik* persists to this day in more remote areas of Russia.

Barong *Southeast Asia*
A spirit king, the leader of the forces of good. He is the tireless opponent of the witch-queen Rangda.

Bastet *Egypt*
The cat-headed goddess of love, sex and fertility. Like the ferocious war goddess Sekhmet, Bastet was originally a lioness deity, but from *c*.900BC she began to be represented as a cat, perhaps because of her gentler nature. She was sometimes depicted with kittens, which symbolized her role as a fertility deity. Mummified cats were often buried near her shrines.

Basuki *Southeast Asia*
A great serpent which lives in the cave of the underworld, according to Balinese cosmology.

Batara Guru *Southeast Asia*
A creator god who, in Sumatran myth, formed the earth and was the ancestor of the human race. One day a swallow told him that his daughter, Boru Deak Parudjar, had jumped from heaven into the limitless sea below. Batara Guru sent the bird down to the sea with a handful of soil to create dry land for his daughter to walk on. The soil became the land, upon which Batara Guru scattered many seeds, from which sprang all the different species of animals.

Batara Guru then sent down a heroic incarnation of himself to defeat Naga Padoha, the serpent ruler of the underworld. The divine hero was rewarded with the hand of Boru Deak Parudjar. They became the parents of the first humans.

Batara Kala *Southeast Asia*
The divine ruler of the cave of the underworld which, according to Balinese cosmology, he rules jointly with the goddess Setesuyara. Batara Kala created light and Mother Earth.

Bedawang *Southeast Asia*
A cosmic turtle which, according to Balinese cosmology, was created through meditation by the cosmic serpent Antaboga. Upon Bedawang rested two coiled snakes, the foundations of the earth, and the Black Stone, the lid of the underworld.

Beli the Great *Celtic regions*
A powerful god who was said to be the ancestor of several of the ancient royal lines of Wales. Beli (whose name means

"light") is probably derived from the ancient Belenus or Belinus, a popular Celtic deity of light and healing. He may be associated with Beltane (1 May), the Celtic festival of light.

Bell Bird Brothers, The *Australia*
Ancestral heroes of the Dreamtime who are associated with Uluru (Ayer's Rock) in central Australia. According to a version of their story related in 1976, the two brothers were once stalking an emu at Antalanya, a rock pool near Uluru. Unknown to them, a young woman was searching for grubs at nearby Wangka Arkal. On her head she carried a collecting dish supported by a pad. The load slipped from her head and disturbed the emu, which ran north toward Uluru with the brothers in pursuit. At the foot of Uluru is an indentation, said to be the girl's head pad, lying where it fell. A little further on is the pool where the emu drank.

Bellerophon *Greece*
A prince of Corinth, the son of King Glaucus and Queen Eurynome of Corinth. Bellerophon tamed the winged horse Pegasus and rode it to kill the monstrous Chimera, which was terrorizing the land of Lycia in Asia

Bellerophon killing the Chimera, based on a stone sculpture, 5th century BC.

Minor (modern Turkey). Bellerophon later attempted to fly on Pegasus to the top of Mount Olympus, the home of the gods. Zeus was irritated by the hero's presumption and sent a gadfly to sting Pegasus, causing the creature to throw Bellerophon to earth. He survived but was lamed for life.

Beowulf *Germanic regions*
A warrior prince, the hero of the 8th-century Anglo-Saxon epic poem of the same name. The events in *Beowulf* are told within a Christian context, but have a strong flavour of pre-Christian Germanic myth.

As a youth, Beowulf came to Denmark from the land of the Geats (in southern Sweden) with a small band of followers to help Hrothgar, the aged Danish king, against the man-eating monster Grendel. Beowulf killed Grendel in a wrestling match, and the monster's mother came to avenge his death. The hero tracked the mother back to her lair and killed her too.

Beowulf returned home and in time succeeded Hygelac as king of the Geats. He reigned peacefully for fifty years until, in his old age, his kingdom was threatened by a ferocious dragon. Beowulf confronted the beast, but his sword could not pierce the dragon's horny skin. The king's companions fled except for one loyal young chieftain, Wiglaf. When the dragon seized Beowulf in its jaws, Wiglaf pierced its underbelly with his sword. Beowulf then drew his knife and together the warriors killed the beast. Beowulf, however, died from the effects of the dragon's poisonous breath.

Bes *Egypt*
A protective deity. Bes, usually portrayed as a hideous but jovial dwarf,

Bell Bird Brothers: *see* ANCESTORS; Dreamtime

Bellerophon: *see* Chimera, The; Medusa; Pegasus

*The Egyptian entertainment and
protector deity, Bes, as depicted in a
Greco-Roman faience.*

was revered as the god of pleasure and
entertainment and as a protector of the
family, especially of children and
women in childbirth.

Bintu *Africa*
A divine antelope, according to the
mythology of the western Sahara region.
The first blacksmith in heaven is said to
have made a hoe from Bintu's skull and
then descended with it to earth in order
to teach people the arts of agriculture.
Heavenly antelopes are often associated
with the invention of agriculture
throughout Saharan Africa.

Black Misery *Tibet and Mongolia*
The black light which, together with its
counterpart Radiant (white light), was
the first thing to exist, according to pre-
Buddhist creation mythology. After
Black Misery and Radiant came into
existence, there arose out of chaos
multi-coloured streams of light which
separated like a rainbow. From their five

colours arose five elements: hardness,
fluidity, heat, motion and space, which
fused to form a huge egg. From this,
Black Misery produced the darkness of
non-being, which he filled with the evils
of the world.

Bladder Festival, The *Arctic regions*
A winter ceremony of the Alaskan Inuit
at which the inflated bladders of all the
sea mammals caught during the year are
pushed through holes in the ice. It is
believed that this act returns the
creatures' souls to the spirit world,
where they rejoin the society of animals
and can be sent out once more as quarry.

Blodeuwedd *Celtic regions*
A beautiful woman conjured out of
flowers by the magician Math, lord of
Gwynedd, Wales, and his nephew
Gwydion. Blodeuwedd (which means
"Flower-Aspect") was created as a wife
for the hero Lleu Llaw Gyffes, whose
mother Arianrhod had sworn that he
would never have a human wife.

Blodeuwedd was unfaithful and with
her lover, Gronw Pebyr, plotted to kill
Lleu. However, they only wounded him
and he escaped in the form of an eagle.
He was later found and restored to
human form by Gwydion, who killed
Gronw Pebyr and turned Blodeuwedd
into an owl. *Blodeuwedd* is the modern
Welsh word for "owl".

Boann *Cetic regions*
The deity, or divine spirit, of the river
Boyne in Ireland. Boann was originally
the wife of Nechtan, a river god, but had
intercourse with the Daghdha, the father
god, to produce Oenghus, the god of
love. When Boann broke a prohibition
by visiting Nechtan's well, its waters
rose and engulfed her and she became
the Boyne.

Bodhbh *Celtic regions*

An Irish sorceress and war goddess. Bodhbh (or Badhbh) brings terror and confusion among warriors with her battle cries, and frequently takes the form of a crow or raven. Her appearance in this guise is often an omen of death.

Bodhisattva *India*

A future Buddha, literally "One whose essence is *bodhi* (enlightenment)". A Bodhisattva has achieved supreme enlightenment but has postponed his entry into the sublime state of

The Bodhisattva Avalokiteshvara, from a 10th-century Sarada inscription.

nirvana in order to assist in the salvation of the human race. It appears that Bodhisattvas were at first aspects of the personality of Siddhartha Gautama (the Buddha). These aspects subsequently developed into individual beings, whose cult was the basis for a flourishing mythology. Among the more prominent of the Bodhisattvas are Amitabha, Avalokiteshvara, Maitreya, Manjushri and Vajrapani.

Bota Ili *Southeast Asia*

A wild woman of the mountains, according to the mythology of the Kédang people of eastern Indonesia. One day Wata Rian, a fisherman, went to the summit of a mountain. He found a hearth and climbed a tree to await the return of whoever had made it. Eventually Bota Ili came back from hunting. After she had rested, she hit her backside on a rock to strike a light but was unable to make fire. She realized that the presence of a stranger was to blame and soon spotted Wata Rian hiding up in the tree.

Bota Ili was angry at first but later relented and Wata Rian came down. She lit the fire and together they cooked their food. Wata Rian poured Bota Ili plenty of wine and when she had fallen into a drunken sleep he shaved her all over. To his astonishment he discovered that the hairy creature was in fact a woman. Later, after Bota Ili had learned to wear clothes, they were married.

Botoque *South America*

A youth who brought fire and the bow and arrow to humanity, according to the Kayapo people of central Brazil. One day Botoque became stranded on top of a high cliff. A jaguar, who was carrying a bow and arrow and all kinds of game, found him and adopted him as a son and hunting companion.

The jaguar took Botoque into his home, where he saw fire and ate cooked meat for the first time. Later the jaguar taught Botoque how to make a bow and arrows. One day, when the jaguar was hunting, his wife threatened Botoque. The boy killed her with the bow and, stealing an ember and some cooked meat, and taking his bow and arrows, he left to return to his village.

Once they had seen Botoque's gifts

Bodhbh: *see*
Cú Chulainn; Morríghan, The

Bodhisattva: *see*
Amitabha; Avalokiteshvara;
Buddha; Maitreya; Manjushri;
Vajrapani

Botoque *see*
CULTURE HERO; JAGUAR

the other men from the village went to the jaguar's house and plundered it. Because of his losses, the jaguar now has to hunt with his claws and he must eat his food raw.

Brahma *India*

A creator deity, the lord of humanity and of the gods and one of the *trimurti*, the Hindu triad of Brahma, Shiva and Vishnu. Brahma is a frequent figure in later Hindu mythology, but usually in a subordinate role to the other two gods. During the early centuries AD, however, he appears to have been the focus of an important cult, presumably as the supreme creator deity.

In the great Hindu epics Brahma, or Pitamaha ("Grand Father") as he is also known, is credited with some of the creation myths associated in earlier texts with Prajapati, the Lord of Progeny. They include the story of how he produced a beautiful young daughter, Sarasvati or Savitri, from his own body. Brahma was smitten with her beauty and, as Sarasvati walked around him in a

Brahma seated in the lotus flower, which appeared from Vishnu's navel.

gesture of respect, his desire to stare at her caused five faces to appear (the fifth face was later destroyed by Shiva). The pair then committed incest and produced Manu, the first man.

As Brahma meditates, he is said to emit both the material elements of the universe and the concepts through which humanity may understand them. The duration of the universe is counted in terms of Brahma's enormous lifespan of one hundred Brahma years (equal to 36,000,000 years of the gods, where one year of the gods is the same as 360 human years). In each day of Brahma the universe is created and in each night it is dissolved.

Eventually Brahma's creative activity became trivialized in mythology into a readiness to grant boons or favours to anyone who performed acts of penance or asceticism. As a result the Asuras (demons) often acquire inordinate power for persistent asceticism until Brahma calls upon the assistance of one of the great gods to restore order.

In much of the mythology surrounding Vishnu, Brahma tends to be presented as a mere demiurge carrying out the intentions of the superior god. According to this tradition, as Vishnu lay on the cosmic serpent Ananta in the primordial waters, a lotus emerged from his navel and opened to reveal Brahma seated within and preparing to send forth the world.

Brân the Blessed *Celtic regions*

A giant warrior, the son of Llyr and brother of Manawydan and Branwen. Brân the Blessed (in Welsh Bendigeidfran) gave Branwen in marriage to Matholwch, king of Ireland, who ill-treated her. To avenge his sister, Brân, who was so huge that no building could contain him, led an army of

BUDDHISM *India*

Buddha ("The Enlightened One"), was the name given to Siddhartha Gautama, founder of Buddhism. Gautama (who lived *c*.560BC) was a prince of the Shakyas, a northern Indian tribal group that occupied Oudh and parts of Nepal. The earliest Buddhist scriptures embellished the story of Gautama's search for enlightenment and release from the eternal cycle of birth, death and rebirth.

Born miraculously from his mother's side as she grasped a tree, Gautama was received by Brahma and the other gods. In myth, the child took seven steps and declared that this was his final birth. He was raised in luxury in the palace of his father, called King Shuddhodhana. He married and had a son. One day

Gautama rode his chariot outside the palace and discovered sickness and death. He decided to search for enlightenment. As he stole away, demi-gods muffled his horse's hooves.

After seven years, Gautama sat under what later became the Bodhi ("Enlightenment") tree, until he had resolved human suffering. Mara, god of death and desire, assailed Gautama with earthly distractions – to no avail. After forty-nine days, Gautama attained enlightenment: he became a Buddha.

Left: *A representation of the Buddha.*

Below: *A map showing the spread of Buddhism from India into Tibet.*

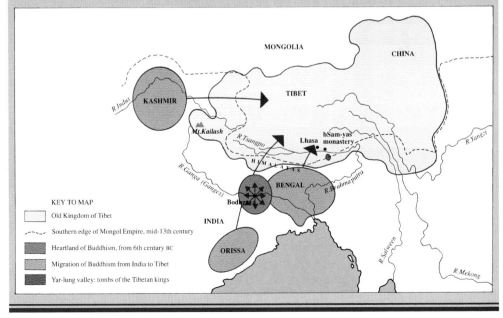

KEY TO MAP

- Old Kingdom of Tibet
- Southern edge of Mongol Empire, mid-13th century
- Heartland of Buddhism, from 6th century BC
- Migration of Buddhism from India to Tibet
- Yar-lung valley: tombs of the Tibetan kings

Britons against the Irish, striding through the sea next to his fleet. The Britons won the battle but only seven of Brân's men survived and Brân himself was mortally wounded by a poisoned spear. He ordered the seven suvivors to cut off his head and bury it on the White Mount in London in order to protect the kingdom from invaders. On the journey to London the warriors spent seven years feasting at Harlech and another eighty years in the blissful otherworld of Gwales. Nevertheless, throughout the journey, Brân's head continued to talk as if he were still alive.

Brer Rabbit *North America*
A trickster rabbit of American folk myth. Brer (meaning "Brother") Rabbit derives from the Hare trickster of west African mythology, who was brought to the southeastern United States by slaves. In his adventures, he is generally seen to out-wit larger and more powerful characters such as Brer Bear and Brer Fox.

Brighid (Brigid, Brigit) *Celtic regions*
An Irish goddess, the daughter of the Daghdha. Brighid may originally have been a goddess of sovereignty: her name is derived from the Celtic root *brig* ("exalted"). She was the patron of poetry and arcane lore, especially divination and prophecy, and the protector of women in childbirth. Brighid was sometimes said to have two sisters of the same name who were associated with healing and crafts. However, the Brighids were commonly treated as three aspects of a single deity.

Brighid was adopted as a Christian saint, St Bride (or Bridget) of Kildare, Ireland's most important female saint and, it was claimed, the founder of the first Irish nunnery, at Kildare. St Bride assumed many functions of the goddess and her cult had a pronounced fertility and pastoral aspect. She even took over Brighid's feast day, 1 February.

BUDDHISM *India*
See panel on previous page

Cadmus *Greece*

The founder of the city of Thebes, son of King Agenor and Queen Telephassa of Phoenicia. When Zeus kidnapped Europa, Cadmus' sister, Agenor sent his three sons to search for her. The Delphic oracle told Cadmus to abandon the hunt for Europa and found a city on the site to which a certain cow would lead him.

The cow took Cadmus to a place in Boeotia, where he killed a marauding dragon. Then, on Athene's instructions, he sowed half its teeth in the ground. From the teeth sprang armed men who fought each other until only five were left alive. These warriors, the Spartoi ("Sown Men"), were the ancestors of the noble families of Thebes.

For killing the dragon, Cadmus spent eight years in the service of its father, the god Ares. At the end of this time he received the hand of Harmonia, the daughter of Ares and Aphrodite. Athene granted Cadmus the title of king and he founded Cadmeia, later called Thebes.

Calais and Zetes *Greece*

Winged heroes, the twin sons of Boreas (the North Wind). Calais and Zetes, known as the Boreades, went on the voyage of the Argonauts and rescued their blind brother-in-law, King Phineus, from the Harpies by flying after them and turning back when the monsters were no longer a threat. However, the Boreades then died, because at their birth it had been decreed that they must catch anyone they pursued or perish.

Calchas *Greece*

A prophet who accompanied the Greeks on their expedition to Troy and made many accurate prophecies about the Trojan War. He predicted that Achilles would cause the destruction of Troy and that it would fall only after nine years.

Callisto *Greece*

A nymph, one of the attendants of the goddess Artemis. One night the god Zeus seduced her. Callisto tried to conceal her loss of chastity, but after some months Artemis noticed that she was pregnant and expelled her from her entourage. Callisto bore a son, Arcas. Later, the goddess Hera, the jealous wife of Zeus, transformed Callisto into a bear

Cadmus: *see*
Aphrodite; Ares; Athene; Europa

Calais and Zetes: *see*
ARGONAUTS, THE VOYAGE OF THE

Calchas: *see*
Achilles; TROJAN WAR, THE HEROES OF THE

Callisto: *see*
Artemis; Hera; ZEUS, THE CONSORTS OF

Can Nü

which was hunted and killed by Arcas. Zeus turned her into the constellation Ursa Major (the Great Bear).

Can Nü *China*

"Lady Silkworm", a girl responsible for the arrival of silk into the world. The girl missed her father greatly when he went away on business. Then while grooming her stallion one day she declared that she would marry anyone who brought her father home. The stallion bolted and galloped away to fetch her father, who hurried home, where he was relieved to find nothing amiss. His daughter remembered her words while grooming the stallion. Furious that a horse should think of marrying his daughter, her father slaughtered the animal and skinned it.

Later, the girl and her friends taunted the skin. It suddenly wrapped itself around her and flew into a tree. In due course her father and his neighbours found her and saw that she had turned into a creature with a horse-like head (a silkworm) which produced a fine glossy thread from its mouth.

Cao Guojiu *China*

The brother of the Empress Cao of the Song dynasty (AD960–1279) and one of the Eight Immortals of Daoist (Taoist) mythology. It is said that Cao became disillusioned with court life and so went into the mountains to seek out the Dao, the path to enlightenment. He came to a river and tried to impress the boatman with his golden tablet for admission to court. The boatman, who actually happened to be the Immortal Lü Dongbin in disguise, asked him how anyone who sought the Dao could try to show superiority. On hearing this, Cao threw his tablet into the river and he was taken by Lü as a disciple.

Cargo cults *Oceania*

In Oceania contact with European civilization led to the creation and alteration of myths to account for the Europeans' place in the cosmos. Melanesians and others were staggered by the amount of material goods which the newcomers brought in their ships and "cargo" became the pidgin word *kago*, which means "goods", "belongings" or "wealth". Melanesians believed that the Europeans must have particularly effective magic to possess such wealth, and started "cargo cults" in an attempt to acquire this lore for themselves. Typically, it was thought that some ancestor, god or other revered figure would bring the *kago*. His arrival would herald a new age of plenty, justice and, some hoped, freedom from foreign control.

Cargo cults persist to this day: for example, Prince Philip, the husband of Queen Elizabeth II, is the focus of a cult on Tanna Island in Vanuatu.

Cassandra *Greece*

A prophetess, the daughter of King Priam and Queen Hecuba of Troy. The god Apollo gave Cassandra the power of prophecy in the hope of winning her heart. However, she failed to return his love, so Apollo, offended by her lack of amour for him, ensured that her prophecies would never be believed.

Cassandra was taken to Greece after the fall of Troy as the concubine of the victorious King Agamemnon. She foretold impending bloodshed and refused to enter his palace. Agamemnon ignored her warnings and was violently assassinated. Cassandra herself was murdered shortly afterwards.

Castor and Polydeuces *Greece*
The sons of the god Zeus (the Dioscuri).

Cathbhadh *Celitc regions*
A druid who features prominently in the stories of the Ulster heroes Conchobar and Cú Chulainn as a great seer and a teacher of heroes.

Centaur *Greece*
A fabulous creature of Thessaly that was part horse and part man. The Centaurs were the hybrid offspring of Centauros, the son of Ixion, and the mares of Mount Pelion in Thessaly. Perhaps because of their illicit origins, Centaurs have often been associated with sexual licence and violence. But some Centaurs were wise and kindly, particularly the centaur Chiron, who educated several heroes.

Centaurs beating a victim, from a vase of the 5th century BC.

At the wedding of King Perithous of the Lapiths, another race of Thessaly, the Centaur Eurytion tried to carry off his bride, Hippodamia. The incident led to an enormously celebrated battle (the Centauromachy) in which the Athenian hero Theseus contributed to the Lapiths' victory. The Centauromachy was a regular subject of Greek art. It was most famously depicted on the friezes of the Athenian Parthenon.

Centeotl *Central America*
A maize god of Aztec myth. Centeotl was the male counterpart of the goddess Chicomecoatl. Meaning the "maize cob lord", Centeotl was associated with maize in particular, while Chicomecoatl represented sustenance which included maize, in general.

Both deities were closely associated with the water goddess Chalchuitlicue, the wife of the rain and fertility god Tlaloc. They were also said to be related to Xilonen, the goddess of the tender young shoots of corn.

Centzon Totochtin *Central America*
The "Four Hundred Rabbits", a group of little Aztec gods associated with the intoxicating beverage called *pulque* or *octli*, which was made from the maguey plant and widely used in public rituals and festivals. Aptly, the Centzon Totochtin include Tepoztecatl, the god of drunkenness. The rabbit is renowned for its fecundity and for its seemingly mischievous antics and this probably explains the creature's association with *pulque*. The liquor was also linked with fertility – sometimes depicted spurting from the breasts of a mother goddess.

Cepheus *Greece*
King of Ethiopia (Joppa), the husband of Cassiopeia and father of Andromeda.

Cerberus *Greece*
A ferocious three-headed dog, one of the numerous monstrous offspring of Echidne and Typhon. Cerberus, who was sometimes said to have a serpent for a tail and dragon heads sprouting from his back and necks, was given to the god Hades to guard the entrance to the underworld, the land of the dead, and to devour anyone who tried to leave. It was said that none could pass him, but

Cerberus was so enchanted by the music of Orpheus' lyre that he allowed Orpheus to enter the underworld and look for Eurydice.

Cerberus returned to the world of the living on only one occasion, when Herakles forcibly dragged the beast before King Eurystheus as his twelfth and final labour.

Ceres *Rome*

The goddess of fertility and crops (the word "cereal" derives from her name). Originally a southern Italian deity of grain, Ceres became largely identified with the Greek goddess Demeter.

Cernunnos *Celtic regions*

"The Horned One", the name given to a male deity with horns or antlers whose image has been found in much of the ancient Celtic world, principally northern and central France (ancient Gaul) and Britain. Cernunnos appears to

Cernunnos, from the Gundestrup cauldron, c.4th–5th centuries BC.

have been a deity of fertility and abundance, a dispenser of fruit, grain and wealth, and a lord of animals. He was sometimes depicted with serpents and the Celtic wheel symbol, which was an emblem of the sun.

Cernunnos had associations with the underworld of the dead: the ancient

Celts placed small wheels in graves in order to provide the deceased with light underground. In one representation he was linked with the Roman gods Mercury, who conducted the souls of the dead to the underworld, and Apollo, who was the god of light.

Cerynean Hind, The *Greece*

A beast with golden horns and bronze hooves that lived on Mount Cerynea in Arcadia. The hero Herakles captured it as the third of his twelve labours.

Cessair *Celtic regions*

The woman who led the first group of people to settle in Ireland, according to the *Book of Invasions*. She was the daughter of Bith, son of Noah, and arrived just forty days before the biblical Great Flood. Cessair and her followers all perished in the Deluge, with the exception of her husband, Fintan mac Bóchra.

Chac, from the Dresden Codex *of the Post-classic period.*

Chac *Central America*

The Maya god of water, rain and lightning. As guardian of the fertilizing rains, Chac presided over agriculture and opened the stone which concealed the first maize. The god is related to the Aztec rain deity Tlaloc.

The Chaos family

Chaos

Gaia   Tartarus   Eros   Erebos = Night

Uranos   Mountains   Pontos   Aither   Day
= Gaia

KEY:
= coupled with

CHAOS: *see*
CREATION; Hun Dun;
Orphism; Pan Gu; *Theogony,*
The

Chaos *Greece*
The first thing to exist, in Hesiod's account of creation in the *Theogony*. It is unclear whether Chaos ("The Yawning Void") was conceived of as a divinity and so whether the next things to form (Gaia, Tartaros, Eros, Erebos and Nyx) were its progeny or unconnected phenomena. In the Orphic creation myth, Chaos sprang from Chronos ("Time"), one of two primal deities present at the start of creation.

In a Chinese creation myth, two emperors decided to repay Chaos (Hun Dun) for his hospitality by giving him the bodily orifices that he lacked. So they bored holes in his body, but killed him in the process. As Chaos died the ordered world came into being.

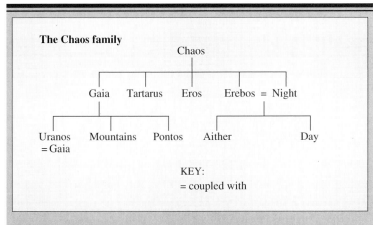

Pan Gu, a creator god of Chinese myth, with the cosmic egg of chaos (see page 52), *from a 19th-century lithograph.*

Chalchiuhtlicue *Central America*
The Aztec goddess of rivers and lakes. Chalchiuhtlicue (which means "Jade Skirt") was the consort of Tlaloc, the rain god, and was regarded as the sister of his entourage the Tlaloque. She was said to possess the power to conjure up hurricanes and whirlwinds and to cause drownings. Some representations of the goddess portray her as a goddess of childbirth, an attribute derived from her association with the waters of birth. In the myth of the five "suns" or ages, Chalchiuhtlicue presided over the fourth age. It came to an end when the world was engulfed by cataclysmic floods.

She has also been linked with the goddess Xochiquetzal, the Aztec goddess of flowers and craftsmen. (*See illustration on page 46.*)

Chalchiuhtlicue: *see*
Five Suns, The; Tlaloc

Chaos

Charybdis: *see*
Scylla and Charybdis

Chicomecoatl: *see*
Centeotl

Chimera: *see*
Bellerophon; Echidne;
Pegasus

Chinawezi: *see*
Chibinda Ilunga: Lueji

*Chalchiuhtlicue (*see entry on page 45*)
from a 16th-century codex.*

CHAOS
See panel on previous page

Charon *Greece*
The boatman of the underworld.
Charon, who was the offspring of
Erebos ("Underworld Darkness") and
Nyx ("Night"), ferried the dead across
the rivers Acheron and Styx to the
kingdom of his employer Hades, the god
of the underworld. He was a testy old
man who refused to take anyone who
could not pay him. For this reason the
Greeks would place a coin in the mouth
of a corpse before burial.

Charybdis *Greece*
A monster resembling a giant whirlpool
which infested the Straits of Messina.

*Chibinda Ilunga, based
on a wooden figure
found in Zaïre.*

Chibinda Ilunga *Africa*
A prince of the Luba-Lunda peoples of
what are now southeastern Zaïre and
northeastern Angola. Chibinda Ilunga
was the grandson of Mbidi Kiluwe, the
forefather of the Luba kings. His face
was said to be white and shining like the
moon. He left the Luba kingdom after
the king, who was jealous of his hunting
prowess, insulted him by declaring that

Chibinda Ilunga had never made war.

One day, Chibinda Ilunga encountered Lueji in the forest. Lueji was the
Lunda queen and granddaughter of the
primordial serpent Chinawezi. She
invited the charming stranger to stay
with her. In due course they were
married and Lueji announced to the
Lunda elders that she was standing
down from her office and that Chibinda
Ilunga would rule in her place. After
handing her husband her bracelet of
office, Lueji began an extraordinarily
long menstruation. Her prolonged flow
of blood meant that she was never able
to bear children. In the end Lueji gave
Chibinda Ilunga another wife, called
Kamonga, who was fertile.

Chicomecoatl *Central America*
A deity of food in Aztec mythology,
especially of maize. She was the female
counterpart of Centeotl.

Chimera, The *Greece*
One of the monstrous offspring of
Echidne and Typhon. The Chimera,
which infested Lycia in Asia Minor
(modern Turkey), had the head and body
of a lion, a serpent for a tail and a third,
goat-like head sprouting from the
middle of its back. The creature came to
represent anything fantastical, hence the
word "chimerical". It was killed by
Bellerophon.

Chinawezi *Africa*
The name given in southern and central
Africa to the primordial cosmic serpent
which features widely in African
mythology. In the beginning, Chinawezi
(also known as Chinaweji), the mother
of all things, divided up the world with
her husband Nkuba, the Lightning.
Nkuba set himself up in the sky with the
heavenly bodies, and his urine became

the beneficial rains. Chinawezi was governor of the earth and the waters: it was said that when the thunder rumbled she responded by causing the rivers to swell. Finally, after some time Chinawezi bore a daughter, Nawezi, and a son, Konde. These offspring married and had three children.

Chiron *Greece*

A Centaur who was untypically famed for his wisdom, kindliness and civilized character. Chiron was educated by Apollo and Artemis in the skills of hunting, medicine, music, poetry and warfare. He counselled the hero Peleus on how to win the hand of the sea nymph Thetis, and later became the tutor of their son, Achilles. Jason was among the other heroes tutored by Chiron, who also taught the demi-god Asklepios, Apollo's son, the art of healing. When Chiron died he became the constellation Sagittarius.

Chitimukulu *Africa*

The first king of the Bemba people of Zambia. According to the Bemba origin myth, Chitimukulu and his two brothers attempted to build a tall tower in their parents' royal village. But the tower collapsed, killing many people, and their father ordered the execution of his sons. However, the three brothers managed to escape to what is now Zambia. It was here that Chitimukulu founded the Bemba kingdom.

Chronos *Greece*

"Time", one of two primal deities (the other being Adrasteia, "Necessity") present at the beginning of creation, according to the Orphic creation myth.

Chronos represents an Orphic reinterpretation of the name Cronos or Kronos, which is of uncertain origin.

Churning of the ocean, The *India*

A great act of creation by the gods (known as Devas) and demons (known as Asuras). It focuses on winning the *amrita*, the elixir of immortality, and illustrates the universal concept of order emerging from upheaval. In this story the Devas and Asuras are clearly distinguished. This, however, is not always the case in earlier myths.

The Devas and Asuras assembled on Mount Meru and pondered how to win the *amrita*. Vishnu suggested that they should churn the ocean to produce the elixir, as well as all the herbs and jewels. The divinities agreed and uprooted Mount Mandara to use as a churning paddle, setting it on the back of a tortoise. They coiled the great serpent Vasuki around the mountain as a rope, with the Devas taking one end and the Asuras the other. They twirled Mandara about, causing its trees to topple and catch fire with the friction as they fell against each other. Indra put out the fire with water from the clouds, but the sap of all the plants flowed into the ocean, turning it to milk and then to butter. In one last great effort, the divinities produced the sun, the moon, the goddess of fortune and other treasures. Finally the physician Dhanvantari emerged from the ocean, bearing the *amrita*.

Vishnu tricked the Asuras into surrendering the elixir and gave it to the Devas to drink. The enraged Asuras offered battle but were defeated by the Devas, who then put Mount Mandara back in its proper place.

Circe *Greece*

A sorceress, the daughter of Helios, the sun god, and the sea nymph Perse or Perseis. Circe, who lived on the island of Aeaea near Italy, was the aunt of the sorceress Medea. When the hero Jason stole the Golden Fleece from Aeëtes, Medea assisted his escape by murdering her half-brother Apsyrtus. Jason and Medea went to Circe for purification.

Circe also features in the story of the hero Odysseus. When some of his crew visited Aeaea, the sorceress transformed them into pigs. One man, Eurylochus, escaped to tell what had happened. Odysseus rescued his crew with the help of the god Hermes, who gave him a special herb as an antidote to Circe's magic. He remained with her for a year and received valuable advice for his onward journey, such as a warning not to approach the Sirens.

Clotho *Greece*
One of the three Fates, the daughters of Zeus and Themis.

Clymene *Greece*
A sea nymph, the wife of the Titan Iapetus and the mother of Prometheus, Atlas, Epimetheus and Menoetius.

Clytemnestra *Greece*
A queen of Argos (or Mycenae), the daughter of King Tyndareos and Queen Leda of Sparta.

However, her father was often said to be the god Zeus, who assumed the form of a swan to have intercourse with Leda. In one account, she subsequently gave birth to two sets of twins from two eggs: Clytemnestra and Castor from one, while Helen (of Troy) and Polydeuces sprang from the other.

Clytemnestra married Tantalus, a son of Thyestes, one of the feuding Pelopid dynasty. Agamemnon, the king of Argos and son of Atreus (Thyestes' brother and enemy), killed Tantalus and his son and claimed Clytemnestra for himself. Tyndareos, who had earlier helped Agamemnon to win the throne of Argos

Clytemnestra and Aegisthus, with Agamemnon trapped under a net.

from Thyestes, forgave him the murders and allowed him to marry Clytemnestra.

Before Agamemnon sailed at the head of the Greek expedition to fight the Trojans, he was obliged to sacrifice his daughter Iphigeneia to the goddess Artemis. Clytemnestra vowed to avenge her daughter's death and became the lover of Aegisthus, the brother of her murdered first husband, who had sworn to seize the Argive throne. Together they plotted the murder of Agamemnon on his return from Troy. When her husband arrived with his entourage, Clytemnestra invited him to take a bath. However, as Agamemnon stepped out of the water, she moved towards him as if to offer him a towel, but instead threw a fine mesh over his head. Aegisthus stabbed the entangled Agamemnon, who collapsed, dying, into the bath. Clytemnestra decapitated the king with an axe, and then struck down his concubine Cassandra. Then Aegisthus assumed the throne.

Orestes was able to escape but returned incognito with his sister Elektra after eight years to take revenge on his father's assassins. He murdered King Aegisthus before cutting off Clytemnestra's head with a single blow.

Coatlicue *Central America*
An Aztec earth goddess, the mother of the god Huitzilopochtli. Coatlicue (which means "Snake Skirt") is said to have conceived Huitzilopochtli at Coatepec (Serpent Hill, near Tula, Mexico) when she was impregnated by a magic ball of down which descended from heaven.

Her existing offspring, the goddess Coyolxauhqui and her four hundred brothers, the Centzon Huitznahua, became angry at her pregnancy and murdered her, cutting off her head and hands. However, at the moment of death Coatlicue gave birth to the fully formed Huitzilopochtli, who immediately killed Coyolxauhqui and then hurled her dismembered corpse to the bottom of Coatepec, before setting out to rout his many brothers.

Coatlicue, the Aztec earth goddess.

Cocijo *Central America*
A Zapotec deity of lightning and rain, who is the equivalent of the great Aztec god Tlaloc.

Cocytus *Greece*
Meaning "River of Wailing", the Cocytus is a river in northern Greece believed in ancient times to flow into the underworld. The unburied dead were said to wander the banks of the Cocytus for a hundred years.

Conán the Bald *Celtic regions*
A warrior and follower of the hero Finn. In 12th-century Irish literature, Conán, the son of Morna and brother of the great warrior Goll, is portrayed as an impulsive and malicious character, whereas later narratives present him as principally a comic figure who is boastful, cowardly and gluttonous. According to one tale, the followers of Finn (the Fian) found themselves stuck to the floor of the Rowan Tree Hostel, a dwelling in the Otherworld, through the sorcery of their enemies. Eventually all of them were released except Conán, who had to be torn from the floor, leaving the skin of his buttocks behind.

Conchobar *Celtic regions*
A king of Ulster, a key figure in the epic *Táin Bó Cuailnge*. Conchobar was the illegitimate son of Nessa, queen of Ulster, and the druid Cathbhadh, who raised him. After the death of Nessa's husband, King Fachtna, Ferghus, his half-brother, succeeded him as king. Nessa agreed to become his lover on condition that Conchobar, then aged seven, be allowed to occupy the throne for one year. Ferghus consented but Conchobar acquired such respect as king that the people would not allow Ferghus to return.

Coatlicue: *see*
Huitzilopochtli

Cocijo: *see*
Tlaloc

Cocytus: *see*
Acheron; Hades; Styx;
UNDERWORLDS

Conán the Bald: *see*
Finn

Conchobar: *see*
Cathbhadh; Cú Chulainn;
Deirdre; Ferghus; Medhbh

A coyote figure from a plate, c.11th–13th centuries AD.

In fact King Conchobar was so popular among his people that whenever an Ulsterman married, he allowed the king to be the first to sleep with his new wife. However, he was less likeable when it came to his treatment of his foster-daughter, Deirdre, once she had eloped to Scotland with her lover Naiose. The couple agreed to return only when Conchobar had guaranteed Deirdre's safety and promised to send Ferghus to escort them. But when they arrived at Emhain Macha, Conchobar's capital, Naoise was put to death and Deirdre was brought before her foster-father with her hands bound. In disgust Ferghus defected to Conchobar's enemy, Queen Medhbh of Connacht, a war ensued and Conchobar was victorious against Medhbh, largely through the deeds of the hero Cú Chulainn, the Ulster king's foster-son.

Conchobar died after being hit by a brain-ball, a projectile so-called because it was made of solidified brains mixed with lime. It lodged in the king's head until, seven years later, he fell into a tremendous rage which caused the missile to split, killing him instantly.

Confucius *China*
A latinization of the name of Kong Fuzi.

Conla *Celtic regions*
One of the Fian, the followers of the hero Finn. One day a woman seen only by Conla appeared before him and bade him go with her to the Plain of Delight or Otherworld, an enchanted land of timeless content. On the orders of Conla's father, King Conn of the Hundred Battles, a druid drove the mysterious woman away, but as she disappeared she threw Conla an apple. The apple sustained him for a whole month without growing smaller. Conla

began to long to see the woman again. Eventually she reappeared and told him that they could travel together in her ship of glass. The youth followed her to a crystal coracle, in which they sailed away, never to be seen again.

Corn, The origin of *North America*
There are many North American myths of the origin of corn. That of the Mikasuki people of Florida tells of two brothers who lived with their grandmother, and one day, tired of meat, asked her for something new to eat. From then on, when they returned from hunting, she served them delicious corn. Their grandmother would not say where it came from, so the younger brother spied on her when she went to the storehouse. To his horror he saw her rub the corn from the sides of her own body. That night the brothers refused the corn, and the old woman could tell that they knew her secret. She announced that she would have to leave them forever, but that she would live on as corn, growing from her grave.

Cornucopia *Greece*
Meaning "The Horn of Plenty", the cornucopia was the horn of the goat-nymph Amalthea, from which poured an unceasing abundance of Nectar, ambrosia and fruit.

COSMOLOGY
See panel on opposite page

Coyote North America
A member of the dog family found from Alaska to Costa Rica, and one of the most popular of all Native American mythical characters. Coyote appears in the myths of the southwest, west and central plains of America in a wide range of roles, particularly as a cunning

COSMOLOGY

According to most accounts of the structure of the universe, the visible world of everyday life is part of some larger whole. Above this world there is an overworld, or heaven, which is the abode of superior beings or divine ancestors, and below it an underworld, peopled by the dead and subterranean spirits. This image is common to the Indo-European traditions, the cultures of the tribal peoples of Asia, Oceania and the Americas, and the peoples of the Arctic regions. Both overworld and underworld may be a mirror image of the middle world in which human beings live. More complicated versions of the three-world cosmos describe seven, eight or even nine levels of both upper and lower worlds.

Many mythologies also describe a central pillar or "World Tree" which is the axis uniting the three worlds. Yggdrasil, the World Ash of Norse tradition, is the best known of these, but the same idea is found in Indonesian Borneo, the Sahara and also among the aboriginal peoples of the Americas.

The lateral structure of the mythical universe is frequently described as being made up of four quarters, corresponding to north, south, east and west. A fifth "direction", the "centre", or "here", is found in the mythology of China, Ireland and North and Central America.

In many regions dwellings are modelled on the cosmos. For example, to the island peoples of Southeast Asia, the left side of the house typically represents the underworld while the right is a representation of the world above, or heaven. The central pole of the house may represent the Tree of Life or cosmic axis, an idea also found in the Amazon and Siberia.

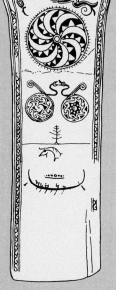

From a memorial stone (c.AD500) of the Cosmos: whirling heavens (top); the sun and moon (below); and the World Tree in the middle. The ship carries the dead.

trickster, as illustrated in one Navajo myth in which Coyote punished a giant that ate children. Under cover of darkness Coyote persuaded a child-eating giant that he could perform a miracle by breaking his own leg and mending it at once. Coyote pounded an unskinned leg of deer until it broke. The giant felt the broken leg and listened as Coyote spat on it and chanted: "Leg, become whole!". Coyote then presented his real leg to the giant, who was astonished that it was apparently restored. Coyote offered to repeat the "miracle" on the giant. He agreed and screamed in pain as Coyote smashed his leg with a rock.

CREATION

See panel on next page

CREATION

Usually in myth, creation is set in motion by some action which occurs either on its own by accident or as the deliberate intention of a creator divinity. In ancient Egypt, the first act of creation was said to have been the rising of a mound of land out of the primordial watery abyss called Nun. The primal watery landscape which is envisaged by the Cheyenne of North America was transformed when a humble watercoot brought up from the depths a beakful of mud which was then transformed into the first dry land by the great deity All-Spirit.

In all mythologies creation signifies, initially, the appearance of separation in place of oneness. Typically, this involves the simplest form of distinction: duality. In Chinese myth, the cosmic giant and divine ancestor Pan Gu (*see illustration on page 45*) grew for 18,000 years inside the cosmic egg (which was thought to embrace all potentiality in many creation myths), until it split into two parts, a light half (the heavens) and a dark half (the earth). In the creation myth of the Maori, the world began when the creator beings Rangi (the male sky) and Papa (the female earth) broke apart from their immobile embrace in the void.

In many traditions creation is the result of a death. In the Chinese account, Pan Gu, exhausted by the long labour of separating earth and heaven, lay down and died. The various parts of his body then became transformed into the features of the heavens and the landscape. In Saharan Africa the world is traditionally said to have been made from the segments of the sacrificed cosmic serpent Minia, which was God's first creation.

Some mythologies formalize the struggle between order and chaos in terms of a perpetual cycle in which worlds are eternally brought into being, destroyed and re-made. The Aztecs told of the successive creation and destruction of five worlds.

However, the most elaborate of all such cyclical schemes is probably that found in Hinduism. One version tells of how the great god Vishnu, resting on the coils of the cosmic serpent Ananta in the waters of chaos, sprouts a lotus from his navel which opens to reveal the creator god Brahma (*see illustration on page 38*). Then from Brahma's meditation the universe comes into being. It lasts for an immense period of time before it dissolves back into chaos, from which a new cosmos emerges in exactly the same way.

Crow and Crab *Australia*

Figures who showed humanity how to die, in the mythology of the Murinbata people of the northeastern Victoria River District. Crow and Crab argued over the best manner in which to die. Crab said that she knew a good way and went off to find a hole in the ground. She cast off her wrinkled old shell and waited in the hole while a new one formed. She returned to their camp with a new shell but Crow declared that he knew a quicker way to die. He promptly rolled back his eyes and fell over backwards. Crab tried to revive Crow with water but could not, because he was dead. According to the Murinbata, people chose to die in Crow's way.

Cú Chulainn *Celtic regions*
An Ulster warrior and the leading hero, Cú Chulainn was the son of Deichtine, the sister of King Conchobar of Ulster, and the warrior Sualtamh. However, he also had a divine father: the god Lugh, who appeared to Deichtine in a dream and announced that he would place in her womb a child named Sétanta. The newborn child had seven pupils in each eye, seven fingers on each hand and seven toes on each foot.

At the age of five, Sétanta went to Emhain Macha, the Ulster capital. When he was nearly seven, King Conchobar took him to a feast given by Culann the Smith, where he was attacked by the host's ferocious hound. Sétanta killed the animal but offered to act as Culann's watchdog until a new hound had been reared. The druid Cathbhadh gave him a new name: Cú Chulainn, "The Hound of Culann".

He was trained in the arts of war by Scáthach, a woman with supernatural powers, who gave him his deadliest weapon, the *gae bolga*, a savagely barbed spear which penetrated every part of the body.

Cú Chulainn was the leading hero in the war between the Men of Ulster and the Men of Ireland (that is, Connacht) recounted in the epic *Táin Bó Cuailnge* (the *Cattle Raid of Cooley*), and demonstrated his prowess and apparent invincibility many times, notably in single combat against his foster-brother Fer Diadh. On the fourth day of gruelling fighting, Cú Chulainn fell into one of his characteristic "fury-spasms" – a fit of uncontrollable rage that caused his body to seethe and swell up – and killed Fer Diadh with the *gae bolga*. On another occasion he saved Conchobar from an assault by Ferghus, Medhbh's chief warrior. Shortly after, the hero

defeated Medhbh, but spared her life because she was female.

Cú Chulainn's death was brought about by the children of Cailidín, a warrior slain by the hero in the war against Medhbh. After Cailidín's death, Medhbh sent his three daughters and three sons abroad to study sorcery. On their return they tracked Cú Chulainn down to the Valley of the Deaf, where Conchobar had ordered Cú Chulainn to remain under the protection of the princesses, noblewomen and druids of Ulster. Normally, no sound could penetrate the valley, but the war goddess Bodhbh conjured up a phantom army whose battle cries could be heard even in heaven, convincing Cú Chulainn that his enemies were plundering the land. He was lured into the open and killed by a magic javelin hurled by one of the sons of Cailidín. Three days later Bodhbh landed on Cú Chulainn's shoulder in the form of a crow, a sign that he was truly dead.

Cuichu *South America*
The Inca god of the rainbow, one of the attendants of Inti (the Sun) and Mama Kilya (the Moon).

CULTURE HERO
See panel on next page

Cupid *Rome*
The Roman god of love, the equivalent of the Greek Eros.

Cybele *Greece and Rome*
A great mother goddess originating in Phrygia in western Asia Minor (modern Turkey). The Greeks came to identify Cybele with the goddess Rhea, the mother of Zeus. She was worshipped in Rome under the name Magna Mater ("Great Mother").

Cú Chulainn with the raven on his shoulder, based on a bronze sculpture.

Cú Chulainn: *see*
Bodhbh; Conchobar; Ferghus; Lugh; Medhbh; *Táin Bó Cuailnge*

Cuichu: *see*
Inti; Mama Kilya

Cupid: *see*
Aphrodite; Eros

Cybele: *see*
Magna Mater; Rhea; Zeus

CULTURE HERO

All mythological traditions feature heroic figures, the roles of whom are to carry out extraordinary acts in the course of laying the foundations of humanity. Frequently, the "culture hero" is male and possesses supernatural or divine qualities. A typical story from Melanesia tells of one primordial culture hero variously known as Sida, Sido, Sosom or Souw, who journeyed through the communities of Papua New Guinea, shaping the landscape, teaching people how to speak, stocking the seas and rivers with fish and providing vegetables for cultivation. Similar stories are widespread in Aboriginal Australia.

Culture heroes are frequently said to be responsible for the discovery or institution of important social rules, such as those governing the hunting of animals and the distribution of food. The origins of religious rites and ceremonies are also attributed to figures such as the mysterious White Buffalo Woman, bringer of the sacred pipe rituals to the Lakota people of North America. The theft of fire by a culture hero is widely seen as a key event in the development of society. In Greek myth, for example, the Titan Prometheus stole fire from the gods for the benefit of humanity.

According to some of the tribal

An illustration based on a painted wooden mask of an ancient culture hero, thought to be Sida. The mask comes from the Torres Strait Islands, Australasia.

mythologies of South America, a young culture hero stole fire from the jaguar. In the Gilbert Islands of the western Pacific, the source of fire is the sun, which was snared by the culture hero Bue again to obtain fire for the human race.

In North America the culture heroes, like the early creator divinities, are quite often represented as animals. For example, along the northwestern coast the local culture hero is the Raven, who was made responsible for the discovery of fire, the tides, the alternation of night and day, and the positions of all the heavenly bodies in the sky. Like his counterparts in other areas of in North America, such as the culture heroes Coyote and Glooskap, Raven also displays many attributes of the trickster.

Culture heroes of the Celtic world take on a more human form than those of North America, and tend to be great fighters and conquerors. Examples are characters such as Cú Chulainn, a figure of incredible strength whose exploits can be found in the *Tàin Bò Cuailnge,* and the hero Finn, the central figure of the body of myths known as the Fenian cycle. Finn was renowned not only for his ability as a warrior but also as a great hunter, and for his supernatural gift of prophecy.

Cyclops *Greece*

"Round-eye", one of a race of monsters or giants often described as possessing a single, round eye in their foreheads. The first three Cyclopes, the sons of the goddess Gaia and the god Uranos, were called Brontes ("Thunder"), Steropes ("Lightning") and Arges ("Bright").

When the Titan Kronos came to power in the heavens, he imprisoned the Cyclopes in Tartaros, the darkest depths of the underworld. They were freed by Zeus, whom they supported in his war against the Titans. As a reward for their assistance, Zeus made the Cyclopes his blacksmiths, responsible for forging his thunderbolts. When Zeus killed Asklepios, demi-god of healing, with a thunderbolt, to assist Hades, god of the underworld, the Cyclopes were slaughtered by Apollo, Asklepios' father.

Another tradition made the Cyclopes the assistants of the craftsman god Hephaistos, the Roman Vulcan. In Homer, the Cyclopes were a tribe of brutal, man-eating shepherds who lived in caves on an island, often identified with Sicily. The most notorious of these Cyclopes was Polyphemus, who captured the hero Odysseus and his crew, but was then blinded by Odysseus during his successful attempt to escape.

Cyclops: *see*
Asklepios; Gaia; Hephaistos; Kronos; Odysseus; TITAN; Uranos; Zeus

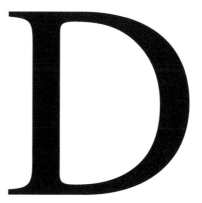

*Daedalus making the
wings for Icarus, from an
antique bas relief.*

Daedalus *Greece*

The greatest of mortal craftsmen. Daedalus was a member of the Athenian royal household, and became famous for his skill as an inventor, painter and sculptor. However, Daedalus fled to Crete after attempting to kill his nephew Perdix, a rival craftsman, out of jealousy at his invention of the saw. There he entered the service of King Minos. At the command of Pasiphaë, Minos' queen, he built a life-size, hollow model of a heifer in which she hid to have intercourse with a bull. As a result of this coupling, Pasiphaë bore the Minotaur, a savage beast that was half-man and half-bull. Minos angrily ordered Daedalus to construct the Labyrinth as a prison for the monstrous hybrid.

Later, Daedalus gave Ariadne, the king's daughter, a ball of twine so that the hero Theseus could negotiate the Labyrinth to slay the Minotaur. Minos was so enraged that he locked Daedalus in the Labyrinth with his young son, Icarus. To escape from Crete, Daed- alus made two pairs of wings from wax and feathers, warning Icarus not to fly too close to the sun, which would melt the wax. But Icarus forgot his father's warning and plummeted to his death into the sea below.

Daghdha, The *Celtic regions*

An Irish god of abundance, fertility, wisdom and magic. The Daghdha ("Good God") was the supreme tribal deity of the Tuatha Dé Danann, the fifth race of people to invade Ireland, and was also referred to as "Great Father" and "The Mighty One of Great Knowledge". The Daghdha's offspring included Oenghus, the god of love, and the goddess Brighid.

The Daghdha possessed a massive club, one end of which was lethal, while the other end brought the dead back to life, and a huge cauldron from which he dispensed never-ending sustenance.

Though revered, the Daghdha had a superhuman appetite which sometimes made him appear ridiculous or even grotesque. On one such occasion, the Fomorians made a vast "porridge" of milk, meal, fat, goats, sheep and pigs in his cauldron. The Daghdha consumed it all and fell fast asleep. He awoke to find a beautiful woman before him but he was unable to make love because his belly was too full.

Daitya *India*
One of a race of demons who were named after their mother, Diti, who was the daughter of Daksha and wife of Kashyapa, one of the Seven Sages. Most of the Daityas were killed in the course of the struggle between the Asuras (demons) and the Devas (gods) on the occasion of the churning of the ocean.

Daksha *India*
A creator deity of the early Vedic pantheon. Daksha ("Ritual skill") was often included among the so-called Seven Sages, who were born from the mind of the god Brahma and were called, like him, Prajapati ("Lord of Creatures"). He sprang from Brahma's right thumb.

Daksha was the father of many of the wives of the gods, such as Sati, the consort of Shiva. He held a horse sacrifice which was attended by all the gods except Shiva, who was forbidden a share in any sacrifice. Angry at his exclusion and goaded on by Sati, Shiva attacked the ceremony and sent Disease to plague the earth. In an alternative account, the sacrifice ended in a great brawl, during which Shiva ripped off Daksha's head and hurled it onto the sacrificial fire. When he had calmed down, Shiva replaced Daksha's head with that of a goat.

Danaë *Greece*
A princess, the mother and mortal lover of the hero Perseus.

Danaïd *Greece*
One of the fifty daughters of Danaus, a king of Argos and descendant of Zeus, and his lover Io. The Danaïds were forced into marriage by their fifty cousins, the sons of Aegyptus, the king of Egypt. On their wedding night, forty-nine of the Danaïds stabbed their husbands to death with daggers received from their father. However, one of the daughters, known as Hypermnestra, genuinely loved her husband, Lynceus, and refused to murder him. The forty-nine murdresses were punished in the underworld by eternally trying to fill a water jar with a sieve.

Danu *Celtic regions*
An Irish mother goddess, about whom little is known except that she was the ancestor of the race known as the Tuatha Dé Danann ("People of Danu").

Dao De Jing *China*
The central scripture of Taoism (Daoism). The *Dao De Jing* (which means "The Classic of the Way and its Power") was attributed to Laozi, the legendary founder of Taoist philosophy, but may have been anonymous.

Dasharatha *India*
A king of the holy city of Ayodhya and father of Rama, the seventh avatar (incarnation) of the god Vishnu.

Dazhbog *Slav regions*
The ancient sun god of the Slavs. Dazhbog ("Giving God") was the son of the supreme elemental deity Svarog and the brother of the fire god Svarozhich. He was often said to live in a celestial eastern land of never-ending light and bounty, from which he rode forth each morning in a chariot drawn by white horses. In some Slavic areas, Dazhbog's consort was said to be the Moon. According to one tradition, Dazhbog was the ancestor of the Russians, the easternmost of the Slav peoples.

The god Daksha, with the fierce aspect of Shiva (Bhairava) seated on his body, from an 18th-century painting.

DEATH, THE ORIGIN OF

After the world has been created it is seen in all mythologies as subject to arbitrary changes. Among the most important of these is the arrival of death to end humanity's original state of immortality. Death's origin is often ascribed to the rivalry between human beings and divinities. In Greek mythology, for example, the gods send the first woman, Pandora, with a "box" (in fact a jar) containing death and disease as a punishment for Prometheus' defiance of Zeus in assuming the protectorship of mankind. As in the story of Pandora, the arrival of death and misfortune is commonly linked with a woman: other examples are the Maori myth of Hine-titama and the story of Abuk told by the Dinka people of the Sudan.

The loss of immortality through a severing of contact with heaven is a common theme in African myth. According to the Luba people of Zaïre, in the beginning humans and the High God lived in the same village. One day,

tiring of their noisy quarrels, the High God expelled his human neighbours to earth, where they encountered death and sickness for the first time.

In Oceania it is widely believed that mortality arrived (or was confirmed) as a result of the sexual shaming of the culture hero. The Daribi of southern Papua relate how a young woman encountered the penis of the hero Souw. It tried to rape her, but she cried out and it withdrew. Humiliated, Souw visited death on humanity. In Polynesia, it is said that humans have been unable to achieve immortality since the hero Maui was killed as he tried to force himself into the goddess of death.

The ecological necessity of death is conveyed in a myth of the Shoshoni people of North America. One day, Wolf and Coyote were discussing death. Wolf said that people could be revived after death, but Coyote argued that if that happened there would soon be no room on earth.

DEATH, THE ORIGIN OF

See panel above

Deianeira Greece

A princess, the daughter of King Oenus and Queen Althaea of Aetolia and the second wife of the hero Herakles.

Deirdre Celtic regions

The daughter of Fedlimid, the bard of King Conchobar of Ulster. When Deirdre (or Deirdriu) was a baby, the druid Cathbhadh prophesied that she would be very beautiful but would bring death and ruin to Ulster. Conchobar had Deirdre fostered in secret, intending to

marry her when she came of age. But as a young woman she fell in love with Naoise, son of Uisneach, with whom she eloped to the wilds of Scotland.

Conchobar invited the couple to return, guaranteeing their safety by sending the great warrior Ferghus to escort them. But when they arrived at Emhain Macha, Conchobar's capital, the king had Naoise put to death by the warrior Eoghan and Deirdre brought before him with her hands bound. Enraged at this display of treachery, Ferghus and his followers ravaged Ulster and transferred their allegiance to Conchobar's enemy, Queen Medhbh of

Connacht. The second part of the druid's prophecy was fulfilled in the ensuing war between Ulster and Connacht.

For a year Deirdre did not smile or raise her head from her knee. Her foster-father asked her whom she hated most, she replied "Eoghan". Conchobar told her that she must live with Eoghan and the next day the two men took her off in a chariot. As the vehicle approached a rock, Deirdre threw herself from the chariot and killed herself.

Demeter *Greece*

A goddess of fertility, the daughter of the Titans Kronos and Rhea and sister of the gods Hades, Hera, Hestia, Poseidon and Zeus. Demeter ("Mother Earth" or "Grain Mother") was believed to protect crops and the bounty of the soil. Her cults also concern female fruitfulness.

The most important myths about Demeter centre on the abduction of her daughter Persephone by Hades, ruler of the underworld. Enraged and grief-stricken, Demeter left Mount Olympus, the home of the gods, and wandered the world disguised as an old woman.

Eventually Demeter came to Eleusis in Attica, where King Celeus hired her as an attendant for his wife, Queen Metaneira. She asked Demeter to nurse her child, whose name was Demophöon. The goddess surreptitiously fed him on ambrosia, the food of the gods, and each

Demeter with her sheaves of corn, based on a terracotta sculpture.

night laid him on a fire to make him immortal. But one night Metaneira interrupted her and screamed in horror at the sight of her child in the flames. Demeter hastily withdrew him and revealed her identity, telling Metaneira that Demophöon would now die like any other mortal. The goddess ordered the establishment of the Eleusinian Mysteries – the most famous mystery cult in the ancient Greek world – in her own honour, and then left her hosts.

Demeter's grief for Persephone returned and she withheld the grain from the earth, threatening to starve humanity unless she saw her daughter again. Zeus sent the god Hermes to bring Persephone back from the underworld. Demeter was delighted to receive her daughter back, but warned that if she had eaten the food of the dead she would have to return to Hades forever. In the underworld Persephone had eaten some pomegranate seeds, but Zeus declared that she could spend two-thirds of the year with Demeter and the remaining third, the winter, with Hades. Mother and daughter rejoiced at this and fruitfulness returned to the land. Before returning to Olympus, Demeter gave seeds, a plough and her dragon-drawn chariot to Celeus' son, Triptolemus, to take the arts of agriculture to all peoples.

Deucalion *Greece*

The son of the Titan Prometheus and his human wife (who is also known in some accounts as Pronoia). As a punishment for the misdeeds of the hero Prometheus in promoting humanity, the great god Zeus decided to destroy the human race by drowning them with a great flood. But Prometheus forewarned Deucalion and his wife Pyrrha, and they built an ark to survive the deluge.

After the waters sent by Zeus had

Demeter: *see*
Hades; Hermes;
OLYMPIANS, THE;
Persephone

Deucalion: *see*
FLOOD MYTHS; Gaia;
Prometheus; Themis; TITAN;
Zeus

Devi: *see*
Durga; Kali; Krishna; Vishnu

Di Jun: *see*
Yi the Archer

Dian Cécht: *see*
Invasions, The *Book of;*
Tuatha Dé Danann

Diana: *see*
Artemis; GREEK AND
ROMAN DEITIES

Diarmaid: *see*
Finn; Oenghus

Dido: *see*
Aeneas; *Aeneid,* The

*The Roman goddess
Diana, based on a life-
size marble statue.*

subsided, Deucalion and Pyrrha went to Delphi to offer thanks to the Titan Themis, who in some accounts was the mother of Prometheus and Epimetheus. Once there Themis told them to throw over their shoulders the bones of the being from whom they were both descended. Bewildered at first, the couple soon realized that Themis was referring to Gaia, the earth, whose bones were the stones in the ground. Each stone thrown by Deucalion turned into a man and each stone thrown by Pyrrha became a woman. in this way the human race was recreated.

Devi *India*
"The Goddess", the name under which the female divinities of the Hindu pantheon are often collectively grouped as different aspects of a single deity. Devi, also known as Mahadevi ("Great Goddess"), is frequently regarded as a major deity on a par with Vishnu and Shiva. In this case she is either linked with Parvati, who was the wife of Shiva, and therefore benign, or is completely independent, in which case her more fearsome aspects, such as Durga and Kali, tend to predominate.

Di Jun *China*
The Lord of Heaven, the supreme sky deity of early Chinese mythology.

Dian Cécht *Celtic regions*
An Irish deity of healing. In the *Book of Invasions,* Nuadhu, king of the Tuatha Dé Danann, lost his right arm at the first battle of Magh Tuiredh and had to renounce the kingship, because the ruler had to be unblemished. However, Dian Cécht fashioned Nuadhu a new arm of silver, enabling him to resume his rule. After the second battle, Dian Cécht sang spells at the head of a well, bestowing

upon its waters the power to heal mortally wounded warriors.

Diana *Rome*
The goddess of hunting and protector of women and animals, who was identified with the Greek goddess Artemis.

Diarmaid *Celtic regions*
An Irish warrior, and companion of the hero Finn. Diarmaid, a young handsome hero, features principally in myth as the lover of Gráinne, the beautiful daughter of the warrior Cormac. Gráinne had reluctantly agreed to marry the ageing Finn, but, at the wedding feast, fell in love with Diarmaid and bound him to her with a magic spell. The couple eloped, and when Finn and his men pursued them they were spirited to safety by Oenghus, the god of love.

Diarmaid and Gráinne wandered through Connacht and Ulster and in due course became true lovers. After seven years Finn pardoned them, and some time later he invited Diarmaid to join a hunt for the magic boar of Beann Ghulbhan (Ben Bulben) in Sligo. This boar had once been Diarmaid's foster-brother, who, it was prophesied, would bring about Diarmaid's death. During the chase, Diarmaid was mortally wounded by the boar and his only chance of life was to receive a draught of water from the hands of Finn. Twice Finn came with water, but each time he remembered Gráinne and let the water trickle away. Diarmaid died and his body was taken by Oenghus to Brugh na Bóinne (ancient burial grounds of Newgrange in Meath).

Dido *Rome*
The queen of Carthage and, according to Virgil's *Aeneid,* the lover of the hero Aeneas. Dido (also known as Elissa)

Dido and Aeneas embracing, from a floor mosaic.

was born at Tyre in Phoenicia (modern Lebanon), the daughter of the local king, Mutto (or Belus in Virgil). She was forced to leave her homeland after the murder of her husband and flee with her sister Anna to North Africa, where she founded a new city, Carthage (in modern Tunisia).

Carthage was nearing completion when the Trojan hero Aeneas and his companions were washed ashore. Dido and Aeneas fell in love. One day, on a hunting trip, they sheltered in a cave from a storm and consummated their love. They lived as man and wife, and Aeneas behaved as if he were king of Carthage. Eventually, however, the gods

reminded him of his duty to found a new Troy in Italy. He left, despite Dido's accusations of treachery. In despair, she stabbed herself with his sword. Later, on his visit to the underworld, Aeneas encountered Dido's shade, but she would not speak to him and slunk off to join her husband, Sychaeus.

Diomedes (1) *Greece and Rome*
A hero of Argos and a leading Greek warrior of the Trojan War. At Troy, Diomedes drove the war god Ares from the battlefield and wounded the goddess Aphrodite with his spear. He came face to face with Glaucus, the leader of Troy's Lycian allies, who was an old friend. They refused to fight, and exchanged armour as a sign of courtesy. Diomedes benefited from the exchange: his armour was of bronze, while that of Glaucus was of gold.

Diomedes was protected by the goddess Athene, who acknowledged that he, unlike many Greek warriors, returned home from Troy swiftly and safely. However, Aphrodite forced him to flee Argos and (in Roman myth) he ended his days in Italy.

Diomedes (2) *Greece*
A king of the Bitones, who were a people of Thrace. Diomedes kept a herd of vicious mares, nourished on human flesh. As the eighth of his twelve labours, the hero Herakles killed Diomedes and fed him to the horses, which he then tamed and led away.

Dionysos *Greece*
Dionysos (known to the Romans as Bacchus) presided over all altered states, such as drunkenness, religious ecstasy and acting. He often appeared disguised as an animal (usually a bull or lion) or a human (male or female).

Diomedes (1): *see*
Aphrodite; Ares; Athene; TROJAN WAR, THE HEROES OF THE

Diomedes (2): *see*
HERAKLES, THE LABOURS OF

Dionysos: *see*
Ariadne; Hera; Pentheus; Persephone; Satyr; Semele; ZEUS, THE CONSORTS OF

Dioscuri, The

Dionysos in a boat with dolphins (the transformed pirates) swimming in the sea.

Alone of the gods on Olympus, Dionysos was of partly mortal parentage. In one account, Zeus and Persephone had a child, Zagreus (an alternative for Dionysos), who, at the prompting of Zeus's jealous wife Hera, was devoured by the Titans. But the baby's heart was saved by Athene and swallowed by Zeus's mortal lover Semele, who conceived Zagreus anew. On her death, Zeus stitched the unborn child into his own thigh and it was born again.

Dionysos was above all the god of wine, which the ancient Greeks revered as a sacred drink. He was the focus of a great mystic cult, whose initiates pursued an ecstatic release brought on by wine, music and dance. The god's mythical male followers, the satyrs, were devoted to wine, revelry and lust. His female followers were called Bacchants or maenads ("mad women"). At Athens two annual festivals were held in honour of Dionysos.

Many of the myths about Dionysos depict him as a newcomer (or "from the east") who travelled among human society establishing his cult, bringing gifts and punishing those who did not accept him, such as Pentheus.

Dionysos was once captured by pirates. They tried to bind him, but the knots untied of their own accord. Still they refused to release him, so the god amazed them with a series of wonders: wine flowed around the ship, vines and ivy grew over the vessel and, finally, Dionysos turned himself into a lion. The pirates leapt into the sea in terror and were turned into dolphins.

Dioscuri, The *Greece and Rome*

"The Sons of Zeus", in Greek *Dios kouroi*, the name given to the heroic brothers Castor and Polydeuces (Pollux to the Romans). The Dioscuri were the semi-divine offspring of Zeus and Leda, queen of Sparta, with whom Zeus had intercourse in the form of a swan. Leda subsequently produced two eggs: from one came Castor and Clytemnestra and from the other Polydeuces and Helen. Some say that Castor and Clytemnestra were the children of Tyndareos, Leda's husband, and entirely mortal.

The Dioscuri were rarely separated in their adventures. Castor gained renown as an expert horseman and Polydeuces became the best boxer in Greece. They journeyed with Jason on the quest for the Golden Fleece and in some sources also took part in Meleager's boar hunt.

The Dioscuri argued with their cousins Idas and Lynceus over the division of the spoils from a cattle raid. Idas mortally wounded Castor with his spear and then speared Lynceus. Zeus, angry at the death of Castor, killed Idas.

Dis Pater *Rome*

The Roman god of the dead and the underworld, identified with the Greek Hades. Meaning "Wealthy Father", Dis

Pater is a translation of the Greek Pluto, an alternative name for Hades. The Celts appear to have adopted this god from Roman myth as an ancestral deity and lord of the dead.

Djunggun *Australia*
A figure in an important Aboriginal myth of the western Kimberley region which explains the origin of non-incestuous marriage. In early times, it is said, incest was commonplace. But two men, Djunggun and Wodoy, married each other's daughters, then Djunggun decided to keep his daughter for himself, so Wodoy knocked his head off with a stick. After that there were no incestuous marriages. Djunggun and Wodoy were turned into birds, each becoming a species of nightjar.

Domovoi *Slav regions*
"House Spirit", a being said to inhabit the homestead. The *domovoi* was usually invisible but those who claimed to have seen him often described him as a hairy old man with a grey beard. He was active at night and families avoided sleeping in his path, leaving food out for him. If they neglected such tasks, he might smash crockery or torment their animals. Domestic prosperity relied upon the *domovoi*'s happiness. In order to ensure this and as a courtesy, new farm animals were introduced to him. If a family moved home the *domovoi* went too, often enticed with coals from the hearth of the old homestead.

Dôn *Celtic regions*
A Welsh ancestral goddess, also known as "Mother of the Gods". Dôn, who is probably related to the Irish Danu, was the sister of Math, the protagonist of the fourth part of the *Mabinogion*. This part is dominated by the actions of Dôn's

family, particularly the doings of her offspring, which included Arianrhod, Gilfaethwy and Gwydion.

Donar *Germanic regions*
The ancient Germanic god of the sky and thunder. Known as Thunor to the Anglo-Saxons, he was related to the later Scandinavian deity Thor.

Donn *Celtic regions*
"The Dark One", the Irish god of the dead. Donn was the ancestral deity of the Gaels, Sons of Míl, the last race to invade Ireland in the *Book of Invasions*. Donn arrived with his people in the southwest of Ireland on the feast of Beltane (1 May) and led them to victory against the Tuatha Dé Danann. But he insulted the earth goddess Ériu and was drowned in the sea as a punishment. Near the supposed spot is the island of Tech nDuinn ("House of Donn"), where Donn resided as lord of the dead. It was here that the dead were said to embark on their journey to the otherworld.

DRAGON
See panel on next page

Draupnir *Germanic regions*
The magic golden ring of the god Odin. Draupnir was forged by dwarfs in order to ensure that the gods had a constant supply of gold. It was said that eight further rings dropped from Draupnir every nine nights.

Dreamtime *Australia*
The primordial creation epoch, a central feature of Aboriginal myth, which was the period in which ancestral beings traversed the Australian continent. They shaped the landscape, determined the form of society and deposited the spirits of unborn children as they went.

Domovoi:: see
Dvorovoi

Dôn: *see*
Danu; Gwydion; *Mabinogion,*
The

Donar: *see*
Thor

Donn: *see*
Invasions, The *Book of;*
Tuatha Dé Danann, The

Draupnir: *see*
Odin; Thor

A depiction of dream-time figures, based on an Aboriginal painting.

DRAGON

The dragon is probably the most universal of all mythical creatures. It is most frequently described as a great flying reptile, a ferocious and untamed (but not necessarily evil) beast which embodies in many cultures the elemental forces of chaos and cosmic order. Many peoples believe that a rainbow is a giant dragon or serpent which encircles the earth, driving away storms and protecting the world from the disorder that lies beyond.

In the West the dragon symbolized the four elements of nature (earth, air, fire and water): it lived in the depths of earth or water, flew through the air and often breathed flame. In the East, it was believed that the dragon's energy bound all the phenomena of nature, bringing benevolent rains but also cataclysmic typhoons.

As the inhabitants of gloomy underground or submarine regions,

The Chinese dragon – a beneficent bringer of rain in early Chinese myth.

dragons are often associated with dark forces. For example, eastern Native American myths tell of great horned dragons, usually malign divinities that live underwater and cause drownings. In many traditions they are linked with the earth-dwelling serpent, a form often seen representing evil. Christian legend pits dragons, which were symbols of the devil, against saints, such as St George or St Michael.

Dragons are frequently depicted in myth as monstrous coveters of treasure and virgins. They are often found presented in combat against great mythical heroes, such as Herakles, Sigurd and Yamato-takeru. The dragon was also known as the guardian of kings. For example, a red dragon was the emblem of King Arthur.

Dreamtime is also a state of being, accessible to participants in ritual. These participants are believed briefly to become the ancestors whose journeys are recreated or whose power is released by striking some sacred site with which the ancestral beings are associated.

Dumuzi *Middle East*

A Mesopotamian god of growth and fertility, also known by the Hebrew name of Tammuz. He has also been identified with the Greek god Adonis.

Although not one of the great gods, Dumuzi was held in high regard in popular religion and his cult was widespread. The divine embodiment of vegetation and the creative forces of spring, Dumuzi spent part of the year, the season of least growth, in the underworld. He is often presented as consort to Inanna (Ishtar).

Durga *India*

A warrior aspect of Devi. Durga is said to be unapproachable by suitors (the name means "Hard to approach") and invincible in battle. Her main role is to combat demons. Sometimes Durga arises from Vishnu as the power of sleep or as the god's creative power; or she emerges from the goddess Parvati, Shiva's consort, when Parvati becomes angry. At other times the male gods pool their attributes to form Durga as a champion against a demon. In one myth, the gods were subdued by the demons led by Mahisha ("Buffalo"). This made Vishnu and Shiva so angry that their wrath coalesced with the energy of the

The Hindu Durga, based on a statuette.

other gods to form a goddess, Durga, riding a lion. The demons attacked Durga, who killed them with her club, noose, sword and trident. Mahisha, in buffalo form, terrorized her troops and then attacked her lion. Durga, furious, caught him in her noose, whereupon he became a lion himself. She cut off its head and Mahisha emerged as a man, sword in hand. Durga pierced the man and he became an elephant. She cut off its trunk and he became a buffalo. Finally, tossing aside the mountains he hurled at her, Durga leaped onto Mahisha, piercing him with her trident. As he tried to struggle free she decapitated him with her sword.

Dvorovoi *Slav regions*

A "Yard Spirit" of Slav folk mythology. The *dvorovoi*'s activities were confined to the farmyard. In all else he resembled the household spirit, the *domovoi*.

Dxui *Africa*

The creator being of the San ("Bushmen") of southwest Africa. One version of the myth tells of how, on the first and second days of creation, when the sun rose, Dxui was a flower and at night, a man. On the third day he was a tree with fruit; at sunset a man again. Next he became a tree bearing fruit, but covered in thorns. When the first woman appeared she tried to take the fruit. The tree vanished, and weeping, the woman lay down and died.

In turn, Dxui became a fly, water, a flower, a bird, and then the snarer and eater of the bird. Soon he became a man again but other men hunted him. He became a great bird and flew to his parents. When his father recognized him, Dxui became a man. Finally, when he died, Dxui became a lizard, said to be the oldest creature of all.

Durga: *see*
Devi; Klai; Shiva; Vishnu

***Dvorovoi*:**: *see*
Domovoi

Ea *Middle East*

The Babylonian (Akkadian) god of wisdom and the waters, equivalent to the Sumerian god Enki. In the Akkadian creation myth, originally Apsu, the sweet-water ocean, and Tiamat, the salt-water ocean, coupled to produce a succession of deities culminating in the great gods known as Anu and Ea. Ea then produced Marduk and killed Apsu in a struggle for supremacy that eventually saw the emergence of Marduk as the greatest of the gods.

Ea (on the left), from the seal of an Akkadian cylinder.

Ea features in myths dealing with death and immortality, such as the story of Adapa and Anu. The Akkadian version of the Mesopotamian flood myth (as told in the epic of the hero Gilgamesh), recounts how the god Enlil sent a flood to destroy humanity. But Ea spared one man, Utnapishtim, and his family, and persuaded Enlil not to destroy all humans but only to punish them when necessary.

Eaglehawk and Crow *Australia*

The two men who were said to be the originators of marriage, according to the Aboriginal mythology of southeast Australia. Eaglehawk (who was also called Biljara) and Crow (or Wagu) are said to have instituted marriage by specifying degrees of kinship within which marriage was permissible.

The two men appear as rivals in tales in which Crow often tries to outwit or trick Eaglehawk. For example, in one story, Eaglehawk burned Crow black and turned him into the bird whose name he bears. Eaglehawk became a bird himself when Crow tricked him into soaring into the sky.

Earth Diver, The *North America*
The name given to the creature which goes to the bottom of the primeval ocean to retrieve mud from which the first land is formed. According to the Cheyenne, the supreme being Maheo ("All-Spirit") created the Great Water together with all the creatures of the water. The water birds soon grew tired of flying and took turns to dive to look for land. Finally the coot returned with a little ball of mud, which he dropped into Maheo's hand. As Maheo rolled the mud in his hand it expanded until only old Grandmother Turtle could carry it. The mud continued to grow on her back: in this way the first land was created.

Ebisu *Japan*
The god of work, who may once have been a deity of fishermen: he is usually shown with fishing line and a fish.

Echidne *Greece*
The offspring of the earth goddess Gaia and her brother Tartarus, god of underworld darkness. Echidne had the upper body of a nymph and the lower body of a repulsive serpent. She lived in a cave and coupled with another monster, Typhon, to produce some of the most famous monsters of Greek myth: the Nemean Lion, the Hydra, Cerberus and the Chimera. Echidne was also sometimes said to be the mother of Orthus, Ladon and the Theban Sphinx.

Echo *Greece*
A nymph of Mount Helicon in Boeotia. Her constant chatter distracted the goddess Hera from catching her husband, Zeus, in an act of infidelity. Hera punished Echo by cursing her to speak only the last words addressed to her. The nymph fell in love with the youth Narcissus, but Hera's curse

frustrated all her efforts at conversation and Echo pined away until only her voice remained. Before her death she cursed Narcissus to fall in love with his own reflection.

According to another myth it was Pan, the god of woods and pastures, who cursed Echo after she had rebuffed his advances. Eventually the nymph's habit of repetition annoyed some shepherds so much that they tore her to pieces, leaving only her voice to reverberate around the mountains.

Ehecatl *Central America*
The Aztec god of wind. Ehecatl, who was a manifestation of the great god Quetzalcoatl, was an important creator deity who assisted in the establishment of the present world order. In the myth of the Five Suns, the Aztec creation myth, the gods gathered at Teotihuacan after the destruction of the fourth sun. Nanahuatzin and Tecciztecatl jumped into a sacrificial fire and became respectively the fifth sun and the moon. However, they were motionless until Ehecatl blew upon them fiercely. At first only the sun rose from the fire into the heavens, but as the sun set then the moon rose also.

Eight Immortals, The *China*
The central figures of Taoist (Daoist) mythology. Of fairly recent origin, the accounts of how each gained his or her immortality date from only the 15th century. However, some of their names are mentioned in earlier sources. The eight, in the order in which they attained immortality, are: Li Xuan, Lü Dongbin, Han Zhongli, Han Xiang, Cao Guojiu, Zhang Guo, Lan Caihe and He Xiangu.

The most famous myth in which the Immortals appear together concerns a voyage to view the undersea world.

A turtle, from a Cheyenne shield, carrying the earth on her back, as in the Earth Diver creation myth.

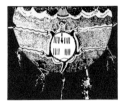

Two of the Eight Immortals: Zhang Guo (on the left) and Han Xiang (on the right), from a woodcut.

Instead of travelling on clouds, their usual method, they demonstrated their magical powers by throwing the objects which they carried into the sea and using them as boats or rafts. During the journey the son of the Dragon King of the Eastern Sea stole Lan Caihe's musical instrument and took him prisoner. He was freed after a fierce battle in which the other Immortals defeated the Dragon King.

Eileithyia *Greece*

The goddess of childbirth, the offspring of the god Zeus and the goddess Hera. Eileithyia (which can also be spelled Ilithyia), determined the duration of a mothers' labour pains and the precise moment of birth. Hera sometimes commanded her to stay away from the births of Zeus's numerous illegitimate offspring, in order to prolong the mothers' agonies. For example, after Zeus made the Titan Leto pregnant with the divine twins Artemis and Apollo, the jealous Hera forced her to wander the world to look for a place to give birth. But wherever she went people were too afraid of Hera to take her in. However, the people of Ortygia (later called Delos) agreed to allow Leto to give birth

El on his throne, from a Ugaritic stele.

on their island. Hera forbade Eileithyia to attend, but the other goddesses sent Iris ("Rainbow"), a divine messenger, to fetch her from Mount Olympus.

El *Middle East*

The supreme god of the Ugaritic (Canaanite) pantheon. Although El is a less active deity than, for example, Baal, he is the highest authority in all mortal and divine matters. He is a creator deity who is described in Ugaritic texts as "the father of gods and men". According to one myth, El had intercourse with two women who probably represent the fertility goddesses Ashera and Anath. They gave birth first to the divinities Shachar (meaning "Dawn") and Shalim (which means "Dusk"), then to the remainder of the Ugaritic pantheon.

The name El is related to the Arabic Allah (meaning "God").

El Dorado *South America*

A mythical land or city of fantastic wealth which was believed by early European explorers and settlers to exist somewhere in the South American interior. El Dorado is Spanish for "The Gilded Man" and once referred to the king of the fabulous land, who was said to possess so much gold that his body was powdered every day with gold dust.

The myth of El Dorado derived from 16th-century eyewitness reports of Amerindian inauguration rites in the highlands of Colombia: the body of the Muisca's new king was smeared from head to foot in resin which was then covered with a fine layer of gold dust.

Elegba *Africa*

The name given by the peoples of Benin to the widespread west African trickster figure known to the Yoruba tribes as the trickster Eshu.

Elysium *Greece*
A paradise to which the great and virtuous went after death. According to earlier Greek mythology, Elysium (also called the Elysian Fields or the Islands of the Blessed) lay beyond the great river Ocean that was believed to encircle the earth. Later, as the Greeks' geographical knowledge increased, a new tradition arose which located the lands of the dead in an underworld in the centre of the earth. In some accounts, the Elysian dead could choose at any time to be reborn on earth: if they attained Elysium three times they won the right to live in the Islands of the Blessed, which were sometimes regarded as a separate, even greater paradise. It was occasionally said that the Titan Kronos governed Elysium after he was overthrown as leader of the gods by his son Zeus.

Emituofo *China*
The Buddhist Chinese name for the Bodhisattva Amitabha.

Emma-ho *Japan*
The ruler of Jigoku, the name given to the Japanese equivalent of hell. When male transgressors descend to Jigoku they are brought to Emma-ho to be judged (his sister passes judgment on female sinners). Before Emma-ho and his court of demons, sinners face a huge mirror in which their misdeeds on earth are reflected. Depending on the category of transgression, the sinner's soul is condemned to one of the sixteen regions of punishment – there are eight zones of ice and eight of flame – which make up Emma-ho's underworld realm.

Enki *Middle East*
The Sumerian god of wisdom and the waters, the equivalent of the Akkadian Ea. Like the other "great gods" Enki was the offspring of the earth goddess Ki and the sky god An. His abode was said to be the subterranean sweet-water ocean, Apsu. Enki was important as the keeper of the *me*, the heavenly decrees which were the foundation of religion and society. To possess the *me* meant to hold supreme power and they were much coveted, for example by Inanna (the Akkadian Ishtar), the goddess of love and war, who travelled from her own city, Erech, to visit Enki. She was welcomed with a great feast at which the god got very drunk and, in his inebrated state gave her the *me*. Enki later tried to retrieve them but failed. This story served to explain how both Erech and Inanna achieved dominant status among the ancient Sumerians.

Enki (or Ea) often appears as the protector of humanity, for example, in the Mesopotamian flood myths.

Enkidu *Middle East*
A hunter and warrior, the companion of the hero Gilgamesh.

Enkimdu *Middle East*
A farmer who appears in one Sumerian myth as suitor of the fertility goddess Inanna (the Akkadian Ishtar). When the goddess decided to marry, Enkimdu and Dumuzi, a shepherd, both sought her hand. Her brother, the sun god Utu, advised her to take Dumuzi, whose animals were the source of more valuable produce than that grown by Enkimdu. The two suitors argued but Enkimdu soon conceded defeat.

Enlil *Middle East*
The national god of the Sumerians and the greatest of the "great gods", the offspring of the earth goddess Ki and the sky god Anu. Enlil was the source of the

Elysium: *see*
Hades; UNDERWORLDS

Emituofo: *see*
Amitabha

Emma-ho: *see*
UNDERWORLDS

Enki: *see*
Anu (1); Atrahasis; Ea; Enlil; Ishtar; Ki; Utnapishtim; Ziusudra

Enkidu: *see*
Gilgamesh

Enkimdu: *see*
Dumuzi; Ishtar

Enlil: *see*
Anu (1); Atrahasis; Enki; Gilgamesh; Ki; Utnapishtim; Ziusudra

ordered cosmos and was responsible for all plant life, cattle, farming tools and the skills of civilization. He lived on a great mountain. It was from this mountain that when angry, he would send storms, floods, famine or pestilence to enforce his will. The god played a crucial role in most versions of the Mesopotamian flood myth, in which he took the initial decision to destroy the human race. However, Enlil was eventually persuaded by Enki, his brother, that humanity should not be wiped out entirely but simply punished when necessary.

Ennead, The *Egypt*

The collective name given to the great deities otherwise known as the Nine Gods of Heliopolis, who feature in the fullest ancient Egyptian account of the creation of the world. The first of the Ennead (from the Greek *ennea*, nine) was the sun god Atum or Ra-Atum, who came into existence on the mound that rose from the Nun, the dark primordial waters. He planned all creation and then put his semen into his mouth, spitting (or sneezing) it out to produce the next two of the Ennead, Shu, the god of air, and Tefenet, the goddess of wetness.

This was the first division into male and female. Shu and Tefenet went to explore the Nun, and Atum, fearing them lost, sent his Eye (a powerful divine force thought to be his daughter) to find them. When the Eye returned with his children, the god wept tears of joy which became the first humans.

Shu and Tefenet had intercourse and produced the next two deities of the Ennead, the earth god Geb and the sky goddess Nut. Geb and Nut also had intercourse but embraced so tightly that their children could not be born until they were separated by their father, Shu.

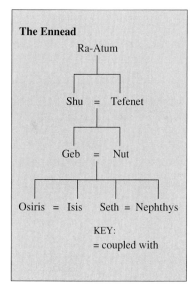

The Ennead

Ra-Atum

Shu = Tefenet

Geb = Nut

Osiris = Isis   Seth = Nephthys

KEY:
= coupled with

The air god supported Nut above the earth with the assistance of eight beings known as the Heh gods, thereby making room for living creatures and giving them air to breathe. Nut eventually gave birth to two sets of divine twins; Osiris and Isis, and Seth and Nephthys. Osiris, who was the eldest child, became the first ruler of Egypt.

Eochaidh mac Eirc *Celtic regions*

The ninth and last king of the Fir Bholg, the fourth race of people to rule Ireland. According to the *Book of Invasions,* Eochaidh was a model ruler, during whose reign there was no rain but only dew, and no year without harvest. Deceit was banished and Eochaidh was the first to establish the rule of justice in Ireland. He was killed on the occasion of the first battle of Magh Tuiredh against the victorious Tuatha Dé Danann, the fifth race of invaders of Ireland. Eochaidh left the field to find water and was set upon by three invaders: all four men died in the fight.

Eos, the goddess of the dawn, shown here in her chariot.

Eos *Greece*
The goddess of the dawn, daughter of the Titans Hyperion and Theia, and sister of the sun god Helios and the moon goddess Selene. In her chariot, Eos (the Roman Aurora) rode before Helios on his daily journey across the sky, announcing his coming in the east in the morning and his arrival in the west each evening.

Epimetheus *Greece*
A Titan, the son of Iapetus and the Oceanid Clymene, and the brother of Prometheus, Atlas and Menoetius. Epimetheus (meaning "Afterthought" or "Hindsight") was hasty and naïve, unlike his brother Prometheus (meaning "Forethought"). The Olympian gods and goddesses sought to punish mankind for Prometheus' protection. Prometheus warned his brother not to accept any gift from the Olympians, but Epimetheus ignored this advice when they sent him the first woman, Pandora, as a wife. She came bearing a sealed jar ("Pandora's Box"), which she opened, releasing its contents (evils and sickness) into the world. The only thing to remain in the jar was hope.

Epona *Celtic regions*
The goddess of the horse, worshipped all over the ancient Celtic world. She was particularly revered by Gaulish members of the Roman cavalry. She was the only Gaulish deity to have Rome grant her the honour of a Roman festival. It was held on 18 December.

Epona was also associated with water, fertility and death, which suggests a possible connection with Celtic earth mother goddesses.

Erebos *Greece*
Meaning "Underworld Darkness", Erebos was one of the primal deities that arose out of Chaos in the very first stages of creation, according to Hesiod's *Theogony*. Erebos coupled with Nyx ("Night") to produce Aither ("Ether", the bright upper air), Hemera ("Day") and, in some accounts, Charon, boatman of the underworld.

Ericthonius *Greece*
A king of Athens, the son of the god Hephaistos and the goddess Gaia, the earth. Hephaistos tried to rape the goddess Athene but she fought him off and he ejaculated on her thigh. She wiped off his semen with a pad of wool and hurled it in disgust onto the ground, thereby impregnating Gaia. Ericthonius (meaning "Born of the Soil") arose from the spot where it landed. He became king of Athens and began the Great Panathenaia, the city's most important annual festival, in honour of Athene.

Erinyes, The *Greece*
The Greek name for the Furies.

Eros *Greece*
Meaning "Desire", Eros was the god of love. To Hesiod, he was a deity who arose out of Chaos, and represented the

Erymanthian Boar, The:
see
HERAKLES, THE
LABOURS OF

Eshu: *see*
Ifa

Eros, as depicted by Alfred Gilbert in a statue of the late 19th century.

primal force of sexual desire.

Another tradition made Eros the offspring of the goddess Aphrodite and her lover, the god Ares. He was known to the Romans as Amor ("Love") or Cupid ("Desire") and was often found accompanying images of Aphrodite (Venus). He was usually portrayed as a handsome young man, but in Roman times Eros/Cupid became the cherub familiar to Latin poetry and later western art. The god was often depicted blindfolded (in order to symbolize love's blindness) and bearing a bow, which he used to shoot the arrows of love and desire.

Erymanthian Boar, The *Greece*
A monstrous boar of Mount Erymanthus in the Peloponnese. The hero Herakles captured the monster as the fourth of his twelve labours.

Eshu *Africa*
A west African divinity who is the most celebrated trickster figure in African mythology. Eshu (also known as Legba and Elegba) is renowned for his cunning and is portrayed as a restless being who inhabits thresholds, crossroads, market places and other places where people are likely to meet. Whenever transition, change and exchange occur, Eshu is said to be in attendance. He is also purported to be the messenger between humans and heaven.

In popular mythology Eshu is above all a bringer of chaos who once even persuaded the sun and moon to swap houses, causing universal disorder. He is blamed for all human arguments and for quarrels between humans and the gods. On one occasion Eshu played a trick on the High God himself, angering him so greatly that he withdrew from earth, where he had lived until then, to heaven. He ordered Eshu to report every evening the goings on in the world. Since that time Eshu has acted as the messenger between heaven and earth.

Etana *Middle East*
A ruler of the city of Kish and, in one Babylonian (Akkadian) myth, the first king. The gods and goddesses chose Etana, who was a humble shepherd, to bring the blessing of kingship to humanity. However, his queen could bear him no heir and he had to go to heaven to get the herb of birth from the goddess Ishtar. On the advice of Shamash, the sun god, Etana rode an eagle to heaven. However, before he reached Ishtar the king was overcome with giddiness and panicked, causing the eagle to plummet to earth. No more of the story is recorded, but, Etana's mission was evidently an eventual success, since Sumerian records list both Etana and his son as historical kings of Kish.

Euphrosyne *Greece*
"Jollity", one of the three Graces.

Europa *Greece*

A princess. Europa was the daughter of King Agenor and Queen Telephassa of Phoenicia. The god Zeus took the form of a white bull to approach Europa as she picked flowers in a meadow not far from the sea. The princess was struck by the gentle creature and sat on its back. The bull strolled down to the seashore, but suddenly ran into the waves and swam out to sea, taking Europa with it. Europa and the bull came ashore on Crete, where Zeus adopted the form of an eagle and had intercourse with the princess. As a result of this coupling Europa bore Zeus three sons: Minos, Rhadamanthus and Sarpedon. Later, she married the Cretan king Asterius, who adopted her sons.

Eurydice *Greece*

A dryad (tree nymph) or naiad (water nymph) of Thrace, the wife of the musician Orpheus.

Eurynome *Greece*

A sea nymph, the mother of the three Graces.

Eurystheus *Greece*

A king of the Argolid (a region of the Peloponnese), the son of King Sthenelus and Queen Nicippe of Mycenae. The hero Herakles was sentenced to serve Eurystheus for twelve years as a penance for killing his wife Megara. During his servitude the king set Herakles twelve arduous tasks, the so-called labours of Herakles.

Europa: *see*
Cadmus; Minos; Sarpedon; ZEUS, THE CONSORTS OF

Eurydice: *see*
Orpheus

Eurynome: *see*
Graces, The

Eurystheus: *see*
Herakles; HERAKLES, THE LABOURS OF

Fafnir *Germanic regions*

A giant of Scandinavian myth. Fafnir killed his father Hreidmar to gain possession of a great horde of treasure and changed into a dragon to guard it. He was later killed by the young hero Sigurd the Volsung.

Faro *Africa*

One of the two primal creator spirits which arose at the beginning of creation, according to the Bambara people of west Africa. After the twin forces of creation (Gla and Dya) arose out of nothingness (Fu), Faro formed the sky while the spirit Pemba formed the earth. They both then established the four cardinal directions. Life appeared on earth and Faro descended to earth and produced twins in the desert. Then the first grass sprang up and the first waters, together with a fish which led Faro and his children to the sea. Once they had arrived there, Faro brought all the creatures of the waters into existence.

Faro called into being every object and creature on earth and gave it its name. He installed night and day and the seasons and ordered all living beings.

He ordained the medical and ritual applications of all plant life. Also he ordered and named all humans, the different tribes and races. Then he returned to the skies.

Fates, The *Greece*

The three divinities of destiny. The Fates (known in Greek myth as Moirai, "The Apportioners") determined a person's birth, lifespan, portion of good and evil, and time of death. They came to be depicted as three old women at a spinning wheel, whose names were Clotho (who span the thread of life), Lachesis (who measured it out) and Atropos (who cut it off).

Father Sky *North America*

A creator deity widespread in traditional Native American mythology. Father Sky (or Sky Father), with his female counterpart and consort Mother Earth (or Earth Mother), are usually described as the offspring of the remote supreme divinity or "Great Spirit". Once Father Sky and Mother Earth appeared, the supreme divinity withdrew from the world leaving them to continue creation.

Faunus *Rome*

An ancient Italian deity of the woodlands who came to be identified with the Greek god Pan.

Fenrir *Germanic regions*

A monstrous wolf, who was the offspring of the trickster god Loki. Fenrir was raised among the gods, of whom only Tyr, the god of battle, dared to go near him to feed him. No chain was strong enough to bind Fenrir, so Odin, who was the chief of the gods, commissioned the dwarfs to fashion a magic unbreakable leash. When the gods tried to place it around Fenrir's neck he insisted that one of them place his arm in his jaws as a guarantee of good faith. Tyr agreed to do this, and Fenrir bit off his hand. As a result, the wolf was bound to a rock with a sword clamped in his jaw as a gag.

Fenrir remained tied to the rock until Ragnarok, the cataclysmic battle that saw the destruction of the old world order. As Loki led the assault against the gods, Fenrir broke his bonds and devoured Odin. Odin's son Vidar tore Fenrir to pieces.

Fer Diadh *Celtic regions*

An Irish warrior, the foster-brother of the great hero Cú Chulainn. Fer Diadh (also spelled Ferdia) and Cú Chulainn were raised together at the court of King Conchobar of Ulster and learned the arts of warfare from the warrior-sorceress Scáthach. During the conflict between Ulster and Connacht, Fer Diadh fought on the side of Queen Medhbh of Connacht but avoided facing Cú Chulainn until persuaded to fight him by Medhbh. Their long duel ended when Cú Chulainn eventually killed Fer Diadh with a blow from the *gae bolga*, his barbed spear.

Ferghus *Celtic regions*

An Irish hero of superhuman size and strength. Ferghus, the king of Ulster before Conchobar, became renowned for his strength, martial prowess and huge sexual appetite.

One of the hero's lovers was Nessa, the mother of Conchobar, who agreed to have intercourse with Ferghus only if her son could become king of Ulster for one year. Ferghus consented, but Conchobar proved so popular that the people would not let Ferghus return. Ferghus accepted this, but following Conchobar's treacherous treatment of Deirdre he defected to the court of Connacht, where he became the lover of Queen Medhbh and fought against Conchobar in the war recounted in the epic *Táin Bó Cuailnge*. During the conflict Ferghus confronted Conchobar, and would have cut him down had not Conchobar's son Cormac persuaded him to spare his life.

The great Ulster hero Cú Chulainn then came to his sovereign's aid. Ferghus had vowed never to fight Cú Chulainn, to whom he had acted as foster-father, and withdrew. This led directly to the defeat of Medhbh.

Ferghus' love affair with Medhbh aroused the jealousy of her husband, King Ailill. The lovers were bathing in a pool one day when Ailill came upon them and killed Ferghus.

Filial Piety, The Twenty-Four Examples of *China*

The name given to a famous collection of mythological tales compiled in the 14th century AD by the author Gui Jujing and designed to inculcate in the young the sacred virtue of reverence for their elders. One story tells of a boy who sliced some flesh from his thigh to make a broth for his sick mother and father.

Faunus: *see*
Pan

Fenrir: *see*
Loki; Odin; Ragnarok

Fer Diadh: *see*
Conchobar; Cú Chulainn; Medhbh; *Táin Bó Cuailnge*

Ferghus: *see*
Conchobar; Cú Chulainn; Deirdre; Medhbh; *Táin Bó Cuailnge*

Filial Piety, The Twenty-Four Examples of: *see*
Can Nü

The wolf Fenrir, from an incised stone tablet.

Another recounts how a son lay naked on a frozen body of water to melt the ice and catch a fish for his hungry parents.

Finn *Celtic regions*

A warrior hero, the central figure of the great body of myths, the Fenian Cycle. Finn and his followers, the Fian or Fianna ("Warriors"), were immensely popular in the Gaelic myth of Ireland and Scotland. "Fenian" derives from the Irish *féinnidh* ("member of the Fian").

Finn was a hunter, warrior and noble prophet of supernatural gifts. In one account, he was the son of Cumhall, the head of the house of Baoisgne and leader of the Fian, an élite band of hunter-warriors loyal to the High King of Ireland. Cumhall loved a woman, Muirne, but her father, a druid, forbade the union and sent the warrior Goll mac Morna to thwart it. Goll killed Cumhal and became leader of the Fian. Muirne was already pregnant by Cumhall and bore a son, Demhne (later Finn).

The thumb-sucking figure on this Celtic stone cross is probably the hero Finn.

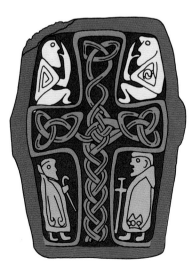

According to a popular tradition, Demhne acquired knowledge of supernatural lore and the gift of prophecy by scalding his thumb on the cooked Salmon of Knowledge. He sucked the thumb to ease his pain: this small taste was sufficient to receive the salmon's gift. His teacher, the poet Finnegas, renamed him Finn and thereafter, whenever Finn chewed his thumb, he learned whatever it was that he wanted to know.

When he had grown to manhood, Finn overthrew Goll and took over as leader of the Fian. The High King of Ireland acknowledged this change after Finn saved the royal seat, Tara, from an evil goblin. There are numerous accounts of Finn's death. According to one, Finn was deserted in his old age by many of the Fian and drowned when trying to leap the Boyne to prove his vigour. Another account relates that the hero still sleeps underground and will rise in Ireland's time of need.

Fir Bholg *Celtic regions*

The name of the fourth race of people to invade Ireland, according to the *Book of Invasions*. After the third race of invaders had been defeated by the monstrous Fomorians, the survivors left Ireland. Some of them were forced into slavery in Greece, their ancestral home, where they acquired the name Fir Bholg ("Men of Sacks") because they were made to create cultivable land by covering rocks with soil carried in bags or sacks. The Fir Bholg held Ireland for thirty-seven years, during which time their five leaders divided it into five provinces: this is the origin of Connacht, Ulster, Leinster, Munster and the former fifth province, Meath. They also established kingship. The Fir Bholg were defeated at the first battle of Magh

Tuiredh by the Tuatha Dé Danann, the fifth race of invaders. Eochaidh mac Eirc, the last Fir Bholg king of Ireland, fell during the battle. The Fir Bholg made peace with the victors and withdrew into Connacht.

Fire, The origin of
See CULTURE HERO

Fireshade and Fireshine *Japan*
The offspring of the god Honinigi and his consort Kono-hana-sakuya-hime. They are called Ho-no-susori and Hiko-hoho-demi in Japanese.

Five Ages, The *Greece*
The ancient Greeks accounted for the development (as well as the progressive degeneration) of the human race in the story of the Five Ages or Races. The people of the first age, the Age of Gold, arose (in some accounts) from Gaia, the earth, in the time of Kronos. They were free from old age, disease and labour and their lives were filled with revelry. They died as though falling into a gentle sleep and after death became benevolent spirits. The second race, in the Age of Silver, was created by Zeus and the Olympians. They lived for a hundred years but were violent, arrogant and in thrall to their mothers. They neglected the gods and were destroyed by Zeus: they too persist as spirits.

Zeus created next the race; the Age of Bronze, who discovered metal and established the beginnings of civilization. But they were brutal and enjoyed making war with their bronze weapons. They all cut each other's throats and perished.

The fourth era, the Age of Heroes, appears in Hesiod. This race, born of divine fathers and mortal mothers, was noble, brave and of superhuman strength. After death the Heroic Race went to the Elysian Fields or Islands of the Blessed. Zeus then made a fifth race, the modern day Race of Iron, who had to labour and for whom good was always combined with evil.

Five Suns, The *Central America*
The name given to the five world epochs, according to Aztec mythology. In the beginning the primordial being Ometecuhtli gave birth to four creator gods: Tezcatlipoca, the supreme deity, Xipe Totec, Huitzilopochtli and Quetzalcoatl (the Four Tezcatlipocas). These gods were joined by the rain god Tlaloc and his consort the water goddess Chalchiuhtlicue. The deities all took part in a great cosmic struggle which saw the successive creation and destruction of five "Suns" or world eras. Tezcatlipoca governed the first Sun, which lasted for 676 years. Quetzalcoatl overthrew Tezcatlipoca and jaguars devoured the world. A second Sun arose, ruled by Quetzalcoatl, who was ousted in turn by Tezcatlipoca and swept away in a mighty hurricane. Tlaloc governed the third Sun, which ended when Quetzalcoatl caused the earth to be consumed by a rain of fire. Chalchiuhtlicue presided over the fourth Sun. This era ended when a great flood destroyed the world.

The present era arose when the god Nanahuatzin jumped into a fire at the sacred city of Teotihuacan and was metamorphosed into the rising sun. However, the sun did not move until the other deities had made a sacrifice of their own blood, an event which underlay the Aztec belief that human sacrifice prolonged the existence of the universe. But such acts could only delay the inevitable end of this Sun, when earthquakes would destroy the world.

Fireshade and Fireshine: *see* Ho-no-susori and Hiko-hoho-demi.

Five Ages of Man, The: *see* Argonauts, The; Elysium; Gaia; Kronos; *Theogony*, The; Troy; Zeus

Five Suns, The: *see* Chalchuitlicue; Huitzilopochtli; Quetzalcoatl; Tezcatlipoca; Tlaloc; Xipe Totec

FLOOD MYTHS

Mythological traditions the world over describe how divine forces seek to punish human beings for their transgressions by destroying them with some form of cosmic disaster, which is most often envisaged as a flood. The best-known example is the Biblical story of Noah, which is probably itself a derivative of older Mesopotamian accounts of a flood sent by the gods to punish humanity, which is wiped out save for one man (variously called Atrahasis, Utnapishtim or Ziusudra) and his family. The "Noah's Ark" theme of these accounts is echoed in the Indian myth of Manu, the first man, who is forewarned by a great fish of a cataclysmic inundation and survives by building a ship.

Similar themes occur in the southern

The Biblical Flood, taken from an illustration in the Nuremberg Bible (1483).

Chinese myth of the Gourd Children, except that the universal flood which destroys humanity is seen as the arbitrary act of the Thunder God. Elsewhere in the world, the cosmic deluge may be prompted by the misdemeanour of a particular individual. For example, in the mythology of the Chewong peoples of Malaya anyone who mocks an animal angers the primal serpent of the underworld. In its rage the serpent releases primeval waters as a great inundation.

The concept of a completely new world emerging from the deluge is common in Central America. For example, in the Aztec myth of the Five Suns, the present world (the fifth) is said to have arisen after the previous world was swept away by a flood.

FLOOD MYTHS
See panel above

Fomorian *Celtic regions*
One of a monstrous race of brigands who, in Irish myth, were descended from Ham, the cursed son of Noah. Because of this curse the Fomorians (or Fomorii) were misshapen, often presented as having one arm and one leg. The Fomorians attacked and oppressed successive races of settlers in Ireland, but were finally defeated at the second battle of Magh Tuiredh by the Tuatha Dé Danann. It has also been

suggested that they were a maritime race who made several expeditions to Ireland before finally settling there.

Frea *Germanic regions*
The chief goddess of the early German pantheon and the consort of the god Wodan, who was the forunner to Odin. Frea (Frig in Anglo-Saxon) gave her name to Friday.

Freyja *Germanic regions*
The great goddess of the Vanir, the Scandinavian deities of earth and water, one of the two divine races who dwelt in

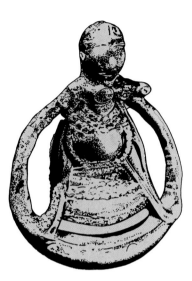

A possible depiction of Freyja, from a Swedish pendant of the Viking period.

Asgard, the home of the gods. Freyja ("Lady") was clearly a powerful figure, venerated by women, heroes and rulers.

Freyja was the sister of the god Freyr and one tradition claimed that they were married (she may be identifiable with Freyr's bride Gerd). The goddess was associated with sexual freedom: she had many lovers among the gods and also among human rulers, whom she protected. Freyja brought fruitfulness to the land and sea and assisted in marriage and childbirth. This generosity explains one of the goddess's alternative names, Gefn, which derives from the verb *gefa*, to give. Freyja was also a goddess of magic and divination.

Like Freyr, Freyja was associated with wealth. She was said to weep tears of gold and to possess a magnificent necklace called Brisingamen.

Freyja had much in common with Frigg, the chief goddess of the Aesir, the race of sky deities. For example, both were associated with childbearing and

could assume the form of a bird. It is possible that they both developed from the early Germanic goddess Frea.

Freyr *Germanic regions*
The chief Scandinavian god of fertility and abundance. Freyr ("Lord") was one of the Vanir, the deities of earth and water. He was the son of Njord, a god of the sea and ships, and Skadi, a goddess of the mountain forests. Freyr's sister, and perhaps also his consort, was the goddess Freyja.

Freyr and the Vanir brought peace and abundance to the land and its rulers, so long as they kept his favour. The god's cult, which laid great emphasis on fertility and which may have involved sexual rites and orgies, was popular throughout Scandinavia during the Viking age. Divination played an important part in the cult.

Although Freyr was not one of the sky gods, he was associated with the sun as a source of fertility. According to one myth, Freyr wooed Gerd, the daughter of a giant, who lived in the underworld. She agreed to marry him when he convinced her that her refusal would arouse the anger of the gods, bringing sterility and destruction. The myth has been interpreted as the sun uniting with the earth to produce abundance.

One of Freyr's symbols was a golden boar, which passed through the sky and beneath the earth as, it was said, did the sun. Another symbol was the ship. Freyr possessed a vessel, *Skidbladnir*, able to carry all the gods, which he kept folded up in a pouch when he did not need it.

Frigg *Germanic regions*
The queen of heaven and chief goddess among the Scandinavian sky deities, the Aesir. Frigg was the wife of Odin, the head of the Aesir and ruler of Asgard,

Freyr: *see*
Aesir, The; Freyja; Vanir, The

Frigg: *see*
Balder; Frea; Freyja; Odin

the home of the gods. She had much in common with the goddess Freyja and they may both have developed from the early Germanic goddess, Frea. Frigg features in myth as the grieving mother of Balder, whom she tried without success to fetch back from Hel, the underworld land of the dead.

Frum, John *Oceania*

The central figure of a Melanesian cargo cult which began in the New Hebrides (modern Vanuatu) during the Second World War. John Frum is said to be an incarnation of Karaperamun, the supreme being worshipped in Vanuatu before the people were converted to Christianity. His coming is believed by his adherents to herald a new age of *kago* ("cargo", that is, "wealth").

Fu *Africa*

The primordial emptiness, according to the creation myth of the Bambara people of west Africa. The process of creation is said to have begun when Gla ("Knowing") arose out of Fu.

Fu Xi *China*

A creator god who features in some of the most ancient Chinese myths, often alongside the creator goddess Nü Gua. From the 4th century BC onward Fu Xi and Nü Gua appear frequently as the creators of the human race and its protectors against calamities, especially floods. During the Han dynasty (202BC–AD220) they came to be presented as husband and wife. They were often depicted with the tails of serpents.

Han scholars reworked many myths as fact to fill in gaps in early Chinese history. Fu Xi was declared to have been the very first emperor, and to have ruled from 2852BC–2737BC. He was hailed as a great culture hero, inventor of musical

Fu Xi and Nü Gua, from a 7th-century painting on hemp, from Turfan, China.

instruments and the first Chinese script. He instructed on how to rear domestic animals and to fish with nets.

Furies, The *Greece*

Fearsome female deities or spirits of the underworld. In most accounts, the Furies (Erinyes in Greek) sprang from the goddess Gaia, the earth, at the spot where the blood of the god Uranos fell after his castration. They were powerful agents of justice, who sought out transgressors on earth and administered and oversaw their torments in the underworld. There were sometimes said to be three Furies: Alecto (which means "Relentless"), Megaira ("Resentful") and Tisiphone ("Avenger of Murder").

Gaia *Greece*

The goddess personifying the earth, one of the primal deities which arose from Chaos in the beginning, according to Hesiod's *Theogony*. Gaia (or Ge) then played the most crucial role in the early stages of creation. She brought forth the god Uranos, the sky, and then the Mountains and the Sea before having intercourse with Uranos to produce the first divine races: the twelve Titans, three Cyclopes and three giants called Hekatoncheires, each with a hundred hands. But Uranos was dismayed by these offspring and forced them back into Gaia. This angered the goddess, who persuaded Kronos, the youngest Titan, to castrate his father and become the ruler of heaven. In some accounts Gaia predicted that Kronos, like Uranos, would be overthrown by one of his children. Kronos therefore devoured each of his offspring as his wife, the Titan Rhea, gave birth. But Rhea concealed the infant Zeus, who was nurtured by Gaia until he was old enough to dethrone his father and become the leader of the gods.

Gaia, causing life to spring from the earth, was also the sacred energy which endowed some sites with oracular powers. Delphi, believed by the Greeks to be the centre of the earth, was the site of Gaia's most famous oracle. It became the chief shrine of Apollo after he had killed the dragon Pytho, which Gaia had set to guard it.

The goddess had many offspring, who included Echidne, Ericthonius, the Furies and Nereus.

Galateia *Greece*

A Nereid (sea nymph) who lived in the sea off Sicily. Galateia loved Acis, a handsome young Sicilian shepherd, but the Cyclops Polyphemus fell in love with the nymph and crushed Acis to death beneath a boulder. Galateia turned her dead lover into a stream which sprang from the rock. In another account (one in which the young Acis is excluded), Polyphemus wooed the nymph and won her heart.

Ganesha *India*

The elephant-headed god, the offspring of the goddess Parvati, the wife of Shiva. Once she had married Shiva,

Gaia: *see*
Apollo; Delphi; Echidne; Ericthonius; Furies, The; Gigantomachy, The; Hekaontcheires; Nereus; Zeus

Galateia: *see*
Cyclops; Nereus

Ganesha: *see*
Shiva; Skanda

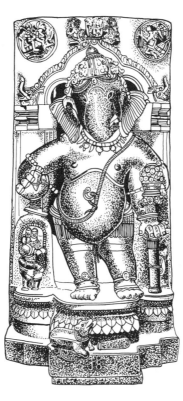

*The elephant-headed god, Ganesha,
from a 13th-century statue.*

Parvati desired a child to guard her from
unwelcome visitors. As she bathed she
created Ganesha from the rubbings of
her own body and set him to watch the
entrance to her chambers. When he tried
to refuse entry to Shiva himself, the god
angrily decapitated him. Parvati insisted
that her son be revived, so Shiva
replaced Ganesha's head with that of an
elephant. He then put Ganesha in charge
of the *ganas*, his goblin-like attendants.

Ganesha was well-known for
overcoming all obstacles and his name
is traditionally invoked before the start
of any enterprise. He is also known as
Vighneshvara ("Lord of Obstacles").

Ganga *India*

"Ganges", the goddess personifying the
river Ganges and the holiest of
Hinduism's three (or, in some accounts,
seven) great river goddesses. Ganga
descended from heaven and in order to
cushion her descent the god Shiva
allowed her to land on his matted hair.
Shiva divided Ganga into seven rivers
(the Ganges and its tributaries) so that
she could arrive on earth without
causing catastrophic floods.

Ganga purifies those who bathe in her
and the ashes of the dead are scattered
on her waters. As a goddess she is often
depicted on her mount, the *makara*, a
water monster.

Ganymede *Greece*

A beautiful youth, the son of King Tros
of Troy. The god Zeus fell in love with
him and sent an eagle to abduct him
(other accounts claim that the eagle was
Zeus in transformed guise). The bird
snatched Ganymede from the Trojan
plain and carried him to the peak of
Mount Olympus, where Zeus granted
him immortality and eternal youth as
cupbearer to the gods.

Garang *Africa*

The first man, according to the Dinka
people of the southern Sudan. He was
the husband of Abuk, the first woman,
who caused death and illness on earth.

Garuda *India*

"The Devourer", the celestial bird which
is the mount of the god Vishnu. Garuda,
often depicted as part human and part
eagle, was the offspring of Kashyapa,
one of the seven divine sages, and
Vinata, the mother of all birds. Garuda
was associated with fire and the sun, and
was regarded as an incarnation of the
fire god Agni. He was the implacable

Garuda in his Buddhist form, from a 16th-century depiction.

the implacable enemy of the *Nagas*, the race of serpents. According to one story, Vinata was enslaved by her sister Kadru, the mother of all snakes. Kadru promised to release her if Garuda brought the elixir of the gods to the snakes. Garuda stole the elixir and placed it on ground where sharp-bladed grass grew. Vinata was freed and the serpents licked the grass, splitting their tongues, which have been forked ever since. The god Indra retrieved the elixir.

Gautama (1) *India*
The name of the Indian prince who, after his enlightenment, became known as the Buddha.

Gautama (2) *India*
One of seven divine sages that arose from the mind of the god Brahma.

Geb *Egypt*
The god of the earth, the offspring of Shu, the god of air, and Tefenet, the goddess of wetness.

Gefion *Germanic regions*
A Scandinavian fertility goddess. The Swedish king Gylfi promised Gefion as much of his kingdom as she could plough in a day, so she transformed her four giant sons into oxen so powerful that their plough wrenched away a great area of the Swedish mainland. This became the Danish island of Zealand, the centre of the goddess's cult. Gefion may have been a manifestation of the goddess Freyja, who was also known by the name Gefn.

Gerd *Germanic regions*
A princess of the underworld race of giants who became the bride of the god Freyr. She may be identifiable with Freyr's sister Freyja, who, according to one tradition, was also his wife.

Gesar Khan *Tibet and Mongolia*
The divine warrior hero of a great Tibeto-Mongolian cycle of myths which contain traces of pre-Buddhist mythological traditions, such as references to numerous local deities. Gesar Khan ("King Gesar") was chosen by the gods to descend from heaven in human form in order to combat the evils arising from a curse laid on humanity by a bitter old woman and her three sons.

The divine war hero, Gesar Khan.

Gautama (1): *see* Buddha

Gautama (2): *see* Ahalya; Brahma; Seven Sages, The

Geb: *see* Ennead, The

Gefion: *see* Freyja

Gerd: *see* Freyr

Gesar was born on earth from an egg and set out on a heroic life of great adventures, defeating evil wherever he and his companions found it. At the end of his life Gesar retreated to the holy mountain Margye Pongri with his followers for a period of meditation and ritual purification for the bloody deeds they had committed as warriors. After this period Gesar ascended to heaven, knowing that one day he would have to return to earth, since evil could never be wiped out completely.

Gigantomachy, The *Greece*
"The Battle of the Giants", specifically the battle between the Olympian deities and a race of giants which sprang from the goddess Gaia, the earth, at the spot where she was spattered with the blood of the castrated god Uranos. The Olympians defeated the giants.

Gilgamesh *Middle East*
An early king of Erech (or Uruk) in Sumer and the hero of the Babylonian (Sumerian-Akkadian) epic of Gilgamesh, the world's oldest extant work of literature (*c*.2000BC or earlier). The most complete version of the epic comes from the library of the Assyrian king Asshurbanipal (*c*.669BC–627BC). In this version, the people of the city of Erech begged the gods to send someone to restrain the repressive hand of their ruler, Gilgamesh, son of the goddess Ninsun and a mortal. So the gods created Enkidu, a hairy barbarian of superhuman strength who lived in the desert. Gilgamesh decided to capture Enkidu and sent a prostitute to seduce him. Enkidu had intercourse with her and let her take him to Erech and civilization.

When Enkidu was brought before Gilgamesh, he at once engaged the king in a bout of wrestling. After this fight

Gilgamesh (left), from a baked clay plaque of the Old Babylonian period.

the two men became companions and journeyed together to slay the monster Humbaba (Huwawa to the Sumerians). When the two men returned in triumph, the goddess Ishtar (the Sumerian Inanna) attempted to seduce Gilgamesh, but she was rejected. The angry goddess sent a fierce bull to kill Gilgamesh, but Enkidu came to his aid and the two butchered the creature. The people of Erech rejoiced, but the deities decided that Enkidu must die for his role in killing Humbaba and the bull. He died in the arms of Gilgamesh.

Devastated by Enkidu's death, Gilgamesh set out on a vain quest to discover the secret of eternal life. He visited Utnapishtim, who was granted immortality after he alone had survived a great flood sent by the gods to destroy humanity. Utnapishtim told Gilgamesh of a plant growing at the bottom of the sea which was said to bring new life to whomever ate it. Accompanied by Utnapishtim's boatman Urshanabi, Gilgamesh found the plant but it was stolen by a snake. At last resigned to mortality, he returned to Erech.

Ginnungagap *Germanic regions*
"The Yawning (or Deceiving) Gap", the primeval emptiness which held all the potential energy of creation, according to ancient Scandinavian cosmogony.

Gitchi Manitou *North America*
"Great Spirit", the name of the supreme deity of the Algonquian people of the northeastern United States and southeastern Canada. Gitchi Manitou conceived and governed the universe, but left its day-to-day running to more active divinities, such as Sun, Moon, Thunder and Wind. His omnipresence manifested itself in the interaction of all life forms, natural and supernatural.

Gla *Africa*
"Knowing", the first thing to emerge from Fu, the primordial emptiness, according to the creation myth of the Bambara people of west Africa. Gla (or Gla Gla Zo) was the prime force of creation. It is said to have emitted a "Voice of Emptiness" from which its twin, Dya, arose. From Gla and Dya sprang a damp matter like cold rust which hardened into icy, shining objects that filled the primal void. The twin beings traversed their vast domain and caused a wind of fire to melt the icy bodies: in this melting all things became potential in silence and invisibility.

Gla and its twin withdrew their energy into themselves and everything solidified anew. Then they melted everything once more. After these two successive fusions, Gla set up a to and fro movement which is the soul of the universe. At the same time the contact between the twin beings caused a cosmic explosion from which a hard, powerful, vibrating matter was ejected. From its vibration emerged, one by one, the signs and names for all things as yet uncreated, each of which began to vibrate gently within itself, each in its own place. Then Gla produced "the foot of humanity", the symbol of human consciousness, which is the "seed" of the universe. This element comm-

unicated consciousness to all things, which were thus able to come into existence. The process of bringing things into being was then assumed by two creator spirits, Pemba and Faro.

Glooskap *North America*
A divine culture hero and trickster figure of the Algonquian people. Glooskap, or Gluskap, was said to have created the stars and planets and humanity from the corpse of his mother, while his evil twin brother, Maslum, produced disease and other ills. The two brothers often conflicted as Maslum endeavoured to counter the benefits which Glooskap brought to the human race. In the end Maslum was defeated.

One myth relates how Glooskap first took the summer to the frozen lands of the north. Glooskap used his trickery to abduct Summer, the beautiful female chief of the little people. He escorted her north and took her into the tipi of Winter. Her warmth caused the giant to melt away. Glooskap then let Summer return to her own people.

Goibhniu *Celtic regions*
The divine smith and founder of craftsmanship. According to Irish myth, Goibhniu ("Smith") headed a group of three deities (the other two being Luchta and Creidhne) who were the craftsmen and arms makers of the Tuatha Dé Danann. A weapon made by Goibhniu was said always to hit its target and cause a mortal wound. He was reputed to be able to forge a weapon with just three blows of his hammer.

Golden Fleece, The *Greece*
The fleece of the golden ram of Colchis, kept by King Aëtes of Colchis and guarded by an unsleeping dragon. It was retrieved by the hero Jason.

Gitchi Manitou: *see*
Wakan Tanka

Gla: *see*
Faro

Glooskap: *see*
CULTURE HERO;
TRICKSTER

Goibhniu: *see*
Fomorian; Tuatha Dé Danann

Golden Fleece, The: *see*
ARGONAUTS, THE
VOYAGE OF THE

Gong Gong *China*

The god of water, sometimes said to be the son of Zhu Rong, the benevolent god of fire and lord of the cosmos. In one myth, Gong Gong, a repellent creature with the body of a serpent and a human head with red hair, envied Zhu Rong's power. He tried to overthrow him, but the fire god's forces were too powerful.

Defeated, Gong Gong flew into a rage and demolished Imperfect Mountain, which supported the heavens in the northwest of the world. The collapse of the mountain left a hole in the sky and caused the world to tilt, causing floods and other disasters. Order was restored when the creator goddess Nü Gua filled in the hole in the sky and propped it up with the legs of a giant tortoise, then mended all the breached river banks.

Gorgons, The *Greece*

Three sisters, Stheno, Euryale and Medusa, the monstrous offspring of Phorcys and Ceto. The Gorgons lived in the far west and were usually depicted as grotesque, grimacing monsters, although in some traditions they were beautiful. They were said to be immortal except for Medusa, who was killed by the hero Perseus. The Gorgons were the sisters of the three Graeae.

Gourd Children, The *China*

The brother and sister who recreated the human race after its destruction in a great flood, according to the mythology of the Yao people of southern China. One day, a farmer captured the Thunder God, who was responsible for storms and floods. He warned his son and daughter not to give the god anything to drink, but the children were merciful. One drop of water revived the god and he burst free from his cage. He gave the children a tooth in gratitude and left.

The children planted the tooth and a few minutes later a plant sprouted producing an enormous gourd. In the meantime, a great flood began to cover the earth. The farmer told his son and daughter to shelter in the gourd while he built a boat and floated on the rising waters to heaven, where he appealed for an end to the deluge. The gods consented, but the flood subsided so rapidly that the farmer's boat plummeted to earth and he was killed.

The children, safe inside their gourd, were the only survivors of the flood. From this point they are referred to as Fu Xi ("Bottle Gourd"). When they were older they married and the sister adopted the name Nü Gua, which also means gourd or melon. Later Nü Gua gave birth to a ball of flesh which they cut into pieces and carried up the ladder to heaven. The pieces were scattered by the wind and as they landed they became people, populating the world.

Graces, The *Greece*

Female divinities embodying beauty, grace, elegance and generosity. The Graces (in Greek myth the Charites) were usually said to be the daughters of the god Zeus and the sea nymph Eurynome. They were often depicted as attendants of Aphrodite. There were generally said to be three Graces, who were Aglaia ("Splendour"), Euphrosyne ("Good Cheer") and Thalia ("Jollity").

Graeae, The *Greece*

Three malevolent hags, known as Deion (meaning "Terrible"), Enyo (which means "Bellicose") and Pemphredo (meaining "Spiteful"), the daughters of Phorcys and Ceto. The Graeae ("Old Women"), who lived at the foot of Mount Atlas, were said to have been born wizened and aged, possessing only

GREEK AND ROMAN DEITIES

The most important gods and goddesses of the Romans were adopted, directly or indirectly (for example, via the Etruscans) from the Greek pantheon. In many cases, the Roman names are those of old Italian deities whose characteristics were assimilated to those of the Greek divinities with which they came to be identified. These are some of the most important parallels:

Greek deity	Roman deity	Influences
Aphrodite	Venus	Love
Apollo	Apollo	Light; the arts; healing
Ares	Mars	War
Artemis	Diana	Hunting; chastity
Athene	Minerva	Wisdom
Demeter	Ceres	Fertility; crops
Dionysos	Bacchus, Liber	Wine; ecstasy
Hades	Dis Pater	Ruler of the underworld
Hephaistos	Vulcan	Forge and fire
Hera	Juno	Queen of heaven; marriage
Hermes	Mercury	Commerce, communication
Hestia	Vesta	Home and hearth
Pan	Faunus	Woodlands
Persephone	Proserpina	Queen of the underworld
Poseidon	Neptune	Ruler of the seas
Zeus	Jupiter	Supreme deity; ruler of the skies

one tooth and one eye between them, which they took it in turns to use. They were the sisters of the three Gorgons.

Gráinne *Celtic regions*
An Irish princess, the daughter of Cormac, the High King of Ireland. Gráinne was betrothed to the great hero Finn but eloped with Diarmaid, one of his warriors.

Great Mother *Rome*
The Roman name of the Near Eastern earth goddess Cybele. She was known in Latin as Magna Mater.

GREEK AND ROMAN DEITIES
See panel above

The Great Mother, based on a stone sculpture of her head.

GREEK AND ROMAN DEITIES: *see* individual names

Gráinne: *see* Diarmaid

Great Mother: *see* Magna Mater

Gu: *see*
CULTURE HERO

Guanyin: *see*
Avalokiteshvara

Gucumatz: *see*
Quetzalcoatl

Gwydion: *see*
Blodeuwedd; Lleu Llaw
Gyffes; Math; *Mabinogion*,
The

Detail of Guanyin, from
a decorative plate.

Gri-gum *Tibet and Mongolia*

The seventh human king of Tibet and the first not to return to heaven at his death. A shaman foretold that Gri-gum would die in combat. The king was furious at this prophecy and challenged his ministers to fight him so that he could prove himself the supreme warrior. The royal groom, Lo-ngam, accepted the challenge and Gri-gum prepared for the duel. To avert bad luck he wore a dead dog and fox about his shoulders and a black turban with a mirror on his brow. He was also accompanied by several yaks which were carrying bags of soot.

The duel commenced and almost immediately the yaks burst the bags with their horns, filling the air with clouds of soot. In the confusion, Gri-gum cut the divine cord by which he, like his royal predecessors, was linked to heaven. Lo-ngam could see nothing in the sooty clouds apart from the mirror on Gri-gum's forehead. He fired an arrow at it and killed the king. Because he had severed his heavenly rope, Gri-gum could not ascend to heaven and in this way became the first Tibetan ruler to be buried on earth.

Gu *Africa*

A divine blacksmith culture hero, the son of the twin creator deities Mawu and Lisa, according to the Fon people of Benin. Lisa, the male twin, took Gu to earth and gave him the task of assisting humanity. He instructed people in the arts of ironworking and toolmaking so that they could practise agriculture and make dwellings and clothes.

Guanyin *China*

The Chinese Buddhist goddess of mercy. The deity Guanyin is derived from Avalokiteshvara, the Indian (male) Bodhisattva of compassion, who in China was considered an embodiment of positive motherly qualities. Mothers also prayed to her to protect their children and she was the goddess of all those in distress.

Gucumatz *Central America*

A Maya deity (who was also known as Kukulkan), who was the equivalent of the Aztec god Quetzalcoatl.

Gwydion *Celtic regions*

A magician, the nephew of Math, lord of Gwynedd, and a prominent character in the fourth branch of the *Mabinogion*. Whenever Math was not at war he had to keep his feet in the lap of a virgin. Gwydion's brother, Gilfaethwy, wanted to seduce the maiden, so Gwydion distracted Math's attention by conjuring up a war with neighbouring Dyfed. When Math returned and discovered his nephews' trickery, he transformed them into animals for three years.

Later, after Gwydion had become human once more, he assisted Math in creating a beautiful woman out of flowers as a wife for the hero Lleu Llaw Gyffes. The woman, Blodeuwedd, was unfaithful to Lleu and with her lover, Gronw Pebyr, plotted to kill him. They succeeded only in wounding the hero and he escaped in the form of an eagle. Gwydion restored Lleu to human form before killing Gronw Pebyr and turning Blodeuwedd into an owl.

H

Hachiman *Japan*
The god of war, the deified Emperor Ojin (died *c.*AD394), who was renowned for his military prowess. In many parts of Japan, men still mark their coming of age by visiting one of the god's shrines.

Hades *Greece*
The god of the underworld, the son of Kronos and Rhea and the brother of Demeter, Hera, Hestia, Poseidon and Zeus. Hades had no home on Mount Olympus and was not generally counted

Hades with Persephone seated at the foot of his couch.

among the Olympians. His name, often used as a synonym for the underworld itself, means "The Unseen". He rarely left the underworld, but the most famous occasion was when he kidnapped Persephone and made her his wife.

Hades presided in grim-faced majesty over his underworld domain, where dead mortals were judged and possibly punished. However, he was also the lord of the riches within the earth, hence his alternative name ("Wealth"). The god's cult stressed this and was sometimes linked with that of the fertility goddess Demeter, the mother of Persephone.

Hammer God, The *Celtic regions*
The name given to a widespread Celtic god, particularly popular in Gaul. His Celtic name is uncertain, but one or two Gaulish representations bear the name Sucellus ("Good Striker"). One of these shows him as consort of the goddess Nantosuelta. He was usually depicted as a bearded man in a tunic and cloak, holding a long-handled hammer in one hand and a pot in the other. The Hammer God had attributes connected with fertility and the goodness of nature.

Hades: *see*
Demeter; Persephone; Zeus

The god Hachiman.

The Hammer God.

Han Xiang

Han Xiang: *see* Eight Immortals, The; Lü Dongbin

Han Zhongli: *see* Eight Immortals, The; Li Xuan

Hanuman: *see* Rama

Hanuman (below), from a stone sculpture.

Hathor, from a mural, c.14th century BC.

Han Xiang *China*
One of the Eight Immortals of Daoist (Taoist) mythology. Han Xiang was said to be the great-nephew of Han Yü, a philosopher and essayist of the Tang dynasty (AD618–907). He embarked on his search for the Dao, the Daoist principle of existence, as the pupil of the Immortal Lü Dongbin, who later escorted him to heaven to eat the peaches of eternal life. Han Xiang began to climb the peach tree, but slipped and plummeted to earth. As he was about to hit the ground he achieved immortality.

Han Zhongli *China*
One of the Eight Immortals of Daoist (Taoist) mythology. Han Zhongli was an elderly man who lived during the Han dynasty (202BC–AD220). He learned the Dao, the Daoist principle of existence, from Li Xuan, the first Immortal, and was the messenger of heaven.

Hanuman *India*
A monkey who became the most loyal companion of Rama and his consort Sita. When Sita was abducted by Ravana, the evil king of Lanka, Rama and his brother Lakshmana set off to find her. They encountered Hanuman, a minister of the exiled monkey king Sugriva. Hanuman led a party of monkeys to continue the hunt for Sita. He heard that she was imprisoned on the island of Lanka and leaped over the sea onto the island. He found Sita and showed her a ring which Rama had given him as a token.

Hanuman allowed himself to be caught by Ravana's son. Ravana then ordered that the monkey's tail be set alight as a punishment for his actions, but Hanuman used his flaming tail to burn down Ravana's kingdom. When Rama and Lakshmana were injured in the ensuing battle, Hanuman went to the Himalaya to fetch healing plants.

Hanuman's dedication to Rama knew no bounds: once he tore open his chest to show Rama and Sita in his heart.

HARES AND RABBITS
See panel on opposite page

Hathor *Egypt*
A powerful and complex goddess with numerous attributes. Hathor was the protector of women, whom she assisted in conception and childbirth. As the guardian of children, she suckled the young god Horus in the form of a cow, and later restored his sight after the god Seth had torn out his eyes. She was also the protector of lovers.

Hathor was associated with death and rebirth. She greeted the souls of the dead in the underworld and offered them refreshments of food and drink.

Haumia *Oceania*
The Maori god of wild vegetables and plants. He was a son of the sky god Rangi and the earth goddess, Papa.

He Xiangu *China*
The eighth of the Eight Immortals of Daoist (Taoist) mythology and the only one who was unambiguously female. She attained immortality after eating a "mother-of-pearl stone" which a spirit told her was to be found on the mountain where she dwelt.

Hebe *Greece*
The goddess of youth, daughter of Zeus and Hera. Hebe ("Youth") lived on Mount Olympus, where she looked after Hera's peacocks, and was cupbearer to the gods. She became the divine wife of the hero Herakles after his death. (*See illustration on page 91.*)

HARES AND RABBITS

The hare or rabbit features in almost every mythology as trickster, culture hero or fertility symbol. The animals are noted universally for their swiftness and playful behaviour, and they occur in myth as cunning jokers who outwit bigger but less agile creatures. The American folklore character of Brer Rabbit represents a fusion of the African trickster hare (brought to North America by west African slaves) and the Native American rabbit trickster of the southeastern states.

The trickster's stratagems often backfire, as in the Japanese story of the White Rabbit, who tricked a family of crocodiles into forming a bridge for him to cross from an island to the Japanese mainland. As he approached the last crocodile in the line he gleefully boasted of his clever trickery, at which the angry crocodile caught him and skinned him alive.

Sometimes the rabbit or hare plays the part of a culture hero, employing trickery to bring benefits to humanity.

The hare in the moon of Chinese myth, mixing the elixir of immortality.

The Muskogean Creek people of Oklahoma (originally of Georgia and Alabama) told how the Rabbit stole fire from the Fire People.

Rabbits and hares are often linked with fertility, lust and vitality. In ancient Greece rabbits were seen as the attributes of Aphrodite, the goddess of love and sexuality. The creatures are widely associated with the moon, itself a symbol of feminine fecundity. The Germanic fertility goddess, who is known as Eostra (from whom the word Easter is a derivative) owned a hare in the moon which laid eggs, symbolizing renewed life, around the time of her springtime festival – hence Easter eggs and the Easter rabbit. In many parts of Asia and the Americas the equivalent of "the man in the moon" is traditionally said to be a rabbit or a hare.

The sexual and tricksterish aspects of the rabbit are brought together in the Aztec deities known as the Centzon Totochtin or "Four Hundred Rabbits".

Hathor: *see*
Bastet; Horus; Sekhmet; Taweret

Haumia: *see*
MAORI PANTHEON, THE; Rangi and Papa

He Xiangu: *see*
Eight Immortals, The; Lan Caihe

Hebe: *see*
Hera; Herakles; ZEUS, THE CONSORTS OF

Hebe (see page 90), *from an antique vase.*

Hector *Greece*

A Trojan prince, the son of King Priam and Queen Hecuba and brother of Paris. Homer's *Iliad* portrays Hector, a leading Trojan warrior, as a man of great fortitude and compassion who is more decisive and righteous than his elder brother Paris.

Hector's rivalry with the hero Achilles, the best Greek warrior, is a central theme of the *Iliad* and forms its climax. When Achilles quarrelled with his commander, Agamemnon, and withdrew from the fighting, Hector took advantage of his absence to push the Greeks back to their ships, wounding and killing many heroes. Patroclus, Achilles' best friend, led a successful Greek counterattack but was killed by Hector, causing Achilles to return to the battle to avenge Patroclus' death. The Trojan warrior Polydamas advised Hector to avoid a confrontation with Achilles but Hector refused to retreat.

Hector: *see*
Achilles; Paris; TROJAN WAR, THE HEROES OF THE; Troy

Achilles pursued Hector three times around the city walls before finally killing him in single combat. He then desecrated Hector's corpse by tying it by the feet to his chariot and dragging it daily around the tomb of Patroclus. Achilles refused to give up the corpse until the gods angrily forced him to accept a ransom from Hector's father. The *Iliad* ends with Hector's funeral.

Hecuba *Greece*

A queen of Troy, the wife of King Priam and the mother of Paris, Hector, Cassandra, Troilus and, according to some accounts, fourteen other children. Hecuba dreamed one night that she gave birth to a flaming torch which set the city on fire, so when Paris was born he was abandoned, setting in motion the events which culminated in the Trojan War. Hecuba remained largely in the background during the conflict except to mourn her son Hector's death. After the fall of Troy and the slaughter of her husband and sons, she was taken into slavery by the victorious Greeks.

Heh and Hehet *Egypt*

A pair of primal deities embodying infinity. They formed part of the group of eight divinities known as the Ogdoad.

Heimdall *Germanic regions*

A Scandinavian deity, also known as the White God. Heimdall was the offspring of nine giant maidens who may have been personifications of waves, and so he probably belonged to the Vanir, the divinities associated with the waters and the earth. He was renowned for his vigilance and acute hearing – he could see at night and hear the sound of grass growing – and kept unceasing watch over Bifrost, the bridge leading to Asgard, home of the gods. Heimdall's

chief opponent was the god Loki, who eventually killed him. This act heralded the beginning of Ragnarok, the cosmic battle ending the old divine order.

Hekate *Greece*

The goddess of sorcery, usually said to be the daughter of the Titans Coeus and Phoebe. Hekate resided in the underworld, where she oversaw ritual purifications as well as magical invocations. Witches, such as Medea, drew power from the goddess. Hekate would sometimes appear on earth at night-time, especially at crossroads, accompanied by baying hounds.

Hekatoncheires, The *Greece*

"One Hundred Hands", the name given to three giants with a hundred hands and fifty heads each. Named Cottus, Briareus and Gyges, they were the offspring of the goddess Gaia, the earth, and the god Uranos, the sky. To prevent their births Uranos forced them back into the earth, together with their brothers, the Cyclopes and Titans. They were released by the Titan Kronos when he overthrew Uranos, but Kronos then reimprisoned them in the underworld. Freed by Zeus, they assisted him in the defeat of the Titans, who, some say, they later guarded in the underworld.

Hel *Germanic regions*

The goddess of the underworld land of the dead, which was itself often referred to as Hel. According to some accounts she was the daughter of Loki and was a sinister figure, said to be half black and half flesh-coloured.

Helen *Greece*

A Spartan princess, daughter of the god Zeus and Leda, the queen of Sparta. Zeus had intercourse with Leda in the form of a swan. As a result of this coupling, Leda produced two eggs. From one of the eggs sprang Polydeuces and Helen, and from the other sprang Castor and Clytemnestra. In some accounts, Zeus was the father of only Polydeuces and Helen.

Helen grew up at the court of Leda's husband, King Tyndareos. Her beauty attracted many princely suitors. One of them, Odysseus, persuaded Tyndareos to make all the suitors swear to uphold the honour of Helen's eventual choice as a husband. She married Menelaus, the brother of Agamemnon and adopted heir of Tyndareos.

A decade later the Trojan prince Paris, who had been promised the hand of Helen by the goddess Aphrodite, visited Sparta. Menelaus, now king, was called away to Crete and returned to discover that the visitor had eloped with his wife. He journeyed to Troy with Odysseus to demand Helen's return; his appeal was rebuffed, and Helen and Paris married.

True to their oath, all Helen's former suitors determined to avenge the insult to Menelaus – and thus began the Trojan War. According to most accounts, after the Trojan War, Helen was reconciled with Menelaus and together they returned to Sparta.

Helios *Greece*

"The Sun", the god personifying the sun, the offspring of the Titans Hyperion and Theia. From his palace beyond the eastern horizon, he was said to drive his chariot westward across the sky. He returned home at night in a great cup that sailed on Ocean, the great river surrounding the world. The daily arrival of Helios was announced by the goddess Eos (meaning "Dawn").

Helios appears in few myths, but most notably in the story of Phaëthon.

Helios in his chariot from a Trojan relief dating from c.300BC.

Hellen *Greece*

The mythical ancestor of the Greek nation, the Hellenes. Hellen was the son of Deucalion and Pyrrha, the only survivors of a great flood sent by Zeus to destroy humanity. Hellen and his wife Orseis had three sons, Aeolus, Dorus and Xuthus, from whom the various Greek peoples were descended.

Hephaistos *Greece*

The god of fire and forge, the divine smith. Hephaistos was the son either of Zeus and Hera or, according to most accounts, of Hera alone. It was said that the goddess bore him without a father in retaliation for Zeus giving birth to the goddess Athene without a mother. However, in other versions Hephaistos, born before Athene, eased her birth by splitting Zeus' head open with his axe. Either way, the two deities were linked as patrons of the arts and crafts.

Hephaistos was born lame and ugly, and Hera felt such shame that she hurled him from Mount Olympus into the great river Ocean which encircled the earth. He was rescued by the sea nymphs Thetis and Eurynome and raised by

Helios: *see*
Eos; Phaethon

Hellen: *see*
Deucalion

Hephaistos: *see*
Aphrodite; Ares; Athene; Cyclops; Ericthonius; Hera; OLYMPIANS, THE

Helen, from an Attic white-ground krater of the 5th century BC.

Hera

*Hera, from a
bas relief in Rome.*

them for nine years, during which time he acquired his knowledge of craftsmanship. The god grew up and sent Hera a beautifully wrought golden throne, but as soon as she sat on it she was bound by invisible cords, which only Hephaistos could loosen. He refused to return to Olympus and free his mother unless he was able to marry the goddess of love, Aphrodite. But, Dionysos got him drunk and led him to Olympus on a mule. The other deities laughed at the sight, but, once home, he freed Hera and married Aphrodite.

Hephaistos was portrayed as milder than the other Olympians and often the butt of their mockery. However, he was not altogether unknown to have violent outbursts: he once tried to rape Athene.

Hephaistos, who was usually shown wearing a craftsman's tunic, created Pandora, the first woman, and made countless other beautiful and magical things. The god's forge was located either on or near Mount Olympus, or underground (especially in volcanic areas), or on Lemnos, one of the god's cult centres. His assistants were the Cyclopes. The Romans identified Hephaistos with Vulcan and claimed that his smithy was beneath Mount Etna.

Hera *Greece*

The supreme goddess of Olympus, the sister and wife of Zeus. Hera (which may mean "Lady") was worshipped as the upholder of the sanctity of marriage and was also associated with fertility and childbirth. She was a great goddess in her own right, but most myths about her concentrate on her tempestuous relationship with her often adulterous husband, Zeus. She is portrayed as jealous and angry, constantly watchful of Zeus and ready to persecute his lovers. Among the victims of Hera's

wrath were Io, Leto and Semele. She also persecuted any offspring of Zeus' affairs, most notably the hero Herakles. Notwithstanding Zeus' adultery, the ancient Greeks called the union of Hera and Zeus the Sacred Marriage and it represented the importance of wedlock in Greek society. Hera always remained faithful to her husband.

Hera bore Ares (god of war), Eileithyia (goddess of childbirth) and Hebe (goddess of youth). She also bore the god Hephaistos, possibly without the participation of Zeus, in revenge for the motherless birth of Athene from the god's head.

Herakles *Greece*

The greatest of all Greek heroes. Herakles (whom the Romans called Hercules) was the offspring of Zeus' adultery with Alkmene, the queen of Tiryns and a descendant of the hero Perseus. Possibly because Alkmene was an unwitting adultress (Zeus had assumed the form of her husband), the wrath of Zeus's wife Hera was directed towards their offspring. Hera sent serpents to devour the infant Herakles and his half-brother Iphikles in their crib, but Herakles throttled them.

Herakles grew to be the strongest man and greatest fighter in the world. He was often in combat, for example against the Lapiths, Centaurs and Amazons. He fought with Death in the underworld to free Alcestis. Herakles joined Jason on his quest for the Golden Fleece. When the expedition neared Bithynia in northern Asia Minor (modern Turkey), Herakles broke his oar and went ashore to make a new one. His squire and lover, Hylas, went to look for water and was captured by water nymphs who dragged him down into the pool where they lived. Herakles was frantic at his lover's

Herakles fighting Achelous, from a Greek red-figure vase.

disappearance and let the Argonauts sail on while he looked for him. But Hylas was never seen again.

Herakles defeated the enemies of Creon, king of Thebes, who in gratitude gave him his daughter Megara in marriage. But one day Hera drove the hero mad and he butchered Megara and their three sons. In penance Herakles served King Eurystheus of Tiryns for twelve years, when he accomplished the twelve tasks known as the labours of Herakles (*see panel on next page*).

Herakles later wrestled with Achelous, a river god, to win the hand of Deianeira, the daughter of King Oenus of Aetolia. Some time later he killed a Centaur, Nessus, who tried to rape Deianeira. As Nessus lay dying, he told Deianeira how to make a potion which would guarantee her husband's fidelity. When Herakles (whose lust was as renowned as his strength) fell for another woman, Iole, Deianeira covered his shirt with the potion and sent it to her husband. But the potion was a poison which ravaged the hero's body, causing him terrible agony and fatal injury. In anguish, Deianeira hanged herself.

The dying hero was borne to Mount Oeta in central Greece by Hyllus, his son by Deianeira, and laid on a funeral pyre. As the flames grew more and more fierce, Herakles ascended to Mount Olympus on a cloud. He was granted immortality by Zeus and was finally reconciled with Hera, and he lived among the Olympians as a god. There he married Hebe, the goddess of youth.

HERAKLES, THE LABOURS OF

See panel on next page

Hermaphroditus *Greece*

A handsome young hunter, the son of the god Hermes and the goddess Aphrodite. A water nymph, Salmacis, fell in love with him, but he rejected her advances. Later, when he bathed in the pool where she lived, Salmacis embraced him so closely that they became fused as one being with a woman's breasts and a man's genitals. As he died, Hermaphroditus prayed that all men who bathed in the pool would acquire both male and female attributes.

Hermes *Greece*

The son of Zeus and the nymph Maia, the daughter of the Titan, Atlas. Hermes was born at sunrise and by noon he had already displayed his divinity by inventing the lyre. In the evening of the same day he stole the cattle of his half-brother, the god Apollo. Apollo caught him and took him to see Zeus for punishment, but agreed to accept the lyre instead.

Hermes was responsible for motion, transfer and exchange. In fact, as the messenger of the gods he was usually depicted in a traveller's hat and wearing winged sandals. He carried a herald's staff which was also his magic wand, the *caduceus*, formed from two snakes entwined around a central pole and usually crowned by a pair of wings.

Hermes, from a Greek vase painting.

HERAKLES, THE LABOURS OF

The TWELVE LABOURS accomplished by Herakles in the service of King Eurystheus of Tiryns were the great hero's most renowned exploits. The first six labours took place in the Peloponnese.

1 The Nemean Lion. Herakles was ordered to kill a monstrous lion which was terrorizing the land of Nemea. No weapon could penetrate its hide, so Herakles beat the creature senseless with a great club and then throttled it. He then skinned the lion with its own claws and donned the pelt to render himself invulnerable.

2 The Lernean Hydra. The hero was sent to kill the Hydra, a great serpent or dragon with nine heads which infested a swamp near Lerna. Whenever he chopped off one head, two more grew in its place. Iolaus, his nephew, solved the problem by cauterizing each neck immediately after Herakles had cut off the head.

Herakles fighting the Nemean Lion from a vase of c.550BC.

3 The Cerynean Hind. Herakles was told to capture this beast, which had golden horns and bronze hooves and lived on Mount Cerynea. It was sacred to the goddess Artemis and the hero dared not cause it harm. He caught the hind after chasing it for a year and slightly wounding it. To escape the goddess's anger he blamed Eurystheus for the creature's injury.

4 The Erymanthian Boar. The hero had to bring back alive a monstrous boar which was laying waste to the area around Mount Erymanthus. He captured the beast and returned to Tiryns. Eurystheus was so frightened at the sight of it that he hid in an urn.

5 The Augean Stables. Herakles had just one day to clean out the cattle stables of Augeas, the son of Helios. The stables had never been cleaned and were piled high with years' worth of dung from Augeas' great cattle herds. Herakles succeeded by diverting the rivers Alpheus and Peneus through the stables.

6 The Stymphalian Birds. Herakles was ordered to get rid of a flock of monstrous man-eating birds with iron claws, wings and beaks which infested Lake Stymphalos in Arcadia. He scared them out of their trees with bronze castanets and then shot them one by one with his bow.

7 The Cretan Bull. Eurystheus sent Herakles to Crete to capture a wild, fire-breathing bull which was terrorizing the island. The hero caught the bull and took it to Greece.

8 The Mares of Diomedes. Herakles went to Thrace to capture a herd of vicious mares owned by Diomedes, king of the Bitones, who fed them the flesh of strangers. Herakles slew Diomedes, fed him to the mares, tamed them and took them back to Eurystheus.

9 The Girdle of Hippolyte. The hero was commanded to fetch the beautiful girdle of Hippolyte, the queen of the Amazons of Asia Minor, for Eurystheus' daughter. Herakles vanquished the Amazons, slew Hippolyte and took the girdle from her body.

10 The Cattle of Geryon. Herakles borrowed the Cup of Helios, the Sun, to sail beyond Spain to the island where Geryon, a three-bodied monster, kept red cattle. He passed through the Straits of Gibraltar (setting up the twin Pillars of Herakles on either side) and into the great river Ocean which surrounded the world. He killed Geryon, his giant herdsman Eurytion and the two-headed watchdog Orthus, and returned to Greece with the cattle.

11 The Apples of the Hesperides. Eurystheus sent Herakles to the far west once again to bring back the golden apples which grew on a tree tended by the Hesperides, nymphs who lived on Mount Atlas. Herakles killed Ladon, the dragon which guarded the tree, and took the apples. They were later returned by Athene, since they had been a wedding present from Gaia to Hera.

12 The Descent to the Underworld. The hero had to capture Cerberus, the three-headed dog which guarded the gates of the underworld. After a struggle he dragged Cerberus before Eurystheus, then sent the dog back to the underworld.

Hermes was the god of travellers and roads and statues of him (*herms*) often stood near crossroads. Hermes oversaw all transactions, both legal and illicit: he was the patron of both merchants and thieves. He carried the divine word of the gods but was also the purveyor of lies and false oaths.

One of the titles given to Hermes was Psychopompos ("Bearer of Souls"), because he was said to escort the souls of the dead to the underworld.

Hesperides, The *Greece*
A group of nymphs, often said to be the daughters of the Titan Atlas. They lived in the far west of the world on Mount Atlas and tended a garden in which grew a tree bearing golden apples.

Hestia *Greece*
The virgin goddess of the hearth, the eldest child of Kronos and Rhea and the sister of Demeter, Hades, Hera, Poseidon and Zeus. Despite being the most senior Olympian deity, Hestia ("Hearth") appears infrequently in myth. However, she was revered as the divine guarantor of domestic stability and prosperity, and was said to be present at the naming and legitimation of children. She was also revered as the protector of social stability.

In Rome, where she was known as Vesta, the hearth goddess became the focus of an important official cult as the protector of the Roman homeland. Her highly respected virgin priestesses, known as the Vestals, tended a sacred eternal flame which was regarded as the "hearth" of the nation.

Hina *Oceania*
A woman who grew the first coconut, according to a Tongan myth. Hina was a noblewoman whose virginity was respected and protected by all the community. An eel had intercourse with her and made her pregnant. Her people caught the eel, chopped it up and ate it, apart from the head, which Hina asked to keep. She buried the head and from it sprouted the first coconut.

Hine-hau-one *Oceania*
The first human being, according to Maori mythology. The creator god Tane, the son of Papa, mother earth, and Rangi, father sky, wanted a wife. His mother turned him down, and on her advice he made the first human, Hine-hau-one ("Earth-Created Maiden"), from the sand of Hawaiki Island. Hine-hau-one was responsible for the first human birth and for the arrival of human mortality: she bore Tane a daughter, Hine-titama, who later became Hine-nui-te-po, the giant goddess of death.

Hine-nui-te-po *Oceania*
"Great Mistress of the Dark", the Maori goddess of the underworld and death. Hine-nui-te-po, originally called Hine-titama ("Dawn Maiden"), was the daughter of Hine-hau-one, the first human being, and the god Tane. Tane married Hine-titama, but when she found out that he was her father she fled in horror to the underworld and became Hine-nui-te-po. She called out to Tane that she would bring death to all his children. This is how the human race became mortal.

The trickster Maui was told by his father that if he passed through the body of Hine-nui-te-po, from her vagina to her mouth, he would become immortal. Maui attempted this act while Hine-nui-te-po slept, but a bird's laughter at the sight awoke her and she killed him (*see* Maui), confirming that human beings would never attain immortality.

*Horus from a wall
painting in the tomb of
an Egyptian ruler.*

Hippolyte *Greece*
A queen of the Amazons slain by the hero Herakles.

Ho-no-susori and Hiko-hoho-demi
Japan
Two famous brothers, the offspring of Honinigi, the grandson of the goddess Amaterasu, and his consort Kon-hana-sakuya-hime. The elder brother, Ho-no-susori (which means "Fireshine"), was a sea fisherman while Hiko-hoho-demi ("Fireshade") was a hunter. Hiko-hoho-demi grew unhappy with hunting and suggested that they swap occupations. Ho-no-susori agreed, but Hiko-hoho-demi fared no better at fishing and lost his brother's prized fish hook. Ho-no-susori insisted on retrieving his hook, so Hiko-hoho-demi went on a long journey to the undersea palace of Watatsumi-no-kami, the sea god.

Watatsumi-no-kami found Ho-no-susori's fish hook in the mouth of a redfish and gave Hiko-hoho-demi his daughter Toyotama-hime in marriage. Later Watatsumi-no-kami let his son-in-law travel home on the back of a crocodile with, as a parting gift, two magic jewels: one to make the sea rise and one to make it fall.

Hiko-hoho-demi arrived home and gave his brother his fish hook. However, Ho-no-susori continued to complain, so Hiko-hoho-demi threw the first jewel into the sea. As the sea rose, Ho-no-susori panicked and pleaded for forgiveness from his brother. Hiko-hoho-demi then threw the second jewel into the sea, causing the water to fall (this is the origin of the tides). Ho-no-susori promised to serve Hiko-hoho-demi for the rest of his life.

Toyotama-hime joined Hiko-hoho-demi and bore a son, Amasuhiko, before returning to her father.

Honoyeta *Oceania*
A serpent deity of the Kalauna people of Goodenough Island in Melanesia. He had two wives, and when they were off at work he would shed his snake's skin to become a handsome young man. One of the wives discovered his secret and destroyed the snake skin. Honoyeta was furious and in revenge brought drought, famine and death to humanity.

Horus *Egypt*
The falcon-headed god, the son of the goddess Isis and the god Osiris. Seth caused the death of his brother Osiris, the first king of Egypt, and seized his throne. Isis retrieved her husband's body and hovered over it in the form of a sparrowhawk, fanning enough life back into him for her to conceive a son, Horus. She knew Seth would harm her child, so she fled to the Nile delta and gave birth to Horus at Chemmis near Buto. With the assistance of other deities, such as the goddesses Hathor and Selqet, Isis raised Horus until he was old enough to challenge Seth and claim his royal inheritance.

The sun god invited Horus and Seth to put their cases before the Ennead. Seth declared that he should be king because only he was strong enough to defend the sun during its nightly voyage through the underworld. Some deities accepted this argument, but Isis persuaded them to change their minds.

Seth refused to proceed with Isis there, so he adjourned the tribunal to an island to which Isis was refused access. However, the goddess bribed Nemty, ferryman of the gods, to take her across. Then she tricked Seth into agreeing that it was wrong for a son to have his inheritance stolen. Seth complained about her trickery and the gods punished Nemty by cutting off his toes.

Further confrontations between Horus and Seth proved inconclusive. In the end the gods wrote to Osiris, who threatened to send demons to the realm of the gods if Horus was not made king at once. The sun god found in favour of Horus.

Horus was seen as a sky god whose left eye was the moon and whose right eye was the sun. The Eye of Horus or Wedjat ("Whole One") was frequently depicted in Egyptian art.

Hreidmar *Germanic regions*

A farmer, the father of the brothers Fafnir, Otter and Regin, according to Scandinavian mythology.

Hrungnir *Germanic regions*

One of the race of giants who were the enemies of the Scandinavian gods. Hrungnir challenged the god Odin to a horse race, but lost. Later, he entered Asgard, the home of the gods, and confronted the god Thor in a mighty duel. The giant hurled a massive whetstone at Thor, part of which lodged in the god's skull. Thor made light of his injury and the destroyed Hrungnir with his hammer.

Huehueteotl *Central America*

The Aztec god of fire and the hearth, probably in origin an Olmec deity (*c*.1500BC–*c*.400BC). Huehueteotl ("Old God") was revered by the Aztecs as the oldest god and the first companion of humanity. He appears to have been above all a domestic deity. From as early as *c*.500BC he was depicted as a hunched old man with few or no teeth, carrying a brazier on his head.

Huitzilopochtli *Central America*

The god of the sun and war, the national god of the Aztecs, also known as the Blue Tezcatlipoca. Huitzilopochtli ("Hummingbird of the South") was a uniquely Aztec god and may have begun as a legendary hero, later deified.

Huitzilopochtli was conceived by magic when a heavenly ball of down entered the womb of his mother, the goddess Coatlicue, at Coatepec (Serpent Hill, near Tula, Mexico). Her existing offspring, the goddess Coyolxauhqui and her four hundred brothers, were angry at her pregnancy and cut off their mother's head and hands. At the moment she died Coatlicue gave birth to the fully formed Huitzilopochtli, who avenged his mother's death by killing Coyolxauhqui and hurling her dismembered corpse to the bottom of Coatepec. He then routed his brothers.

The god was said to have guided the Aztec people from their place of origin, Aztlan, on a great southward trek to the future site of Tenochtitlan, the capital of the Aztec empire (modern Mexico City). A historical migration in fact lasted from *c*.AD1150 to *c*.AD1350.

Huitzilopochtli, the lord of the Fifth Sun, the current world epoch, was a forbidding deity closely associated with war and death (hummingbirds were said to be the souls of fallen warriors). He was central to the Aztec cult of human sacrifice, which was believed necessary to feed Tonatiuh, the sun, with whom the god was identified. His most important shrine, at the top of the Templo Mayor (Great Temple) in Tenochtitlan, was the site of human sacrifices, often on a massive scale.

HUMANITY, THE ORIGIN OF
See panel on next page

Hun Dun *China*
"Chaos", the protagonist of a creation myth written down *c*.350BC. In this myth the primordial chaos and the two

Hreidmar: *see* Fafnir; Loki; Odin; Sigurd

Hrungnir: *see* Asgard; Odin; Thor

Huitzilopochtli: *see* Aztlan; Coatlicue; Five Suns, The

Hun Dun: *see* CREATION; Yin and Yang

Huehueteotl, from a stone sculpture found in Tenochtitlan.

Huitzilopochtli, from the Codex Borbonicus of the 16th century.

HUMANITY, THE ORIGIN OF

Surprisingly few mythologies recount the origin of humanity in great detail. One concept found almost worldwide is that humans were formed from earth or clay by a particular creator deity. For example, the Bible recounts how God created Adam ("Man") "of the dust of the ground", and according to Chinese myth the goddess Nü Gua created humanity from drops of watery mud. In Rwanda the High God is believed to form babies from clay in the womb, and women of childbearing age are careful to sleep with a pot of water next to the bed for God to use in order to mould his clay.

Usually, but not universally, man is said to have arrived before woman, a mythic tradition that often goes hand in hand with the belief, seen in the story of Adam and Eve, that women also brought misfortune to humanity. The Greeks related how the first woman, Pandora, took into human society a jar (known as "Pandora's Box") in which were contained all the evils of the world. Myths like these have served to justify the inferior position of women in patriarchal societies.

However, a number of cultures claim that the first human was, in fact, a woman. For example, according to Iroquois and Huron mythology the ancestor of the human race was called Ataentsic, a woman who fell from the heavens to earth. Maori myth recounts how the god Tane wanted a wife and created the first woman Hine-hau-one ("Earth-Created Maiden"), from the sand of Hawhaiki island.

A particular type of human origin story widespread throughout the Central and South Americas is the "emergence myth". For example, the Incas believed that the creator deity Viracocha created humans from clay. He then told them to descend into the earth and emerge from caves. Thus the ancestors of the Incas emerged from three caves at Pacariqtambo ("Place of Origin") near Cuzco, the Inca capital.

opposing but complementary forces of the universe are personified as three emperors. Hu, the emperor of the Southern Sea, met Shu, the emperor of the Northern Sea, in the land of Hun Dun, the emperor of the Centre. Hun Dun showed Hu and Shu great hospitality and they discussed how to show their gratitude. They realized that everyone except Hun Dun had seven bodily orifices. Hu and Shu therefore decided to repay their host's hospitality by making seven holes in his body. Using chisels and drills they bored one orifice a day. After seven days the emperors finished their task – only to discover that they had killed Hun Dun.

The ordered universe then came into existence at the moment Chaos died.

Hunaphu *Central America*

One of the so-called Hero Twins, the other twin being Xbalanque. The most complete version of their story appears in the *Popul Vuh*, the sacred book of the Quiche Maya. It recounts their lives from their games with the gods of the underworld to their eventual rebirth as the sun and moon.

Hydra *Africa*

The offspring of Echidna and Typhon, the Hydra was a multi-headed dragon or water-snake slain by the hero Herakles as the second of his twelve labours. The monster was sometimes said to have the body of a hound.

Hymir *Germanic regions*
A giant who, in Scandinavian myth, sailed on a celebrated fishing expedition with the god Thor. During the expedition Thor, using the head of one of Hymir's oxen as bait, hooked the World Serpent, a fierce, poison-spitting dragon which lived in the depths of the ocean. The god hauled the dragon's head out of the water but as he raised his hammer to strike it, Hymir, terrified at the sight of the creature, cut Thor's line. Thor was furious and hurled Hymir into the sea.

Hyperion *Greece*
A Titan, the son of Gaia and Uranos. Hyperion married his sister Theia and their offspring were Helios (the Sun), Selene (the Moon) and Eos (the Dawn). In later tradition Hyperion, which means "Going Above", became another name for Helios.

Hypsipyle *Greece*
A queen of the island of Lemnos and a lover of the hero Jason.

Hymir: *see*
Dragon; Thor

Hyperion: *see*
Eos; Helios; Selene; Titan

Hypsipyle *see*
ARGONAUTS, THE VOYAGE OF THE

Icarus strapped to the
wings made by his
father, based on a bronze
figurine.

Icarus *Greece*

The son of the craftsman Daedalus and a slave woman. When Daedalus and Icarus were imprisoned in the Labyrinth by King Minos of Crete, their only possible escape was by air. Daedalus made two pairs of magical wings from wax and feathers. Before they took off he warned his son not to fly too close to the sun, but Icarus forgot this advice and the sun's heat melted the wax in his wings, causing them to disintegrate. He plummeted into the sea and drowned. Daedalus retrieved his son's body from the ocean, thereafter called the Sea of Icarus or Icarian Sea, and buried him on a nearby island, thereafter called Icaria.

Ifa *Africa*

The west African god of order and control, who was sent down to earth to teach humans the secrets of healing and prophecy. Ifa (his Yoruba name: he is known as Fa among the neighbouring Fon) often appears in myth as the companion of, and counterbalance to, the trickster god Eshu, who tries to disrupt the regular order of things. Before people embark on an important enterprise or piece of work it is customary to make an offering to Ifa. However, the first taste of the offering is always presented to Eshu in order to ensure that things proceed smoothly.

Ifa is said to have established the Ifa oracle, a system of divination which is widespread throughout Africa.

Iliad, The *Greece*

The title of a great verse epic written *c*.750BC and traditionally attributed to Homer, a blind poet said to have lived on the island of Chios in the Aegean. The *Iliad* covers events in the Trojan War toward the end of the conflict, from the withdrawal from the battlefield of the Greek hero Achilles to the death and funeral of the Trojan hero Hector. The title of the epic is derived from Ilion or Ilium, an alternative name for Troy.

Ilyap'a *South America*

The Inca god of storms and weather. Ilyap'a was greatly revered as the god of the fertilizing rains, which he was said to draw from the waters of the celestial river (the Milky Way). Ilyap'a's sister had a jug in which she kept the water, which would fall as rain when Ilyap'a smashed the jug with a bolt of lightning hurled from his slingshot. The crack of Ilyapa's sling was heard as thunder and his gleaming attire was glimpsed as flashes of lightning as the god moved through the heavens.

Imhotep *Egypt*

An architect and priest-minister of the pharaoh Djoser (27th century BC). Imhotep, a historical figure, was revered as a demi-god of wisdom, medicine and magic. His parents were apparently the creator deity Ptah, the god of crafts and intellect, and a human mother.

Inari *Japan*

The god of rice. Inari is the patron of rice farmers and is said to ensure the success of their harvest. In addition he is revered, especially by merchants, as the deity who brings wellbeing. The god was also considered in ancient times to be the patron of swordsmiths. Inari is depicted as a bearded old man with two foxes, who were his messengers.

Indra *India*

The warrior king of the gods and the head of the early Vedic pantheon. Indra was the champion of the gods against the forces of evil and the races of demons, known as the Asuras and the Rakshakas, and the protector of the Aryan invaders of India.

The tawny-haired son of Heaven and Earth, he was said to be huge and powerfully built, with massive arms for wielding his weapons, which included the thunderbolt (*vajra*). Whenever he drank *soma*, an intoxicating drink which was central to ancient Vedic ritual, he swelled to such an enormous size that he filled the heavens and the earth. The *soma* gave him the power to make the

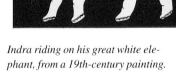

Indra riding on his great white elephant, from a 19th-century painting.

sun rise and to perform the great deeds of a mighty divine warrior. He was often depicted riding a white elephant.

A famous story about Indra relates how he fought and killed the dragon-demon Vritra, lord of chaos and drought, allowing the ordered world to exist. By killing the dragon, Indra separated the waters from the land, the lower regions from the upper, and caused the sun to rise every morning.

Indra appears to have been a rival of the god Varuna, whom he may have ousted as the ruler of the gods. Indra himself declined in prestige in later Hinduism. For example, the myth of Vritra was reworked so that the dragon became a brahman, whom it was a grave sin to kill, and Indra had to do penance for his transgression. As a sinner, Indra lost his strength and fine appearance and the younger deities often humiliated him. Krishna persuaded Indra's followers to cease worshipping him. Indra's chief function in the mythology of classical Hinduism was as the god of rain, a role derived from his ancient association with thunder.

Ing *Germanic regions*

An early Germanic god who was known to the Anglo-Saxons and (as Yngvi) to the Swedes. Ing, who appears to have been a fertility god, was associated with a waggon for journeying round the land. The Ynglings, who were a historical line of Swedish kings, claimed him as the founder of their dynasty. The name Yngvi-Freyr was used for the Ynglings' protector, Freyr.

Inti *South America*

The Inca sun god and lord of life. Inti was revered as the divine ancestor of the Inca, who called themselves "children of the sun". The god was held in great awe and eclipses of the sun were considered to be a sign of his anger. He was the focus of many important official rituals as well as his chief festival, Inti Raymi, which took place annually at the June solstice. The centre of Inti's worship was the massive Coricancha or Temple of the Sun at Cuzco, the Inca capital. The god's shrine there contained the mummies of deceased emperors and its walls were covered with gold, a sacred metal considered to be the sweat of the sun. Inti was usually depicted as a great disc of gold with a human face, from which emanated sun rays.

Invasions, The *Book of* *Celtic regions*

A 12th-century prose collection of myths which claim to relate the history of Ireland since the Biblical Flood. The *Book of Invasions* (in Irish *Leabhar Gabhála*) probably relies on earlier works. As its fuller title, The *Book of the Conquest of Ireland*, suggests, it recounts the successive invasions of Ireland by six peoples: Cessair and her followers; Parthalón and his followers; Nemhedh and his followers; the Fir Bholg; the Tuatha Dé Danann; and finally the Sons of Míl or Milesians, the Gaels. The book focuses on two conflicts, the first and second battles of Magh Tuiredh (Moytirra).

Io *Greece*

A princess, the daughter of King Inachus of Argos and his wife Melia. Io was a virgin priestess of the goddess Hera. Zeus, Hera's husband, had intercourse with Io in the guise of a cloud. When Hera grew suspicious, Zeus turned Io into a beautiful white heifer. Not decieved, Hera asked for the heifer as a gift. The goddess set Argus, an unsleeping giant with one hundred eyes, to guard her.

Zeus asked the god Hermes to help free his captive lover. Hermes told Argos many stories, lulled him to sleep, then cut off his head. However, before Zeus could restore Io to human form Hera sent a gadfly which plagued her constantly and pursued her round the world as she tried to escape its sting. Eventually she reached Egypt, where Zeus finally turned her back into a human. As he did so Io became pregnant with a son, Epaphos.

Iolofath *Oceania*

A culture hero and trickster figure of Micronesian mythology, also known as Olifat. Often identified with the sun, he is credited with bringing fire to humans. For example, in the central Caroline Islands, Olifat is said to have sent a bird to earth with fire in its beak.

On Ulithi atoll, Iolofath, the sun, is said to be the son of the sky god Lugeilang and a woman, Thilpelap. Iolofath lived on earth but one day decided to visit the sky. Iolofath was killed in a battle with his sky relatives, but Lugeilang revived him and allowed him to stay among the gods.

Irik *Southeast Asia*

One of two primordial bird spirits (the other being Ara) which, according to the Iban people of Borneo, were the first beings to exist (*see* Ara and Irik).

Ishtar *Middle East*

The great Babylonian goddess of love, sex and fertility, the daughter of either the god Anu or the god Sin. Ishtar (this is her Akkadian name: she was called Inanna by the Sumerians) was also a great war goddess, often referred to as "the Lady of Battles". In this aspect she was presented as a formidable figure, for example in the epic of Gilgamesh. Ishtar-Inanna was identified with the planet Venus.

The most important myth in which Ishtar-Inanna is the central figure recounts her descent to the underworld land of the dead, possibly in order to sieze power there. According to the longer Sumerian account, the goddess told her vizier Ninshubur to go to three gods for aid if she did not return from the underworld. Inanna travelled through the underworld, passing through seven gates, at each of which she had to remove a piece of clothing. When she finally arrived before her sister Ereshkigal, who was the queen of the underworld, Inanna was naked. She tried to overthrow Ereshkigal, but failed and was executed, and her corpse was hung on a nail.

Realizing that some disaster must have occurred, Ninshubur went to Enki (the Akkadian Ea), the god of wisdom. He made two asexual beings which descended to Inanna and revived her, but she was only allowed to leave the underworld on condition that she found a substitute. She returned to earth and declared that her substitute would be her husband Dumuzi. He tried to escape, but

was captured by underworld demons. The poem ends with a speech, possibly by Inanna, declaring that Dumuzi would spend one half of the year in the underworld and his sister, Geshtinanna ("Lady of the Vine"), the other.

Isis *Egypt*

A great goddess, the consort and sister of Osiris, the sister of Seth and Nephthys, and the mother of Horus. Isis, one of the nine great deities known as the Ennead, features in myth principally as the devoted wife of Osiris, the first king on earth, and mother of Horus. As the divine exemplar of the dedicated wife and mother, Isis was the centre of an important cult which spread farther afield than Egypt.

The goddess's adversary was her brother Seth, who brought about the death of Osiris and usurped his throne. Isis retrieved her husband's corpse and protected it from Seth, using magic powers to halt or reverse its decay. In one account, Isis hovered over the body as a sparrowhawk and fanned enough life into Osiris with her wings to enable her to conceive a son, the god Horus. Isis protected Horus from Seth and assisted him to regain his birthright, the kingship, from his uncle.

Islands of the Blessed, The *Greece*

A region of the underworld, usually identified with Elysium but sometimes seen as a separate paradise.

Itzamna *Central America*

The lord of heaven, the supreme deity of the Maya pantheon. Itzamna ("Lizard House") was the inventor of writing and learning and the first priest. He was also revered as a deity of medicine and his consort was Ix Chel, the goddess of medicine, childbirth and weaving. The

Ishtar: *see*
Ashera; Astarte; Dumuzi; Ea; Enki; Enkimdu; Gilgamesh

Isis: *see*
Anubis; Horus; Osiris; Seth

*Isis (*below*), from a 19th-dynasty mural in Set I's temple at Abydos.*

Islands of the Blessed, The: *see* Elysium

Itzamna: *see* Ahau Kin

*Itzamna (*below*), the supreme god of the Maya pantheon.*

god was variously represented as an enthroned monarch, a scribe, an old man, and sometimes a great sky serpent. Itzamna appears to have been associated with the sun god, Ahau Kin: representations of the two gods can be seen to bear a close resemblance. He was also known as simply Zamna and may have been the God K.

Ivan the Fool *Slav regions*
A figure of Russian folk mythology who reflects the theme of ancestor worship. He was the guardian of the hearth and upholder of family tradition. According to the well-known tale of Silver Roan, Ivan the Fool was the youngest and most scruffy of three brothers. Shortly before his death, their elderly father asked his sons to keep watch over his grave for three nights. The two elder sons ignored this request and sent Ivan, who was dirty and lay on the stove all day, to guard the grave on his own. At midnight on the third night, the dead father appeared and rewarded Ivan for his vigil with Silver Roan, a magic horse who breathed smoke from his nostrils and flashed fire from his eyes.

Later, the Tsar announced that he would give his daughter in marriage to any man who could snatch her veil at a great height. Ivan summoned Silver Roan with a magic spell, climbed into his ear and became a handsome young man. He won the Tsar's contest on the third occassion and then turned back into the usual dirty Ivan and disappeared. The monarch held a great banquet in order to find the youth who had earned his daughter's hand. Ivan, dirty and in rags, sat behind the stove in the feasting hall. He was recognized when he used the veil to wipe his tankard. To the annoyance of his brothers, he was given his prize.

This redrawing is taken from a wall-painting in a temple at Tulum, thought to show Ix Chel.

Ix Chel *Central America*
The goddess of fertility, childbirth, medicine and weaving in Maya myth, as well as the wife of the supreme deity Itzamna. Ix Chel (meaning "Lady of the Rainbow") was sometimes depicted as an old woman with serpents in her hair and occasionally with the eyes and claws of a jaguar. She was particularly revered by women, and was also known as Ix Kanleom meaning "The Spider's Web that Catches the Morning Dew".

Ixion *Greece*
A king of the Lapiths, who were a race of Thessaly, and a notorious sexual transgressor of Greek myth. Ixion tried to rape the goddess Hera, the wife of Zeus. However, she tricked him by making an image of herself from a cloud and putting it in her bed in her place. While drunk, Ixion had intercourse with the cloud, which consequently gave birth to Centauros, who became another sexual transgressor and as such the father of the Centaurs. Zeus punished Ixion for attempting to rape Hera by condemning him to be tied to a burning wheel which would rotate eternally in the underworld.

IZANAGI AND IZANAMI
See panel on opposite page

King Ixion of the Lapiths on the burning wheel, from a bowl.

IZANAGI AND IZANAMI *Japan*

The primal creator couple of Japanese mythology, in full Izanagi-no-Mikoto ("August Male") and Izanami-no-Mikoto ("August Female"). According to the *Kojiki*, five primordial divinities, the Separate Heavenly Deities, came into existence when the world was young. Seven further generations of divinities culminated in Izanagi and his sister Izanami, also his wife. The other deities commanded the couple to form the land. They stood on the Floating Bridge of Heaven and stirred the oceans with a jewelled spear. The water drops that fell from the spear became the first land, the island Onogoro.

Izanagi and Izanami descended to the island and built a heavenly pillar and a palace. They devised a wedding ritual: they each walked around the pillar, Izanami from the right and Izanagi from the left. When they met they exchanged greetings and then had intercourse. As a result Izanami gave birth to a deformed child, Hiruko ("Leech-Child"), which they abandoned. An assembly of the gods decided that the birth was Izanami's fault because she had spoken first at the pillar. The couple repeated the ritual and Izanagi spoke first. Izanami then gave birth to many offspring, beginning with a series of islands (Japan). She bore gods and goddesses, including the gods of mountains, winds and trees. But as the fire god Kagutsuchi (or Homusubi) was born, Izanami was burned and died, producing more deities in her urine, excrement and vomit.

Izanagi wept tears of grief, from which sprang more divinities. Angry at his loss, he cut off the fire god's head: yet more deities arose from Kagutsuchi's body. Determined to bring his beloved back to life, Izanagi went to Yomi, the underworld realm of the dead. In the shadows, Izanami promised to ask if she could return with him, but warned Izanagi not to look on her. His desire to see his wife was too great, and he used the tooth of a comb to make a torch. He saw at once that Izanami was already a rotten corpse and fled in horror. His wife, furious that he had ignored her wishes, sent demons, fierce underworld gods, after him. Finally she became a demon and joined the chase. Izanagi shook off his pursuers and blocked the entrance to Yomi with a boulder. From either side of the boulder the couple declared themselves divorced.

Izanagi felt contaminated by his contact with Yomi and bathed in a stream in northeastern Kyushu island as an act of purification. Gods and goddesses sprang from his clothes as he undressed and others arose as he washed his body. Finally Izanagi produced three great deities: the sun goddess Amaterasu from his left eye; the moon god Tsuki-yomi from his right eye; and the storm god Susano from his nose. Izanagi divided his kingdom among them. Each of them accepted their father's decree except Susano, whom Izanagi banished for his defiance. Izanagi then withdrew to heaven, where he is still said to reside in the "Younger Palace of the Sun".

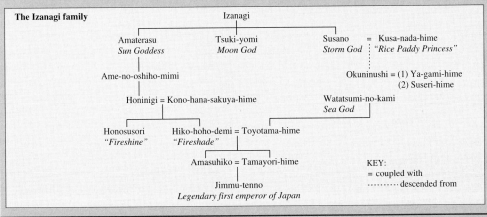

The Izanagi family

Izanagi

Amaterasu *Sun Goddess* — Tsuki-yomi *Moon God* — Susano *Storm God* = Kusa-nada-hime *"Rice Paddy Princess"*

Ame-no-oshiho-mimi

Okuninushi = (1) Ya-gami-hime / (2) Suseri-hime

Honinigi = Kono-hana-sakuya-hime

Watatsumi-no-kami *Sea God*

Honosusori *"Fireshine"* — Hiko-hoho-demi *"Fireshade"* = Toyotama-hime

Amasuhiko = Tamayori-hime

Jimmu-tenno *Legendary first emperor of Japan*

KEY:
= coupled with
·········· descended from

Jade Emperor, The *China*

The divine ruler of heaven, also known as Yuhuang. In earlier times the supreme heavenly deity was known by various names, but by the Song dynasty (AD960–AD1279) the Jade Emperor was widely accepted as the ruler of heaven. His cult contained elements of both Daoism (Taoism) and Buddhism.

The emperor lived in a palace and, like his earthly counterpart, the emperor of China, governed his realm through a vast celestial civil service. The emperor of China was the only human being to have direct personal dealings with the Jade Emperor. All other humans were the responsibility of the heavenly bureaucrats. His chief minister, known as Dongyue Dadi ("Great Ruler of the Eastern Mountains"), ran seventy-five departments of state, each of which was headed by a minor deity. The emperor's consort was Wang Mu Niang Niang, another name for Xi Wang Mu, the Queen-Mother of the West, who lived on the sacred Mount Kunlun.

JAGUAR

See panel on opposite page

Jambudvipa *India*

The name of the circular continent at the centre of the world, according to Hindu and Jain cosmology. In the very middle of Jambudvipa stands Mount Mandara (or Meru) which was used by the Asuras and Devas to churn the ocean. The continent is ringed by the great Salt Ocean and by another seven continents alternating with seven seas.

Janaka *India*

A king of Videha and the father of Sita, who was the wife of Rama.

Janus *Rome*

The god of entrances and exits, a role symbolized by his representation as a man with two faces, one of which looks forward while the other looks backward. Janus presided over every door and entry, including the *jani*, the great triumphal arches and other ceremonial gateways. He was the god of commencements and was usually the first deity invoked in any religious liturgy. Janus gave his name to January, the first month of the year, in which his festival took place (9 January).

JAGUAR

The jaguar, the largest and most ferocious cat of the Americas, features prominently in the mythology of Central and South America. It occurs in the art and religion of all pre-Columbian American civilizations and is still important today in the beliefs of many indigenous peoples. The creature itself stands for royalty, sovereignty, power, fertility and the earth and, as a nocturnal animal, is also closely associated with the forces of the spirit world. The ancient concept of the "were-jaguar", a human being who had magically transformed into a jaguar, links the part-man, part-feline sculptures of the Olmecs (c.1500BC–c.400BC) with the present-day South American tribal jaguar-shamans, each of whom are believed to be able to change into a jaguar. Jaguar-shamans conduct rituals in order to cure disease, to bring success at hunting or even to divine the future.

The jaguar itself is often revered as a divine figure and the possessor of knowledge. For example, the jaguar was believed to be a manifestation of Tezcatlipoca, the supreme deity of the Aztecs. The Maya sun god, Ahau Kin, was said to become the Jaguar God, the lord of darkness, when he travelled at night through the underworld from west to east. The Kayapo people of central Brazil relate how the human society did not possess fire or the bow and arrow before the hunter Botoque stole them from the jaguar.

Jaguar: see Ahau Kin; Botoque; Tezcatlipoca

Jason *Greece*

A prince of Iolcus in Thessaly, the son of King Aeson. Aeson was overthrown by his brother Pelias. Jason's mother sent him for safety to Mount Pelion, where he was educated by the wise Centaur Chiron. When he was twenty Jason set out for home. On the way he helped an old woman (the goddess Hera in disguise) across a river, and won the goddess's protection throughout his subsequent adventures. In helping Hera Jason lost a sandal and arrived at Iolcus with one bare foot. Pelias was alarmed when he saw him, because an oracle had warned him to beware a stranger with one shoe. To get rid of his nephew, Pelias said he would cede him his throne if he travelled to Colchis at the far end of the Black Sea and brought him the famous Golden Fleece.

Jason accepted the challenge and succeeded in his dangerous mission. He returned to Iolcus, to find that Pelias had executed Aeson. In revenge Jason's wife, the sorceress Medea, persuaded the usurper's daughters that if they chopped up their father and cooked him, he would become a young man once more. They followed her instructions, only to discover that she had tricked them into murdering Pelias.

The gruesome way in which Pelias had been killed caused public outrage and Jason and Medea were forced to flee Iolcus. They settled in Corinth and had many children. Years later, King Creon of Corinth offered Jason the hand of his daughter, and Jason, attracted by a good political alliance, proposed divorce to Medea. She was furious and sent Creon and his daughter robes impregnated with venom which caused them both to die in agony. To hurt Jason further she then slit the throats of their children and fled to Athens, leaving Jason alone in

Jason: see ARGONAUTS, THE VOYAGE OF THE; Chiron; Medea

Jason being rescued by Athene, from a red-figure vase.

his misery. He is said to have died many years later when a section of the *Argo*, which had been set up in a temple, fell on his head.

Jataka *Buddhist regions*

"Birth story", the Sanskrit name given to the countless popular myths about former lives of the Buddha. Usually didactic and often amusing, Jataka stories occur in all regions where Buddhism is established.

Jimmu-tenno *Japan*

The legendary first emperor of Japan, whose dates are traditionally 660BC–585BC. Jimmu-tenno (who was also known as Kamu-yamato-iware-biko) was the grandson of Hiko-hoho-demi ("Fireshade") and the great-great-great-grandson of the goddess Amaterasu.

Jimmu and his elder brother, Itsu-se, marched eastward from the region of Hyuga in northeastern Kyushu island on a great expedition to conquer new lands. Japanese chroniclers claimed that the expedition began in 607BC, but there is evidence to suggest that a historical invasion of Yamato from the west

occurred *c.*AD300–AD400. Itsu-se died in battle on Honshu, but after burying him, Jimmu pressed on to pacify the Land of the Reed Plain (Yamato). Receiving the homage of local rulers as they went, Jimmu and his army marched eastward, guided by a great heavenly crow. Finally, when he reached Yamato, Jimmu called a halt to the expedition. He built a palace and married Isuke-yori-hime, a local princess descended from the god Susano.

Jizo *Japan*

A Buddhist deity, the protector of children, in particular of those who have died. Jizo looks after anyone in pain and is also believed to bring souls back from hell. Together with Amida and Kannon he is one of the three most popular deities of Japanese Buddhism. Temples to Jizo are found all over Japan.

Jimmu-tenno, the legendary first emperor of Japan, setting out to conquer new lands.

Jocasta *Greece*

A queen of Thebes, the wife of King Laius and later, unwittingly, of her own son, Oedipus.

Jotunheim *Germanic regions*

The land of the race of giants, according to ancient Scandinavian cosmology. Jotunheim ("Home of the Giants") was said to lie among the roots of Yggdrasil, the cosmic ash tree which united the heavens, the earth and the underworld.

Juno *Rome*

The chief goddess of the Roman pantheon as well as the sister and wife of Jupiter. An ancient Italian deity in origin, Juno was identified early on with the Greek goddess Hera, the wife of Zeus. She was the patron of women, marriage and motherhood, and was an embodiment of Roman matronly values.

Jupiter *Rome*

The supreme deity of the Roman pantheon, usually spelled Juppiter by the Romans and also known as Jovis ("Jove"). Like his Greek counterpart, Zeus, with whom he early on came to be identified, Jupiter was probably a sky and weather god in origin (his name means "Sky Father"). From ancient times the cult of Jupiter was central to Roman religion: he was worshipped as the protector of the Roman state and of its rulers and as the upholder of honour and justice. His greatest temple,which was founded *c*.500BC and dedicated to Juppiter Optimus Maximus ("Best and Greatest Jupiter"), stood on the Capitoline Hill in Rome. Most stories about the god are adapted from the mythology of Zeus.

Jurupari *South America*

A child of the sun who overthrew the rule of women, according to the Tupi people of Amazonian Brazil. In their version of a myth which occurs widely from the Amazon to Tierra del Fuego, the Tupi recount how originally women, not men, ruled the world. The sun grew angry at this state of affairs and took a wife, Ceucy, a virgin whom he made pregnant by the sap of the cucura tree. Ceucy bore Jurupari, who ordered an end to the dominance of women and transferred all power and sacred wisdom to men. Jurupari told men to celebrate their power by holding feasts from which women were excluded on pain of death, and, to set an example, he even caused the death of his own mother. To this day Jurupari is said to wander the world looking for the perfect wife for his father, the sun.

Jocasta: *see*
Oedipus

Jotunheim: *see*
Yggdrasil

Juno: *see*
GREEK AND ROMAN DEITIES; Hera

Jupiter: *see*
Zeus

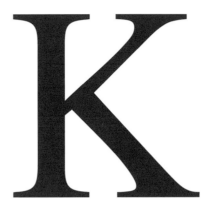

Kachina *North America*

One of a class of ancestral spirits, according to the Pueblo peoples of the southwestern United States, such as the Hopi and Zuni. Kachinas are revered as intermediaries between humans and the great elemental gods and as bringers of harmony and prosperity.

Kagutsuchi *Japan*

The god of fire, who was also known as Homusubi. Kagutsuchi was the son of the Japanese primal creator deities Izanagi and Izanami.

As his mother Izanami gave birth to him, she suffered such terrible burns to her genitals that she died in agony. Izanagi's grief soon turned to anger and he cut off Kagutsuchi's head for causing the death of his beloved consort. As Kagutsuchi died, eight deities sprang from his blood and a further eight from the parts of his body.

Kaintangata *Oceania*

A sky goddess of Maori mythology. She married a cannibal chief, Whaitiri, and subsequently gave birth to Hema, the father of the hero Tawhaki.

Kalala Ilunga *Africa*

A quasi-historical hero king in the mythology of the Luba people of Zaïre. Once a prince called Mbidi Kiluwe journeyed west to hunt in the land of Nkongolo, the great Rainbow King. Nkongolo was very hospitable and allowed Mbidi to sleep with his twin sisters, Bulanda and Mabela. Both sisters became pregnant and Bulanda bore a son, Kalala Ilunga, while Mabela had twins, a boy and a girl. Nkongolo claimed Kalala as his own son and, after they had had an argument, Mbidi left Kalala Ilunga to go home.

Kalala became the best dancer and runner in the kingdom and the jealous Nkongolo decided to kill him. He ordered a concealed pit full of sharp stakes to be made in the dancing area and then invited Kalala Ilunga to a dance contest. Kalala's drummer Kahia warned him of the danger and he escaped, with Nkongolo and his men in pursuit, across the Lualaba river to the land of his real father. Mbidi greeted him warmly and lent him an army to defeat Nkongolo, who fled west with Bulanda and Mabela to Kaii mountain.

But the sisters betrayed him to Kalala's men, who cut off his head. Kalala Ilunga became king and founded the second Luba empire in what is the modern day southeastern Zaïre.

Kali *India*

The goddess of death, the destroyer of demons and the most terrifying of all Hindu goddesses. Kali ("The Black One" or "Time") is dark-skinned and emaciated, with great fangs. She wears a tiger skin and a gruesome necklace of

Kali, from a wall painting.

severed heads or skulls and appears most often on battlefields or at cremation grounds. She is said to spring from the forehead of the warrior goddess Durga when she grows angry. Her ferocity is boundless and in battle she is liable to become so intoxicated with blood that she is in danger of causing the destruction of the world.

According to one myth Durga summoned Kali to kill the demon Raktabija, who produced replicas of himself from every drop of his blood that touched the ground. Durga and her companion goddesses, the seven Matrikas ("Little Mothers"), had wounded him many times, only to find themselves facing an ever-increasing number of Raktabijas. When Kali appeared she caught all his blood before it landed on the earth, devoured all the replica demons in a single mouthful and finally sucked Raktabija dry. The goddess's most famous temple is at Kalighata in Calcutta.

Kaliya *India*

A venomous many-headed serpent which infested the sacred river Yamuna (Jumna). The youthful Krishna subdued Kaliya by dancing on its heads and banishing it to the ocean, together with all its serpent companions.

Kalkin *India*

The future tenth avatar (incarnation) of the god Vishnu. Kalkin is a messianic figure whose advent will herald the end of the present cosmic age of evil, the Kali Yuga, and the beginning of a new golden age, or Krita Yuga. It is said that he will be manifested as a warrior on a white horse, or (according to South Indian popular belief) as the horse itself.

Kamimusubi *Japan*

One of the five primordial "Separate Heavenly Deities", the first divinities to come into existence before the earth had been formed.

Kamsa *India*

The evil king of Mathura and the enemy of Krishna.

Kannon *Japan*

A Buddhist deity, who was the *bosatsu* (Bodhisattva) to whom worshippers would turn to find mercy and wise counsel. Kannon is derived, like his

Kali: *see*
Brahma; Devi; Durga

Kaliya: *see*
Krishna

Kalkin: *see*
VISHNU, THE AVATARS OF

Kamimusubi: *see*
Separate Heavenly Deities, The

Kamsa: *see*
Krishna

Kannon: *see*
Amida; Avalokiteshvara; Bodhisattva; Guanyin

Karaperamun: *see*
CARGO CULTS; Frum, John

Kariki: *see*
Tawhaki

Kek and Keket: *see*
Ogdoad, The

Keret: *see*
Anath; Ashera; Baal; El

Khepry: *see*
Atum; Ra; Ra-Atum; SUN,
MOON AND STARS

Khnum: *see*
Amon; Atum; Imhotep; Ptah

Kannon, from a sword-guard dating from the late 19th century.

Chinese equivalent Guanyin, from the Indian Bodhisattva Avalokiteshvara.

His cult was introduced from Korea a short while after Buddhism reached the Japanese archipelago. He is revered as the protector of infants and women in childbirth, as well as being the protector of the souls of the dead.

In his popular manifestation as Senju Kannon ("Thousand-Armed Kannon"), the deity is said to dispense compassion from each of his thousand hands. He is often regarded as the companion of the *bosatsu* Amida.

Karaperamun *Oceania*
The supreme being worshipped in Vanuatu (formerly the New Hebrides) before the islanders were converted to Christianity. The cult of Karaperamun was revived in 1940 with the arrival of the cargo cult figure of John Frum, who was believed to be his reincarnation.

Kariki *Oceania*
The brother of the Maori hero Tawhaki. Kariki is portrayed as gauche and stupid, in contrast to his borther who is shown to be heroic and clever.

Kek and Keket *Egypt*
A pair of primal deities embodying darkness. They formed part of the group of eight divinities known as the Ogdoad.

Keret *Middle East*
A famous king of Ugaritic (Canaanite) mythology. King Keret was anxious for an heir and married seven times, but each of his wives died childless.

In a dream, the supreme god El told him to invade the neighbouring kingdom and marry Huray, the daughter of its ruler. Keret embarked on his mission and vowed to present the fertility goddess Ashera, the wife of El, with several times Huray's weight in gold if he succeeded. Keket won his bride, and El promised that Huray would have eight sons and that the eldest would be weaned by two goddesses, Ashera and Anath.

Huray bore the eight sons, but then Keret fell ill, probably because he had failed to fulfil his promise to Ashera. He was unable to administer justice and the land grew dry and infertile. However, a ritual was held in honour of the storm god Baal and the rains returned. Keret recovered his health and suppressed a rebellion by one of his sons.

Khepry *Egypt*
A divine scarab beetle which was the dawn manifestation of the sun god. Khepry is typically represented pushing the sun up into the sky, an image derived from the scarab rolling a ball of dung. To the Egyptians, the scarab beetle was a symbol of rebirth, regeneration and transformation.

Khnum *Egypt*
One of the four principal creator gods of the Egyptians, the others being Amon-Ra, Atum and Ptah. Khnum was

envisaged as a potter who moulded deities, humans and animals from clay on his potting wheel, and then breathed life into them. He was usually depicted as a man with the head of a ram, his sacred animal and a symbol of male creative power. Khnum was believed to control the rising of the waters of the Nile, an annual phenomenon crucial to the fertility of the land.

Khori Tumed *Tibet and Mongolia*
The name of a man who married a swan maiden, according to the mythology of the Buriat people of Siberia. One day Khori Tumed saw nine swans fly down to the island of Oikhon in Lake Baikal, where they undressed to reveal nine beautiful maidens. As they bathed in the lake, Khori Tumed took away the feather dress of one swan, so that she could not fly away with the eight other swan maidens. She became his wife and bore him eleven sons.

They were happy, but one day she asked to try on her old swan dress, which Khori Tumed kept hidden. He agreed, thinking that he could stop her if she tried to escape through the door of their *yurt* (a round tent of skins). However, as soon as his wife donned the dress she flew up through the smoke hole in the *yurt*'s roof. Khori Tumed held her feet and asked her to name their sons before she went. She did so and they became men. She then flew around the *yurt* many times bestowing blessings, before finally disappearing into the sky.

Ki *Middle East*
The Sumerian earth goddess. She was the daughter of Nammu, the primeval sea, and the consort of An, the supreme deity (known to the Mesopotamians as Anu). The coupling of Ki and An produced Enlil (the Akkadian Ea) and Enki, as well as the other great gods of the Sumerian pantheon.

Kigwa *Africa*
The mythical divine ancestor of the kings of Rwanda. The supreme lord of heaven, Nkuba the Lightning, had a barren wife. One day the wife killed one of her husband's cows and hid its heart in a pot. Carefully she nourished the heart on milk for nine months until it became a baby boy. This child, called Kigwa, spent time growing up in heaven and eventually fell to earth. He had a son, Gihanga, who invented the first metal tools and weapons, and became the first king of Rwanda.

Kikimora *Slav regions*
A household deity of Russian folk mythology. The *kikimora*, which takes the form of a small female being with flowing hair, is believed to be a manifestation of the soul of a dead person. It is said that if a housewife is lazy the *kikimora* will cause trouble and require propitiating. The appearance of the deity is sometimes taken as a portent of misfortune.

Kingu *Middle East*
The son of the god Apsu, the sweet-water ocean, and the goddess Tiamat, the salt-water ocean, according to the Akkadian (Babylonian) creation myth. After the god Ea killed Apsu, Kingu led his mother's demon army against Ea's son Marduk. Kingu was slain by Marduk, who mixed his blood with earth to make the first humans.

Kintu *Africa*
An ancestral hero who founded the royal dynasty of Buganda, according to the Ganda people of Uganda. Kintu, a

Ki: *see*
Anu (1); Enki; Enlil

Kikimora: *see*
Bannik; Domovoi; Dvorovoi

Kingu: *see*
Apsu; Ea; Marduk; Tiamat

Kintu: *see*
DEATH, THE ORIGIN OF; Nambi

foreigner, went to heaven for a wife. The High God gave him his daughter Nambi and told Kintu to hurry home or her brother Walumbe (Death) would come with them. They left at once, but Nambi realized that she had no grain with which to feed her chicken.

In spite of Kintu's pleading she insisted on going back and when she returned Death was close behind her. He accompanied them home and lived beside them on earth. Since then all humans have had to face Death.

Kitchen God, The *China*

The most important of all Chinese domestic deities. The image of the Kitchen God (alternatively known as the Hearth God) usually stood above the family stove, from where he would observe the household. Every New Year he was said to visit heaven to give an account of the behaviour of the family in

Krishna dancing on the head of the snake demon Kaliya, from a 10th-century Indian bronze.

The Kitchen God and his wife, from a woodblock print.

the past year. Before he left, sweet paste or honey was smeared over the mouth of his image in order to prevent him from speaking ill when he arrived (other accounts say that this was done to please him and make him speak sweet words). To speed the god on his journey the image was ceremonially burnt.

Kojiki, **The** *Japan*

An 8th-century AD compilation which is a primary source for Japanese myth. The *Kojiki* (Record of Ancient Matters), was commissioned by the empress Gemmei in AD711 and written by a courtier, Ono Yasumaru, who presented it to the empress in AD712.

Kong Fuzi *China*

"Master Kong", a philosopher better known in the West as Confucius, the latinized form of his name. Kong Fuzi (551BC–479BC) founded Confucianism, which stressed above all education, ritual, filial piety and devotion to the members of one's family, particularly the elderly and ancestors. Kong Fuzi himself came to be regarded as a divine figure who ranked after Heaven, Earth, the Imperial Ancestors and the Gods of Grain and Soil in the hierarchy of deities of the imperial Chinese state.

Krishna *India*

A divine hero, the eighth avatar (incarnation) of the god Vishnu, but also an important figure in his own right. When Kamsa, the evil king of Mathura, heard a prediction that the eighth child of his sister Devaki would kill him, he imprisoned Devaki and her husband Vasudeva, and ordered each of their children to be killed at birth. However, Vasudeva smuggled the eighth child, Krishna ("Dark"), out of the birth chamber and exchanged him for the newborn daughter of the cowherds Nanda and Yashoda, who lived across the river Yamuna (Jumna).

Outsmarted, Kamsa ordered the terrible goddess Putana to devour any newborn that might be Krishna. But when she offered Krishna her poisonous breast, he sucked the life out of her.

As a child Krishna became renowned

for his pranks, especially for stealing milk and butter. He encouraged his foster-father to cease worshipping Indra, who, in retaliation, sent a deluge to flood the land. But Krishna lifted Mount Govardhana as an umbrella to protect the cowherds and their cattle. He also defeated Kaliya, a many-headed serpent infesting the Yamuna.

Krishna liked to play tricks on the *gopis*, the young women of the cowherd tribe. On one such occasion he stole their clothes as they bathed in the Yamuna. The *gopis* adored the enchanting youth and left their homes to join him by the river in an ecstatic dance. The beautiful *gopi* Radha captured Krishna's heart. Traditions vary as to whether she was one of Krishna's wives, or his mistress, but their passion symbolizes the intimate relationship between deity and worshipper.

Eventually word of Krishna's deeds reached King Kamsa, who summoned him. Krishna killed the bull-demon Arishta, the horse-demon Keshin and a champion wrestler, before finally hurling Kamsa against a wall and killing him. Then he led his followers, the Yadavas, to a new city called Duaraka.

Krishna had many wives. One, Rukmini, bore a son, Pradyumna, who also had a son Aniruddha. Aniruddha was captured by the demon Bana. In Krishna's fight to retrieve him it seemed that the world would be dissolved, but Shiva, Bana's ally, recognized Krishna as the highest god. Krishna spared Bana and freed his own grandson.

Krishna's death was brought about when some young Yadavas offended a group of sages, by asking them what sort of child they thought Samba (another grandson who they had dressed as a woman) would bear. Incensed, the sages cursed Samba to bear a pestle that

would destroy the Yadavas. The pestle was ground to dust and thrown into the sea, where it turned to reeds. One lance-like reed was eaten by a fish and then caught by a hunter. In a drinking bout, Krishna, Balarama and the Yadavas picked the reeds, killing each other with them. As Krishna sat lost in thought, the hunter, mistaking him for a deer, shot him in the foot with the reed he had found in the fish, and killed him. Krishna then resumed his divine nature.

Kronos *Greece*

A Titan, the son of the goddess Gaia, the earth, and Uranos, the sky. When Gaia bore the Cyclopes, Hekatoncheires and Titans, their huge size alarmed Uranos, who forced them back into her womb. Gaia persuaded Kronos, the last-born Titan, to castrate his father when he next had intercourse with her. Uranos died and Kronos became the ruler of heaven.

Kronos feared being overthrown by his children and devoured each of his offspring as soon as his wife, Rhea, gave birth. But Rhea concealed the sixth child, Zeus, and instead gave Kronos a rock wrapped in swaddling clothes. Zeus grew up in the care of Gaia and plotted the overthrow of Kronos.

First, the goddess Metis ("Wise Cunning") gave Kronos a drink that made him regurgitate the brothers and sisters of Zeus (Demeter, Hades, Hera, Hestia and Poseidon). Zeus and his siblings fought Kronos and defeated him. Kronos went to the underworld and became, some say, ruler of Elysium.

In the Orphic creation myth, the name Kronos (which is of uncertain origin) was reinterpreted as Chronos ("Time").

Ku *Oceania*

The Hawaiian name of the Polynesian god of war, known elsewhere as Tu.

Kronos: *see*
Chronos; Cyclops; Hekatoncheires, The; Orphism; TITAN; Zeus

Ku: *see*
Tu

Ku with a ferocious expression, from a Hawaiian sculpture.

Kukulkan

Kukulkan *Central America*
A Maya deity (also called Gucumatz), equivalent to the Aztec's Quetzalcoatl.

Kumarbi *Middle East*
The father of the gods, according to Hittite mythology. In the beginning the ruler of heaven was Alalu, but he was deposed by the god Anu. Kumarbi (the equivalent of the Sumerian deity Enlil) in turn overthrew Anu and bit off his penis, but at the same time was impregnated by Anu's sperm. He gave birth to three "terrible gods", probably three different aspects of the weather god Teshub.

The sources are incomplete, but Teshub apparently overthrew Kumarbi, who then sought to avenge his downfall. He coupled with the Sea, representing the forces of chaos, and produced a son, Ullikummi, who grew to an enormous size on the shoulders of the sea-giant Upelluri. Ullikummi forced Teshub to abdicate. Teshub went to the wise god Ea, who separated Ullikummi from Upelluri, destroying his strength. The struggle between Kumarbi and Teshub was then renewed.

Kungarankalpa *Australia*
The Aboriginal name for the ancestral heroines known as the Seven Sisters.

Kurma *India*
A tortoise, the second avatar (incarnation) of the god Vishnu. Kurma supported Mount Mandara on his back during the churning of the ocean by the Devas and Asuras.

Kusa-nada-hime *Japan*
The wife of the storm god Susano. Kusa-nada-hime ("Rice Paddy Princess") was the youngest of eight sisters, seven of whom had been devoured by Yamato-no-orochi, an eight-headed dragon. The creature was due to come for her when Susano arrived at the house of her elderly parents, on the river Hi in Izumo, Honshu island. The god killed the dragon and, with her parents' consent, married Kusa-nada-hime.

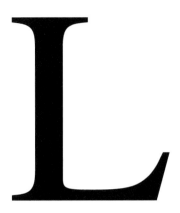

Lachesis *Greece*
One of the three Fates, the sister of Clotho and Atropos.

Laius *Greece*
A king of Thebes, and the husband of Jocasta and father of Oedipus.

Lakshmana *India*
The brother and companion of the divine hero Rama, the seventh avatar of the god Vishnu. Lakshmana assisted Rama in many of his exploits.

Lan Caihe *China*
One of the Eight Immortals of Daoist (Taoist) mythology. Lan Caihe was sometimes depicted as a young woman or, as one writer expressed it curiously, "a man who did not know how to be a man". One day, when she (or he) was picking herbs in the hills, she came across a beggar covered in sores and tended his wounds. He turned out to be Li Xuan, one of the Immortals, who rewarded her by granting her eternal youth. Thereafter she toured the country as a minstrel, telling people to seek the Daoist path.

Lang *Oceania*
The realm of the sky in the mythology of Ulith atoll in Micronesia.

Laozi *China*
Meaning "Old Master", the legendary founder of Daoism (Taoism) and supposed author of the *Dao De Jing* ("Classic of the Way and its Power", *c.*550BC), the chief work of Daoist scripture. Nothing certain is known about the life of Laozi, who came to be regarded as a deity.

Lapiths, The *Greece*
A people of Thessaly in northern Greece. The Lapiths make several appearances in Greek myth, most notably in the story of the Centauromachy (the Battle of the Centaurs), which took place after the Centaurs disrupted the wedding feast of Perithous, the Lapith king, and attempted to run off with his new bride, Hippodamia. The great Athenian hero Theseus, who was a guest at the wedding, helped the Lapiths gain their victory. The battle was famously depicted on the Parthenon at Athens.

From an incense burner thought to show Laozi.

*A lar, based on a
statuette.*

Lar *Rome*

A guardian divinity of the household. Many Roman houses had a shrine to its Lar (plural Lares) depicting a small youth in a short tunic (*see* illustration in the margin). Offerings were made to the Lar on family occasions, such as weddings and funerals.

Latinus *Rome*

A king of Laurentum in Latium who assisted the hero Aeneas when he arrived in Italy.

Lavinia *Rome*

The daughter of King Latinus and second wife of Aeneas. He founded a town, Lavinium, named after her.

Leda *Greece*

A queen of Sparta with whom the god

Leda with the swan who is really the god Zeus in transformed guise.

Zeus had intercourse in the guise of a swan. She was the mother of Helen of Troy, Clytemnestra and the Dioscuri (Castor and Polydeuces).

Leech-child *Japan*

The misshapen first offspring of the primal deities Izanagi and Izanami.

Lernean Hydra, The *Greece*

A many-headed dragon killed by Herakles as the first of his labours.

Leshii *Slav regions*

A forest spirit of eastern Slav folk mythology. He is the guardian of trees and forest animals and resembles a peasant. He may be as tall as a tree or as short as the grass, depending where he lives. He can change shape, such as into an animal or a relative, especially when he intends mischief. A peasant entering a forest would ward off the *leshii* by praying or turning his clothes inside out.

Lethe *Greece*

"Forgetfulness", one of the rivers of the Greek underworld. The dead were obliged to drink its waters to erase memories of their past life.

Leto *Greece*

A Titan, the daughter of Coeus and Phoebe. She had intercourse with Zeus and became pregnant with the twins Apollo and Artemis. The jealous Hera, the wife of Zeus, caused Leto to wander the world in agony looking for a place to give birth. She eventually bore the divine twins on the island Ortygia, later called Delos. In some accounts these were different islands and Artemis was born on Ortygia and Apollo on Delos.

Lha-tho-tho-ri *Tibet and Mongolia*

A legendary king of Tibet (ruled AD433–AD493). One day the sky filled with rainbows, and Buddhist images and texts fell onto his palace. Lha-tho-tho-ri worshipped the objects without understanding them: it was prophesied that their meaning would become clear after five generations: Tibet was converted to Buddhism by King Srong-lde'u-btsan in the 8th century AD.

LION

As the king of beasts, the lion is above all a symbol of royal authority and prestige. In myth, the animal is often associated with divinity as a symbol of supreme power. It is not necessarily benign: for example, the Egyptian lion-headed goddess Sekhmet was a terrifying deity who was once sent by the Sun God to destroy a rebellious race of human beings. Her messengers were believed to appear in the form of all kinds of varied infectious diseases. It was for this reason that her priests were also doctors. The Hindu god Vishnu became incarnate as Narasimha, a creature half man; half

Lions guarding the sun door, from a papyrus illustration in the Ancient Egyptian Book of the Dead.

lion, to destroy a demon that could not be killed by a man or a god. The lion is the mount of the goddess Parvati, the wife of Shiva, and as such represents her more frightening aspect as the warrior goddess Durga.

Unsurprisingly the lion also features as a symbol of invincibility, such as in the myth of Herakles and the Nemean lion.

But the lion does not always have things its own way. In Africa, for example, where the powerful beast would otherwise be revered for its royal status, the lion is often outwitted in myths by smaller and more cunning creatures, such as the hare.

Li Xuan, based on a 19th-century porcelain statue.

Li Xuan *China*
The first of the Eight Immortals of Daoist (Taoist) myth. Li Xuan ("Iron Crutch") had a club foot and was said to have learned the Dao, the principle of existence, from the goddess Xi Wang Mu, the Queen-Mother of the West, who gave him an iron crutch.

Liber *Rome*
An Italian agricultural deity. He was identified with the Greek god Dionysos.

Lilith *Middle East*
The demonic first wife of Adam, in Hebrew mythology. Lilith may have been derived from the Mesopotamian fertility goddess Ninlil. (*See illustration on page 122.*)

LION
See panel above

Llama *South America*
Llamas were among the Incas' most valuable sacrificial animals, and were closely associated with the heavens and rain. They were sacrificed to the new moon and, by tradition, black llamas were deliberately starved during the month of October so that the gods would hear their bleating as a plea from earth for rain.

It was also said that when the constellation Yacama (the Llama, which is found near the Milky Way) disappeared from view at midnight, it was preventing flooding by drinking water from the earth.

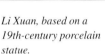

Li Xuan: *see*
Eight Immortals, The; Xi Wang Mu

Liber: *see*
Bacchus; Dionysos; GREEK AND ROMAN DEITIES

Lilith: *see*
Enlil; Ninlil

Lion: *see*
Ahau Kin; Durga; HERAKLES, THE LABOURS OF; Sekhmet; VISHNU, THE AVATARS OF

*The Hebrew Lilith (*see
entry on page 121*).*

*Possibly Loki, based on
a furnace stone.*

Lleu Llaw Gyffes *Celtic regions*

"Shining One of the Skilful Hand", a divine warrior-magician of Welsh mythology, probably related to the old Celtic god Lugus and the Irish hero Lugh. According to the *Mabinogion,* Lleu's mother Arianrhod, daughter of the goddess Dôn and sister of the magician Gwydion, gave birth to twin boys. One was called Dylan but she vowed that the other would have no name until she named him herself. His uncle Gwydion tricked her into calling him Lleu Llaw Gyffes. She forbade Lleu to bear arms until she had armed him; again Gwydion tricked her. Finally, Arianrhod forbade Lleu to have a human wife and so Gwydion and his uncle, Math, made him a magic wife of flowers, Blodeuwedd.

Lleu was magically gifted in the arts, could also change shape at will, and it was almost impossible to contrive his death. Blodeuwedd and her adulterous lover, Gronw Pebyr, succeeded in doing so once, but Lleu escaped, wounded, in the form of an eagle.

Llyr *Celtic regions*

The divine head of a family which dominates the second branch of the *Mabinogion.* Llyr was the father of Branwen, Brân the Blessed and Manawydan. In Geoffrey of Monmouth's *History of the Kings of Britain* (1136) Llyr appeared as Leir, one of the mythical early kings of Britain. This Leir was the ultimate source of Shakespeare's *King Lear.*

Loki *Germanic regions*

A trickster deity of Scandinavian mythology. It is uncertain whether Loki is a god or a giant, one of the gods' enemies. He caused mischief among the gods, such as the death of Balder, but also assisted them, such as when he helped Thor retrieve his mighty hammer from the giants.

Loki was the father of Hel, the queen of the underworld land of the dead, and of Sleipnir, Odin's eight-legged horse. He also bore the monstrous wolf Fenrir and the venomous World Serpent which swam in the depths of the ocean surrounding the world.

In punishment for causing the death of Balder, the gods chained Loki to three rocks. He eventually broke free and led the giants against the gods at the apocalyptic battle of Ragnarok. Loki came face to face with the god Heimdall and both were killed in the ensuing duel.

Lono *Oceania*

The god of the sky, peace and agriculture, the Hawaiian equivalent of the god known elsewhere as Rongo. Lono came into the ascendancy in Hawaii every year during the four-month long Makihiki festival, which began with the appearance of the constellation of the Pleiades on the evening horizon and the arrival of the autumn rains. During Makihiki, which the god was said to have founded, an image of Lono was taken around the Hawaiian islands and homage was paid to him in return for fertility and abundance. At the end of the Makihiki festival Lono was ritually "killed" at his chief temple and was then said to leave for Kahiki, his invisible land, until the following autumn. The remainder of the year was dedicated to Ku, the god of earth and warfare.

Lü Dongbin *China*

One of the Eight Immortals of Daoist (Taoist) mythology. Lü Dongbin dreamed that he enjoyed great prosperity for fifty years but then suffered disgrace and ruin. It convinced him that worldly ambition was futile and he followed Han Zhongli, whom he had met at an inn, into the hills to seek the Dao, the Daoist principle of existence. Among his disciples were the Immortals Han Xiang and Cao Guojiu.

Lueji *Africa*
A legendary queen of the Lunda people, the descendant of the primordial serpent Chinawezi and wife of the hero Chibinda Ilunga.

Lugh *Celtic regions*
"The Bright One", the name of a divine Irish warrior-hero probably identifiable with the Welsh figure Lleu and the old Celtic deity Lugus.

According to the *Book of Invasions*, Lugh was the grandson of Balar of the Evil Eye, the leader of the monstrous Fomorians. Balar, it was foretold, would be killed by a grandson, so he imprisoned his only daughter, Eithne, in a cave on Tory island. Kian, one of the Tuatha Dé Danann, the enemies of the Fomorians, secretly seduced her and she had triplets. Balar drowned them all except Lugh, who was saved and reared by a smith.

Many years later Lugh, a handsome young warrior, arrived at the court of Nuadhu, the king of the Tuatha Dé Danaan. His skills in all the arts – warfare, healing, prophecy, magic, music, poetry and others – made such a great impression that Nuadhu abdicated in his favour. Lugh led the Tuatha Dé Danann against the Fomorians at the second battle of Magh Tuiredh and killed Balar.

The ancient festival of Lughnasad, held on 1 August, was said to have been introduced by Lugh.

Lugus *Celtic regions*
A deity widely popular throughout the ancient Celtic lands. His name means "Bright" or "Shining" and he is related to the Irish Lugh and Welsh Lleu. Lugus was probably the god whom Julius Caesar referred to when he said that "Mercury" was the chief deity of the Gauls and "inventor of all the arts".

The Emperor Augustus chose Lugdunum ("Fort of Lugus", modern Lyon) as the capital of Gaul in 12BC. He inaugurated a festival in his own honour on 1 August, the date of the local festival of Lugus (the Irish Lughnasad).

Lynceus (1) *Greece*
A son of King Aphareus and Queen Arene of Messenia. He was one of the Argonauts and was said to have such keen sight that he could even see beneath the earth.

Lynceus (2) *Greece*
A king of Argos, the son of Aegyptus and husband of Hypermnestra. He and Hypermnestra were ancestors of the hero Perseus.

Lugh: *see*
Balar; Fomorian; *Invasions,* The *Book of;* Lleu Llaw Gyffes; Lugus; Nuadhu;

Lugus: *see*
Lleu Llaw Gyffes; Lugh

Lynceus (1): *see*
Dioscuri, The

Lynceus (2): *see*
Danaïd; Perseus

Maat *Egypt*

The goddess of truth and justice. Maat, the daughter of the sun god and wife of Thoth, embodied divine order and harmony. She was depicted standing or squatting, with her symbol, an ostrich feather, in her headdress. In the underworld, the heart (that is, the conscience) of a dead person was weighed against the feather of Maat. If the heart was burdened by sin so that it was heavier than the feather, the deceased was devoured by a monster. If the scales balanced, the deceased became a spirit among the gods.

Mabinogion, **The** *Celtic regions*

A collection of Welsh mythological tales. The *Mabinogion* is the principal source of ancient Welsh and British myths, even though these are overlain by many later elements. There are four sections or "Branches" to the main narrative of the *Mabinogion.* These deal with the stories of the families of Pwyll (First and Third Branch), Llyr (Second Branch) and Dôn (Fourth Branch). Pryderi, the son of Pwyll, appears in each Branch, and there are numerous

other interrelationships. Outside the main narrative are other tales, such as the story of Culhwch and Olwen.

Within the stories there are parallels with Irish myth, such as the families of Danu (the Tuatha Dé Danann) and Dôn, and the figures of Lugh and Lleu.

Mael Dúin *Celtic regions*

An Irish hero who went on a great sea voyage. Mael Dúin sailed away to kill the man who had slain his father. However, he took more crew members than a druid advised him to, and when the ship reached the murderer's island a storm blew it far off course. They encountered many fabulous lands and monsters, including ants the size of foals, blazing hot swine, vanishing maidens and the Land of Women, an island of perpetual feasting and pleasure where old age was unknown.

Mael Dúin and his crew eventually returned to Ireland.

Magh Tuiredh, The battles of
Celtic regions

Two conflicts at Magh Tuiredh (Moytirra, County Sligo) which serve as the focal points of the *Book of Invasions*, the account of the mythical conquest of Ireland by successive races. The divine race, the Tuatha Dé Danann, defeated their predecessors, the Fir Bholg, in the first battle of Magh Tuiredh and the monstrous Fomorians in the second battle.

Magna Mater *Rome*
Meaning "Great Mother", Magna Mater is the Roman name of the earth and fertility goddess Cybele. Her worship was introduced to Rome from Asia Minor (modern Turkey) in 204BC, on the instructions of the oracle at Delphi. Her cult involved ecstatic music and dancing and her priests were self-castrated eunuchs, in memory of her lover Attis. He was sworn to fidelity, but later proposed marriage to a nymph. As a result, Cybele drove him mad and he castrated himself, dying of the wound. Regretting his death, she later instituted a cult in his honour.

Mahabharata, The *India*
A great Sanskrit verse epic composed *c.*400BC–*c.*AD400. Vast in extent and scope (Homer's *Iliad* and *Odyssey* combined are just a tenth of its length), the *Mahabharata* relates a dynastic feud between two related families, the Pandavas and the Kauravas. In the course of the narrative, many myths are recounted, alongside other aspects of Hindu religion, ritual and philosophy.

Mahadevi *India*
"Great Goddess", an alternative name for Devi, "The Goddess".

Mahendradatta *Southeast Asia*
An 11th-century queen of Bali exiled for sorcery who may be the origin of the mythical witch-queen Rangda.

Mahisha *India*
"Buffalo", the name of a demon killed by the goddess Durga.

Maia *Greece*
One of the Pleiades, the seven daughters of the sea nymph Pleione and the Titan Atlas. Maia lived in a cave, where the god Zeus had intercourse with her, without his wife Hera noticing, so Maia did not suffer Hera's jealous anger. The offspring of this coupling was the god Hermes. Maia and her sisters became the constellation bearing their name.

Main *Arctic regions*
The guardian of the sun, according to the Evenk people of Siberia. One day, in the upper world above this one, an elk ran to the top of a hill, caught the sun in his antlers, and ran down again into the forest. The middle world, where humans live, became dark, so Main donned winged skis and flew to the upper world, where, at midnight, he shot the elk with his bow. The sun rose above the hills again and light returned. These events have been repeated every night since.

Maitreya *India*
The Bodhisattva embodying *maitri*, meaning "friendliness". He resides in the Tushita heaven and is the Buddha of the future age, but until its arrival he is said to visit earth in various guises to bring salvation and instruction. (*See illustration on next page.*)

Maka *North America*
"Earth", a creator goddess, who is an aspect of the deity Wakan Tanka.

Makosh *Slav regions*
The goddess of fertility, abundance and moisture. Makosh, also spelled Mokosh, was the centre of a fertility cult that was

Magna Mater: *see* Rhea

Mahabharata, The: *see* *Puranas*, The; *Ramayana*, The; *Vedas*, The

Mahadevi: *see* Devi

Mahendradatta: *see* Rangda

Mahisha: *see* Durga

Maia: *see* Hera; Hermes; ZEUS, THE CONSORTS OF

Main: *see* SUN, MOON AND STARS

Maitreya: *see* Bodhisattva; Buddha

Maka: *see* Wakan Tanka

Possibly a represen-tation of Makosh, from an embroidered Slav design.

Mama Kilya: *see*
Inti

Manannán: *see*
Manawydan

Manasa: *see*
Ananta; SNAKES AND
SERPENTS; Vishnu

Manawydan: *see*
Branwen; Brân the Blessed;
Llyr; *Mabinogion*, The;
Manannán; Pryderi; Pwyll;
Rhiannon

*The Bodhisattva Maitreya (*see entry on
page 125*), based on a porcelain statue.*

widespread among the eastern Slav
peoples (Belorussians, Russians and
Ukrainians). Makosh was also revered
as the protector of women's work, as
well as the protector of maidens.

Malaveyovo *Oceania*
A voracious cannibal found in the
mythology of Goodenough island
(Papua New Guinea).

It is said that Malaveyovo used to
wander through the interior of the
island, enthusiastically consuming
anyone he encountered and thereby
causing serious depopulation. So the
islanders made offerings of garden
produce to him in the belief that the
more vegetables he ate the fewer people
he would devour. These offerings led to
abutu, a competition in which present-
day islanders challenge one another to
make the largest gifts of vegetables.

Mama Kilya *South America*
The Inca moon goddess, the sister and
wife of the sun god Inti. She was revered
as the mother of the Inca people and as
the deity whose waxing and waning
marked the passing of time. During an
eclipse of the moon it was believed that
Mama Kilya was being attacked by a
mountain lion or giant serpent, which
people would drive off by causing a
great din.

Manannán *Celtic regions*
An Irish divinity of the sea, the son of
the sea god Lir and one of the Tuatha Dé
Danann. Manannán was regarded as the
protector of Ireland, which he embraced
with the ocean. He had great magic
powers and assisted some of the heroes
of Irish myth. For example, he helped
Lugh to secure a Tuatha Dé Danann
victory against the monstrous Fomorian
invaders by giving him a magic boat,
horse and sword.

Manannán was said to have been the
first king of the Isle of Man, which was
named after him (Mannin in Manx).

Manasa *India*
A serpent goddess, the sister of Ananta,
the serpent upon which the god Vishnu
is said to rest between cosmic
emanations. Manasa is greatly revered
in Bengal, where she is believed to ward
off poisonous snakes.

Manawydan *Celtic regions*
A Welsh hero-magician, the son of Llyr.
Manawydan is the protagonist of the
Third Branch of the *Mabinogion*, which
relates how his homeland, Dyfed, was
placed under a spell that caused all
people and beasts to disappear.
Manawydan travelled to England with
his wife Rhiannon, stepson Pryderi (lord
of Dyfed) and Pryderi's wife Cegfa.

After many magical adventures he discovered that the spell had been cast by a bishop, Llwyd, in revenge for a wrong done to a friend by Pryderi's father Pwyll. Eventually, Llwyd lifted the spell and Manawydan returned home with his companions.

Manawydan may be identical in origin to the Irish Manannán.

Manco Capac *South America*

The mythical ancestor of the Inca emperors. Manco Capac was one of three brothers and three sisters who emerged into the world from caves at Pacariqtambo. After a journey of some distance with Mama Oqlyo, his sister and wife, Manco Capac came to an auspicious site and stuck his golden staff in the ground. They founded a settlement there which became Cuzco, the Inca capital, and their offspring became the Inca imperial family. Later, Manco Capac became a stone – one of the Incas' most venerated treasures.

Manitou *North America*

The supreme deity of the Algonquian people. The name means "spirit".

Manjushri *India*

"Amiably Majestic", the Bodhisattva who is said to eradicate ignorance from the world.

Mantis *Africa*

An insect which appears widely as a trickster and culture hero. Both roles are evident in the fire origin myth of the Khoisan peoples of southwestern Africa. Originally, Ostrich kept fire tucked under his wing. Mantis persuaded him to reach for some fruit at the top of a plum tree. As Ostrich opened his wings to balance himself, Mantis took the fire.

The Bodhisattva, Manjushri, based on a gilded bronze statue, 17th century.

The Khoisan also claim that it was Mantis who was first to give everything its name.

Manuk Manuk *Southeast Asia*

The blue cosmic chicken which initiated the creation of the world, according to Sumatran mythology. God possessed Manuk Manuk instead of a wife. The chicken laid three eggs, from which hatched three gods who created the three levels of the universe: heaven, this world and the underworld.

MAORI PANTHEON, THE

See panel on next page

Maponus *Celtic regions*

A youthful god revered in ancient Gaul and Britain. Maponus ("Divine Son" or "Divine Youth") appears to have been associated with music, poetry and hunting. He was probably identical with the Welsh Mabon ("Son"), who figures

Manco Capac: *see*
HUMANITY, THE ORIGIN OF; Pacariqtambo

Manitou: *see*
Gitchi Manitou

Manjushri: *see*
Bodhisattva

Mantis: *see*
ANIMALS

Manuk Manuk: *see*
Batara Guru; COSMOLOGY

Maponus: *see*
Apollo; Oenghus; Olwen

Maponus, from a Roman carving on a well in Southwark, London, 3rd century AD.

Marduk

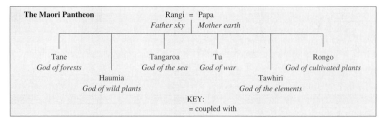

The Maori Pantheon

Rangi = Papa
Father sky | Mother earth

Tane
God of forests

Tangaroa
God of the sea

Tu
God of war

Rongo
God of cultivated plants

Haumia
God of wild plants

Tawhiri
God of the elements

KEY:
= coupled with

in the story of Olwen and Culhwch as a boar hunter with divine powers, and the Irish Mac Óc ("Young Son"), otherwise known as Oenghus, the god of love.

Marduk *Middle East*

The supreme god of Akkad and its capital, Babylon. The creation myth of the Akkadian people recounts how the primal deities Apsu and Tiamat coupled to produce a succession of divinities

Marduk and his snake-dragon, from a lapis lazuli cylinder.

culminating in Ea, from whom sprang Marduk. A power struggle arose in heaven: Ea killed Apsu and in revenge Tiamat (who was envisaged as a dragon embodying primordial chaos) unleashed a host of monsters headed by her son Kingu against the younger deities. The latter elected Marduk as their champion. He killed Tiamat by cutting her body in two, forming the earth from one part and the sky from the other. Then he took from Kingu the Tablets of Destiny, the divine decrees which conferred supreme power on their possessor. He killed Kingu and mixed his blood with earth in order to form the human race. The gods acknowledged Marduk as supreme deity and built him a great sanctuary, Esagila, in Babylon.

After the conquest of Sumer by the Akkadians *c.*1900BC, Marduk became the supreme god of Mesopotamia. His temple in Babylon contained a great *ziggurat* (stepped pyramid), perhaps the original of the Biblical Tower of Babel.

Mariyamman *India*

The name by which the local goddess of a southern Indian village is often known. Mariyamman was a high-caste brahman. An untouchable (one of the lowest caste) wooed her in the guise of a brahman, but after her marriage to him she discovered the deception and so killed herself. She at once became a goddess and punished her former husband by burning him to cinders or otherwise humiliating him.

Mariyamman is often regarded as the "wife" and protector of a village. She may also be responsible for causing and controlling disease.

Mars *Rome*

The god of war and agriculture. Mars was originally the god of agriculture and the divine guardian of the land. He presumably grew more warlike in character as the expanding Roman state became itself more aggressive and militaristic. Mars enjoyed far greater prominence than the Greek war god Ares, with whom he came to be identified, and not all his myths were adapted from Greek ones. According to the most important of these native myths, Mars was the father of Romulus and Remus, the founders of Rome.

Mars was the champion of the Roman nation and its armies and his official cult was second in importance only to that of Jupiter. However, the god retained the role of the protector of farmers and herdsmen. He was popular in Gaul and Britain, where many Celtic protector deities (not only those of war and agriculture) were identified with him.

His chief festivals took place in March, which is named after him (in Latin *Martius*)

The Roman god of war, Mars, shown riding a chariot.

Math *Celtic regions*

The magician-lord of Gwynedd and protagonist of the Fourth Branch of the *Mabinogion*. Math, the son of Mathonwy and brother of Dôn, had to keep his feet in the lap of a virgin whenever he was not at war. His nephew Gilfaethwy wanted to seduce one of these maidens, so his brother Gwydion got Math out of the way by conjuring up a war with Pryderi, lord of Dyfed. When Math returned and discovered his nephews' trickery, he transformed them into animals for three years.

Math needed a new virgin, so his niece Arianrhod, the sister of Gwydion and Gilfaethwy, submitted to a virginity test. She stepped over Math's magic wand and failed the test by giving birth at once to twins, Dylan and Lleu Llaw Gyffes. Among the prohibitions she imposed on Lleu was the stricture that he should never have a human wife. Later, Math and Gwydion created a beautiful woman out of flowers, called Blodeuwedd, as a wife for Lleu.

Maui *Oceania*

The most famous trickster and culture hero of Polynesian mythology. Maui was born prematurely and, some say, thrown into the sea by his mother, but the sun saved him. One of his first exploits was to slow down the sun with the jawbone of his dead grandmother, either to give people more time to cook their food, or to give his mother more light for making bark-cloth (*tapa*).

On a fishing trip with his brothers, Maui fished up the first land (that is, island), in one account the island of Hawaiki or Te-ika-a-Maui (which means "Fish of Maui"), New Zealand. He brought humanity fire, which he stole from its keeper, Mahui-ike, an ancestral heroine of the underworld.

Mars: *see*
Ares; Jupiter; ROME, THE KINGS OF; Romulus

Math: *see*
Blodeuwedd; Dôn; Gwydion; Lleu Llaw Gyffes

Maui: *see*
CULTURE HERO; Hine-nui-te-po; TRICKSTER

On another trip to the underworld Maui attempted to pass through the body of the sleeping Hine-nui-te-po, the goddess of death, because he believed that this would render him immortal. But the goddess awoke and killed him. Since then no human has been able to achieve immortality.

Mbidi Kiluwe *Africa*

A prince, who was the father of the hero Kalala Ilunga.

Mboom *Africa*

A creator deity and one of the first two gods, according to the Kuba people of Zaïre. Mboom and his companion deity, Ngaan, created the world, which was dark and covered with water. Each was king of half the earth, but one day they fell out and left the world. Ngaan went beneath the waters and Mboom went to the heavens. There he spewed up the sun, moon and stars. The sun dried the earth and land appeared. Then Mboom spewed up animals and humans to live on the land. Among the first humans was Woot, royal ancestor of the Kuba.

Medea *Greece*

A sorceress, the daughter of King Aeëtes of Colchis and the sea nymph Idyia, and the wife successively of Jason and Aegeus, the father of Theseus. When the Argonauts sailed from Iolcus to Colchis, Medea fell in love with Jason and helped him win the Golden Fleece. She assisted his escape by murdering her own brother, Apsyrtus.

Later, Jason and Medea went to Medea's aunt, the witch Circe, to be purified for the murder of Apsyrtus, but Circe was appalled at the crime and cursed them. They returned to Iolcus, to find that Jason's uncle, King Pelias, had executed Aeson, Jason's father and the

Medea demonstrating to Pelias, based on a late 6th-century BC vase painting.

rightful king. Medea brought Aeson back to life and then convinced the usurper and his daughters to cut up their father and stew him, so that he would become young again. They followed her instructions, to discover that Medea had tricked them into murdering Pelias.

The gruesome manner of Pelias' death caused outrage and Jason and Medea fled to Corinth. They had many children. Later, King Creon of Corinth offered Jason his daughter in marriage. Jason agreed and told Medea that he proposed to divorce her. Furious at this betrayal, Medea sent Creon's daughter poisoned robes, killing both her and her father. She then slit the throats of her children and fled to Athens.

In Athens she married King Aegeus and they had a son, Medus, Aegeus' heir presumptive. But Aegeus had an elder son, Theseus, whom he had never seen, born to a princess of Troezen. One day Theseus arrived in Athens and Medea, who recognized him through her magic powers, persuaded Aegeus that the stranger planned to kill him. Aegeus agreed that she should poison his wine, but at the last moment he recognized Theseus and knocked the wine from his hand. Realizing Medea's treachery, Aegeus banished her and Medus.

According to one account, Medea and Medus finally returned to Colchis, where Aeëtes had been overthrown by his brother Perses. With his mother's aid Medus killed Perses and took the throne.

Medhbh *Celtic regions*
A divine sorceress, who was the queen of Connacht and the chief adversary of the Ulster heroes Conchobar and Cú Chulainn in the war in *Táin Bó Cuailnge* (*The Cattle Raid of Cooley*). She was the lover of many kings and the only woman to satisfy the sexual appetite of the hero Ferghus, said to be seven times that of other men. She died after being hit by a piece of hard cheese hurled in a slingshot by her nephew Furbaidhe, whose mother she had murdered.

Medusa *Greece*
One of the three Gorgons, the monstrous daughters of the sea divinities Phorcys and Ceto. The hero Perseus was charged with bringing Medusa's head to King Polydectes of Seriphos, who held his mother Danaë captive. Medusa's direct glance turned anything living to stone, so Perseus cut off her head either while looking in a mirror or, in another

Perseus decapitating Medusa, from a black-figure wine-jug, 5th century BC.

account, by letting his protector, the goddess Athene, guide his hand. He put the head into a bag, later using it to turn his enemies to stone before finally giving it to Athene, who wore it on her *aegis* (breastplate). From Medusa's blood sprang a son, Chrysaor, and the winged horse Pegasus.

Megara *Greece*
The daughter of King Creon of Thebes and the first wife of the hero Herakles, who killed her in a fit of madness caused by the goddess Hera, Herakles' mother.

Meleager *Greece*
A prince of Calydon in Aetolia, the son of King Oenus and Queen Althaea. When Meleager was born, the Fates told Althaea that he would die when a certain piece of wood on the fire had been burned up. To save her son Althaea removed it from the fire and hid it.

Years later, at a hunt for a monstrous boar that was ravaging Calydon, Meleager fell in love with Atalanta and after the hunt awarded her the boar's pelt because she had drawn first blood, although he had finally killed it. This decision provoked a row with his uncles, the brothers of Althaea, and Meleager slew them. When Althaea heard of her brothers' death she put the old piece of wood on the fire and Meleager died. She later regretted her deed and hanged herself.

Menelaus *Greece*
A king of Sparta. Menelaus was the son of Atreus, brother of Agamemnon and first husband of Helen of Troy.

Menoetius *Greece*
A Titan, the son of Iapetus and Clymene and brother of Prometheus, Atlas and Epimetheus. He appears little in myth.

Menelaus and Helen meeting, from a black-figure amphora, 5th century BC.

Mercury *Rome and Celtic regions*

The god of communication and commerce. Mercury was the divine messenger and the guide of the dead into the underworld. Originally a god of trade, Mercury came to be identified with the Greek god Hermes.

According to Julius Caesar, a god he called "Mercury" was the most widely worshipped deity of the Gauls and Britons. Caesar called this Celtic Mercury the inventor of the arts and a god of commercial success. He may in fact have been referring to the god Lugus. In Roman Gaul and Britain, many shrines were dedicated to the Celtic manifestations of Mercury.

Meresger *Egypt*

A snake goddess of the mountain peak overlooking the royal tombs of Thebes (modern Luxor). She was generally benevolent and had the power to cure disease, but she could also inflict sickness on sinners.

Merlin *Celtic regions*

A magician and prophet. The Merlin of Arthurian legend derives ultimately from the figure of Myrddin or Merddin, a seer or madman with prophetic gifts who was said to have lived in the Caledonian Forest in British-speaking southern Scotland. He is said to have gone mad after seeing a terrible vision in battle. Other versions of the Myrddin story are the Irish myth of the Frenzy of Suibhne (Sweeney) and the Scottish myth of Lailoken (or Llalogan).

The story of Myrddin was brought to Wales after c.AD500 by British migrants from Strathclyde and developed in the 9th and 10th centuries. The character of the Arthurian Merlin was fixed by Geoffrey of Monmouth, whose Latin *History of the Kings of Britain* (1136) introduced a seer-magician called Merlinus Ambrosius, based on another, unrelated, legendary character, the wonder-child Ambrosius. Parallels have also been drawn between the tales of Merlin and those of the Irish hero Finn.

Merlin as a boy. From an illustration of the 13th century in Geoffrey of Monmouth's Prophecies of Merlin.

Metis *Greece*

An Oceanid (sea nymph), the daughter of Okeanos and Tethys and first wife of Zeus. Metis ("Wise Cunning"), assisted Zeus in the overthrow of his father Kronos by serving Kronos an emetic drink that made him spew up Zeus' brothers and sisters, whom he had swallowed at birth. Together with Zeus they fought and defeated the Titans, establishing Zeus as lord of the heavens. Zeus then married Metis and she became pregnant by him.

The goddess Gaia predicted that Metis would bear a goddess equal to Zeus in wisdom as well as a god who would overthrow him and become lord of heaven and earth. Wishing to avoid the fate of his father, Zeus swallowed Metis and thereafter possessed her cunning wisdom, which meant that he could never be tricked as Kronos had been. Of Metis' predicted children, the god was never born, but the goddess – Athene – eventually sprang, fully formed and armed, from Zeus' head.

Mictlan *Central America*

The Aztec land of the dead. Mictlan was a terrifying place but not solely a region of punishment, because everyone, sinner and virtuous alike, was destined to pass through it unless they had died violently (in which case they went straight to one of the celestial regions). The souls of the deceased encountered various perils, such as sharp knives and turbulent waters, on their way to Mictlan where the god Mictlantecuhtli and his consort Mictecacihuatl presided over the dead.

The god Quetzalcoatl was said to have travelled into the underworld to steal bones from which he fashioned a new race of humans. Mictlantecuhtli chased him, causing him to drop some of the stolen bones, a number of which broke. As a result of this, the new race of humans became all different sizes.

Milesians, The *Celtic regions*

The sixth and final race to conquer Ireland, according to the *Book of Invasions*. The Milesians (the Gaels or Celts) are also called the Sons of Míl, after their leader, Míl Espaine, whose name comes from the Latin Miles Hispaniae ("Soldier of Spain"). It is said that they landed in southwest Ireland from Spain on 1 May, the feast of Beltane. They defeated the Tuatha Dé Danann and the land was divided in two: the Milesians ruled Ireland above ground and Tuatha Dé established a new domain in the subterranean Otherworld.

Mimi Australia

A trickster being in the Aboriginal mythology of western Arnhem Land. The *mimi* are said to live in crevices in the rock face of the Arnhem Land escarpment and on the whole are benign: for example, they taught people the art of hunting. But *mimi* are hostile if surprised by the sudden presence of strangers, and anyone wandering in the bush calls out to let the *mimi* know that a human is nearby. People who startle them may be punished with sickness. A tame-looking wallaby should not be approached in case it is the pet of a *mimi*: its owner will kill anyone who harms the animal. Ancient Aboriginal cave paintings are often said to be the work of the *mimi*.

Minakshi *India*

A warrior goddess worshipped at Madurai as the consort of Shiva. She was said to have been born with three breasts and raised as a boy by her parents, who were a king and queen. She

Redrawn from a bark painting, thought to show mimi *tricksters.*

Minerva

The goddess Minerva.

succeeded her father as ruler and conquered the world, then went to the sacred Mount Kailasa to challenge the god Shiva. On meeting the great god, however, she became shy and reserved, losing her third breast. The story contrasts with the myth of Parvati, whose gentler nature subdued the fierce and warlike Shiva.

Minerva *Rome*
The goddess of wisdom, learning, arts and crafts. Probably of Etruscan origin she seems to have been identified with the Greek goddess Athene before being adopted into the Roman pantheon.

Minia *Africa*
A cosmic serpent of northern African mythology. In the Sahara and Sahel it is widely said that Minia was the first thing made by the divine creator. The serpent's head was in the sky and its tail was in the waters beneath the earth. Its body was divided into seven parts. The god then used these parts to form the world and all life.

Minos *Greece*
A king of Crete, the son of Europa and Zeus. After her affair with Zeus, Europa married Asterius, king of Crete, who adopted Minos, Sarpedon and Rhadamanthys, her three sons by Zeus. Minos succeeded Asterius following a quarrel with his brothers, who left Crete. To affirm his power Minos prayed to the sea god Poseidon for a suitable sacrificial beast; a magnificent bull emerged from the sea. But the beast was so beautiful that Minos would not sacrifice it, angering Poseidon, who caused Minos' wife Pasiphaë to commit adultery with the bull. In consequence, Pasiphaë bore the Minotaur, a monster which was half bull and half man.

During his reign Minos conquered much of Greece. But, failing to take Athens, he prayed for a plague to strike the city. This epidemic was relieved only by the payment, by King Aegeus of Athens, of an annual tribute of seven boys and seven girls, who were fed to the Minotaur. This subservience ended when Aegeus' son, Theseus, sailed to Crete and killed the Minotaur.

Minos employed the great craftsman Daedalus. Following imprisonment for his part in killing the Minotaur, Daedalus fled to King Cocalus of Sicily. Minos followed him and demanded that Cocalus hand him over. However, while staying at Cocalus' palace, Minos was

Theseus attacking the Minotaur, from an Athenian jar of the 6th century BC.

killed by a contraption invented by Daedalus, causing him to be drenched in boiling water in the bath and scalded to death. Minos went to the underworld and became a judge of the dead. Among his children were Euryale, Orion's mother, and Phaedra, a queen of Athens.

Minotaur, The *Greece*
A monster, part bull and part man, the offspring of Queen Pasiphaë of Crete and a bull. King Minos, the husband of Pasiphaë, prayed for a bull to sacrifice to the god Poseidon. The bull which appeared was so marvellous that he did not want to kill it, angering Poseidon so much that the god made Pasiphaë fall passionately in love with the animal. To satisfy her lust she enlisted the help of the royal craftsman Daedalus, who constructed a hollow life-sized model of a beautiful heifer to attract the attentions of the bull. Pasiphaë positioned herself in this model to have intercourse with the beast. She became pregnant and bore the Minotaur (literally "Bull of Minos"), sometimes called Asterius or Asterion.

Furious at his wife and craftsman, Minos ordered Daedalus to make a prison for the savage hybrid. He built the Labyrinth, an underground maze of tunnels from which it was impossible to escape. In the centre of this was the Minotaur's lair.

Every year King Minos demanded tribute of seven boys and seven girls from Aegeus, the king of Athens, to be devoured by the Minotaur. One year, however, the victims were accompanied by the hero Theseus, the son of Aegeus. Ariadne, the daughter of Minos, fell in love with Theseus and when the terrified children were sent into the Minotaur's lair she gave the hero a ball of twine. With this he could enter the Labyrinth and later find his way out. Unravelling the twine as he went, Theseus followed the sound of the bellowing Minotaur and reached the centre of the Labyrinth. He wrestled with the Minotaur and beat it to death, then led the children out of the Labyrinth to safety.

Mithra *Middle East*
A Persian god of justice, war and the sun. Mithra was originally the divine personification of *mitra* ("contract") and the upholder of order and truth. As a god of war he rode in a golden chariot drawn by four horses to combat demons and their followers, and was associated with the sun (often being envisaged in myth, for example by the Greeks, as a deity riding a chariot through the sky).

Under the Roman Empire, Mithra became the focus of a mystery cult particularly popular among the Roman soldiery. Mithraic shrines were characterized by an image of Mithra slaying a bull in an ancient Persian rite said to have been established by the first man, Yima. For the followers of Mithraism this rite symbolized the renewal of creation. In killing the bull it was believed that Mithra brought back

Minotaur, The: *see*
Aegeus; Daedalus; Minos; Poseidon; Theseus

Mithra, based on a marble sculpture of c.2nd century AD.

Miyazu-hime

Yima's rule over a world where hunger and death were yet unknown. The rite bestowed immortality upon Mithra's worshippers, hence its appeal to troops facing the dangers of combat.

Miyazu-hime *Japan*
A princess, and the wife of the hero Yamato-takeru.

Mjollnir *Germanic regions*
The name of the magic hammer-axe that was the chief weapon of the god Thor. It was said to cause lightning.

Mnemosyne *Greece*
A Titan, the daughter of Gaia, the earth, and Uranos. Mnemosyne ("Memory") coupled with Zeus to produce the Muses, nine goddesses of the fine arts, history and astronomy.

Monkey *China*
The alternative title of the 14th-century novel *Journey to the West*, about the mythological figure Sun Wukong, the Monkey King.

Monkey King, The
The character, also called Sun Wukong, who stole the peaches of immortality from empress Wang Mu Niang Niang.

Moon Spirit, The *Arctic regions*
One of the three great spirit forces in Inuit belief, together with the Air Spirit and the Sea Spirit. The Moon Spirit (Tarqeq: *see illustration on page 198*) is a male deity and a great hunter. He dwells in the land of the sky, presiding over fertility, morality and, to the Inuit of Alaska, animals. The Moon Spirit is inherently benevolent but is perceived as threatening as he responds to human misdeeds by sending sickness, bad weather, and failure in hunting.

The Monkey King with the peaches of immortality, from a decorative plate.

Morríghan, The *Celtic regions*
An Irish war goddess, who is sometimes manifested as three goddesses. The Morríghan (which means "Phantom Queen") was one of a number of powerful female Irish war deities. Like the others she was an awesome presence on the battlefield, although she did not participate in combat. Before a battle she could possibly be found by a ford. There she would wash the armour of those warriors whose destiny it was to die in the fray.

The goddess possessed magic powers and could change shape at will, especially into a raven or crow, which was regarded as a herald of death. In some accounts it was the Morríghan (rather than Badhbh) who landed on the corpse of the hero Cú Chulainn to show that he was dead. Also associated with fertility and sexuality, the goddess tried to seduce Cú Chulainn in the guise of a young maiden, and stood astride her ford to have intercourse with the Daghda, the father god of the Tuatha Dé Danann, on the feast of Samhain.

Mot *Middle East*
The Ugaritic (Canaanite) god of death, a primal deity embodying the earth. Mot, who represented the destructive power of sterility and drought, features in the important cycle of Ugaritic myths about the storm god Baal. When Baal, who represented the life-giving power of rain and water, became king on earth, his rule was challenged by Mot. Even after a protracted struggle Baal was unable to vanquish Mot, who as the personification of death could never be defeated. However, the supreme god El intervened and persuaded Mot to accept Baal's overlordship.

Mother Earth *North America*
In Native American mythology, Mother Earth (or Earth Mother), with her male counterpart and consort Father Sky (or Sky Father), is usually the offspring of the remote supreme divinity or "Great Spirit". Once Mother Earth and Father Sky appeared, the supreme divinity withdrew from the world and left them to continue with the task of creation. According to some peoples of the American southwest, Mother Earth and Father Sky coupled to produce the first living beings, including the first humans who emerged from within the earth.

Moyang Melur *Southeast Asia*
A moon spirit, who was half tiger, half man, who kept the rules of society in a bag, according to the Ma'betisék people of Malaya. In the beginning, humans lived like animals with no rules of behaviour. They were constantly found committing incest, cannibalism and murder. Moyang Melur enjoyed leaning out of the moon to watch the chaotic state of human society. One night he leaned too far and fell out. When he landed on earth, he encountered a hunter, Moyang Kapir. He vowed to the hunter that he would kill all humans unless he could return at once to the moon. Moyang Kapir threw a liana rope up to the moon and the pair climbed up to Moyang Melur's dwelling. The spirit's wife, Moyang Engko, invited the hunter to stay for dinner, but Moyang Kapir suspected that she intended to cook him. While she was preparing the meal he escaped back to earth with the bag containing the rules of behaviour, which he had found under a mat. Moyang Kapir cut the rope to the moon to prevent Moyang Melur from following him, and gave out the rules to his kinsfolk. From that time humans knew how to behave and were punished when they broke the rules.

Moytirra *Celtic regions*
The location in County Sligo, Ireland, of the first and second battles of Magh Tuiredh. Moytirra is an anglicized spelling of Magh Tuiredh.

Mudungkala *Australia*
A blind old woman responsible for the arrival of the first people, according to the Tiwi people of Melville and Bathurst islands off northern Australia. In the creation period or Dreamtime, Mudungkala emerged from the ground at the southeastern end of Melville island. She was carrying three children, the first people, who populated the islands. Mudungkala crawled across the featureless primeval landscape and, as she went, water sprang up in her track. Eventually the water level rose so much that the islands were cut off from the Australian mainland.

Mot: *see*
Baal; El; Yam

Mother Earth: *see*
CREATION

Moytirra: *see*
Magh Tuiredh, The battles of

Mudungkala: *see*
Dreamtime; Purukupali

MUSES, THE: *see*
Apollo; ZEUS, THE
CONSORTS OF; *Aeneid,* The

MUSES, THE *Greece*

Nine goddesses of the arts, history and astronomy, the offspring of Zeus and the Titan Mnemosyne ("Memory"). The Muses featured little in myth but they were often invoked by writers, poets and other artists as the sources of inspiration. They were among the retinue of the god Apollo, the patron of music and the arts, who possessed the title Musagetes, "Leader of the Muses". Althought traditions varied, they were often said to reside on Mount Helicon near Thebes or on Mount Parnassus near Delphi. Their names and the branches of the arts over which they presided came to be widely accepted as follows:

The epic poet, Virgil, seated between Melpomene, muse of tragic drama (right), and Calliope, muse of epic poetry (left). From a Tunisian mosaic.

Name	Meaning	Branch of the arts
Calliope	Beautiful voice	Epic poetry
Clio	Fame	History
Erato	Lovely	Lyric poetry
Euterpe	Joy	The flute
Melpomene	Singing	Tragic drama
Polyhymnia	Many Songs	Mime
Terpsichore	Joyful Dance	Dance
Thalia	Good Cheer/Plenty	Comic drama
Urania	Celestial	Astronomy

Muromets, Ilya *Slav regions*

"Ilya of Murom", a Russian folk epic hero, or *bogatyr*. He was the son of a peasant and was said to have been a weak, sickly child. For thirty-three years Ilya was so poorly he could not even stand, but then one day a pair of travelling musicians offered him a draught of honey which conferred great strength upon him. With the blessing of his ageing parents Ilya went off to become a great hero, protecting his people against monsters and other perils. He was said to possess a horse which flew through the air and a magical bow and arrows which could shatter a tree into small many pieces. These possessions link Ilya with Perun, the old Slav god of lightning and war.

One famous episode recounts how Ilya overcame the monster known as Nightingale the Brigand, a creature half bird and half human which lived in a tree and waylaid travellers on the road to Kiev. Nightingale could conjure a great screaming wind which could kill humans as well as flatten trees and plants. Ilya urged his horse to ignore the noise of the wind and shot Nightingale in the head. He tied him to his stirrup and carried him triumphantly into Kiev.

When Ilya knew that it was time to die he ordered the construction of a great cathedral at Kiev. When it had reached completion, he died and his body was transformed into stone.

MUSES, THE *Greece*
See panel on previous page

Mweel *Africa*
The sister and consort of Woot, mythical ancestor of the Kuba kings and people of southeastern Zaïre. Woot and Mweel had intercourse, as a result of which she bore Nyimi Lele, ancestor of the neighbouring Lele people.

Mwetsi *Africa*
"Moon", the first man, according to the creation mythology of the Shona people of Zimbabwe. Mwari, the high god, created Mwetsi, who lived at first beneath the waters. Mwetsi went to live on earth, but it was a desert and he started to lament. Mwari sent him a wife, Morning Star, who gave birth to all the trees and plants of the earth. The trees touched the sky and it began to rain, making the land fertile. Mwetsi and Morning Star made a house and tools and cultivated the land.

When two years had passed, Mwari replaced Morning Star with a second

wife, Evening Star, and warned Mwetsi that he faced disaster. That night Mwari and Evening Star had intercourse and produced goats, sheep, cattle, chickens and antelopes, then girls and boys who grew to adulthood in a single day. On their fourth night together Evening Star warned Mwetsi that his life was in peril, but still he had intercourse with her and on the following day she gave birth to lions, leopards, scorpions and snakes. That evening, however, she did not want intercourse with Mwetsi and suggested that he take their daughters. He took this advice and coupled with his daughters, who the next morning had babies who became adults by evening.

In this way Mwetsi became king of a populous nation. But Evening Star had intercourse with a serpent and became barren. The snake bit Mwetsi and he fell ill from its poison. As Mwetsi's health grew worse, so too did the health of the land: the rains stopped, the rivers and lakes dried up and death stalked the nation. To put an end to all the suffering, Mwetsi's children strangled him and chose another king.

This myth probably served to account for the ritual murder of the Mambo (king) of Monomotapa in medieval Zimbabwe. To ensure the uninterrupted prosperity of the land, the Mambo was not permitted to grow old but was ritually slain after ruling for four years and a replacement chosen.

Mweel: *see* Woot

Naga India

One of the race of serpents, the offspring of Kadru, the daughter of the god Daksha. The *nagas* often appeared as malign, for example the multi-headed serpent Kaliya who was subdued by the god Krishna. However, not all *nagas* were hostile or destructive. Among the kings of the *nagas* was the many-headed Vasuki, whom the gods and demons used to twist Mount Mandara during the churning of the ocean. Elsewhere the world is said to rest on his many heads (however, when he moves he causes earthquakes). Another *naga*, Ananta, is the resting place of Vishnu in the periods between the absorptions and emanations of the cosmos.

The *nagas* were the particular enemy of Garuda, whose mother Vinata, the ancestor of all birds, was Kadru's sister. *Nagas* are often depicted as cobras.

A naga, based on a bronze figure from Angkor Wat in Kampuchea.

Naga Padoha Southeast Asia

The serpent ruler of the underworld, in the Sumatran creation myth. Naga Padoha, of Hindu origin, was confined to the lower depths of the universe by a heroic incarnation of the god Batara Guru, to make the newly formed earth a safer place for the creatures who lived there. Batara Guru gave his daughter Boru Deak Parudjar to the divine hero as a reward for his deed.

Nambi *Africa*
The woman responsible for the arrival of death on earth, according to the Ganda people of Uganda. Nambi was the daughter of the High God, who gave her in marriage to Kintu, the mythical founder of the royal dynasty of Buganda, when he went to heaven to find a wife. The High God warned Kintu that he must hurry back to earth, or Nambi's brother Walumbe (Death) would follow them. The High God gave the couple a chicken as a wedding gift and they duly departed.

However, on the journey Nambi realized that she had forgotten to bring any grain as chicken-feed and insisted, despite Kintu's pleas, on going back to fetch some. When she returned Death was following close behind her. Death accompanied the couple home and since then all people have been mortal.

Nammu *Middle East*
The Sumerian goddess embodying the primeval ocean. Nammu was the first deity and origin of all things. She gave birth to the earth goddess Ki and the sky god An, who in turn coupled to produce the great gods of the Sumer, including Enlil and Enki.

Namorodo *Australia*
A race of trickster beings in the Aboriginal mythology of western Arnhem Land. Frightening figures with long claws, their bodies consist only of bones and skin held together by sinew. The creatures move at night, flying through the air with a swishing sound. They may kill anyone they hear with one of their claws: particularly the injured and the ill.

If the Namorodo captures the spirit of a dead person, it can never join the clan's totemic ancestors, but instead turns into a hostile being that wanders through the bush. The Namorodo have also been linked with sorcery and shooting stars.

Nanna (1) *Middle East*
The Sumerian moon god. Nanna (the Akkadian Sin) was greatest of the trinity of astral deities, comprising himself and his offspring Inanna and Utu. He was revered as the god who measured time and, because he shone in the night, also as the enemy of dark forces and of wrongdoers. Nanna was renowned for his wisdom by the other gods, who would visit him regularly for advice.

Nanna (2) *Germanic regions*
The daughter of the god Balder. When Balder was killed, Nanna was so overcome with grief that she died. She was burned beside him on his funeral pyre.

Nantosuelta *Celtic regions*
A goddess of rivers and possibly also of fertility and abundance. Her name means "Winding Stream" and is known from a single Gaulish stone relief from Sarrebourg, on which she is depicted as the consort of Sucellos, the Hammer God. She carries what looks like a house on a pole, so she may be connected with the home and domestic prosperity.

Nareau *Oceania*
The primordial deity, according to the mythology found in the Gilbert islands (in Micronesia). Nareau initiated the process of creation by persuading an eel to separate the sky and the earth.

Nataraja *India*
"Lord of the Dance", a title of the god Shiva. As Nataraja, Shiva is said to be the source of movement in the cosmos. (*See illustration on next page.*)

Nambi: *see*
DEATH, THE ORIGIN OF;
Kintu

Nammu: *see*
Anu (1); Enki; Enlil; Ki

Namorodo: *see*
Argula; Mimi; Ngandjala-Ngandjala; TRICKSTER;
Wurulu-Wurulu

Nanna (1): *see*
Ishtar; SUN, MOON AND
STARS; Utu

Nanna (2): *see*
Balder

Nantosuelta: *see*
Hammer God, The

Nataraja: *see*
Shiva

*Nataraja (*see previous page*), based on a copper statue of the 9th century* AD.

The great mother goddess Neith, based on a figurine.

Naunet *Egypt*

A primal deity embodying the primeval waters. Naunet and her male counterpart Nun formed part of the Ogdoad, eight divinities which personified the forces of chaos.

Nauplius *Greece*

A king of Nauplia, a port city founded by his ancestor (also called Nauplius) who was a son of the god Poseidon. Nauplius the younger was an Argonaut and the father of Palamedes, a Greek warrior at Troy who was stoned to death by his comrades after being framed for treachery by Odysseus. In revenge for his son's death, Nauplius urged the wives of the Greeks to commit adultery. He later lit beacons which lured many of the Greek ships returning from Troy onto dangerous rocks during a storm, causing many to sink with their crews. The ensuing outrage forced Nauplius to flee Nauplia. According to one account, he drowned after he too was lured onto rocks by a bogus beacon.

Nechtan *Celtic regions*

A water god and the husband of Boann, the goddess of the river Boyne. Nechtan was said to possess a sacred Well of Knowledge, which only he and his three cupbearers were permitted to approach.

Nehalennia *Celtic or Germanic regions*

A sea goddess of the coastal Netherlands. Nehalennia was particularly revered as the goddess of seafarers and was worshipped at two sanctuaries, one on the island of Walcheren and one (now submerged) at Colijnsplaat. Here many altars were erected, upon which offerings were made both to ensure a good voyage and to thank the goddess for a safe return. There is some debate over whether Nehalennia was in origin a Celtic or Germanic goddess. However, her cult flourished in the 3rd century AD, when the sanctuaries were in the region occupied by the Morini, a Celtic tribe under Roman rule. Her worshippers appear to have come from all over the western Roman Empire.

Neith *Egypt*

The great mother goddess. According to one account, she emerged from the Nun, the primordial waters, and created deities and humans. When she spat into the Nun her spittle became Apep, the serpent of chaos. She was also the mother of Sobek, the crocodile god.

During the struggle of Horus and Seth over the kingship, the gods and goddesses wrote to Neith seeking her advice. She replied that to compensate for giving up the throne to Horus, Seth should receive Anat and Astarte, two goddesses of foreign origin, as wives. This judgment probably implies that Neith considered Seth unworthy of marriage to native goddesses.

Neith was a formidable figure who was also associated with hunting and warfare. Her emblem was a shield displaying two crossed arrows. The centre of her cult was at Sais (modern Sa el-Hagar) in the Nile delta.

Nekhbet *Egypt*

The vulture goddess of the southern city of Nekheb (modern el-Kab) and the patron goddess of Upper Egypt. With Wadjet, the patron goddess of Lower Egypt, Nekhbet was the protector of the Egyptian king (*pharaoh*) and was often depicted as a vulture hovering with her wings spread above the royal image. She was also the goddess of childbirth, and was identified by the Greeks with the goddess Eileithyia.

Nemhain *Celtic regions*

"Frenzy", an Irish warrior goddess. Like other female war deities, such as the Morríghan, Nemhain took no part in combat, but was a terrifying presence on the battlefield. She caused warriors to panic and once, during the final battle in the war between Ulster and Connacht related in the epic *Táin Bó Cuailnge*, her howling caused a hundred Connacht warriors to die of fright.

Nemhedh *Celtic regions*

The leader of the third people to conquer Ireland in the *Book of Invasions*. Nemhedh, the son of Agnomen of the Scythian Greeks, arrived with four women thirty years after the destruction through plague of the second race of invaders, whose leader was Parthalón. The newcomers settled and multiplied, and cleared more plains for settlement and cultivation, a process begun by Parthalón. More lakes arose and the land of Ireland became fully formed.

Nemhedh came into conflict with the monstrous Fomorians, and fought them successfully until plague wiped out most of the Nemedians. The survivors and their descendants continued to be oppressed by the Fomorians, who forced them to pay a heavy tribute every year, on the feast of Samhain (31 October–1 November): two-thirds of their corn, two-thirds of their milk and two-thirds of their children.

Eventually the Nemedians, who were led by Ferghus, attacked the Fomorian stronghold on Tory Island. Ferghus killed Conan, the Fomorian king, but most of the Nemedians were slain, except for thirty men – one boatload – who went into exile. Some of them then settled in Britain, some in the "Northern Islands of the World", and some in their ancestral homeland, Greece. The descendants of those who went to Greece (the Fir Bholg) and to the northern isles (the Tuatha Dé Danann) subsequently returned to Ireland as the fourth and fifth races of invaders, respectively.

Nephthys *Egypt*

A goddess, the daughter of Geb and Nut, sister of Isis, Osiris and Seth. Nephthys,

The Egyptian goddess Nephthys (on the left).

Neptune

less prominent in myth than her siblings, married Seth but produced no children, so she committed adultery with Osiris and consequently bore the god Anubis. She deserted Seth after he had brought about the death of Osiris and then she lamented with Isis over their brother's corpse. It was the custom at Egyptian funerals for two women to impersonate Nephthys and Isis and lament over the mummy of the deceased.

Neptune *Rome*
The god of the sea, identified with the Greek god Poseidon.

Nereid *Greece*
One of the fifty divine sea nymphs who were daughters of "The Old Man of the Sea", Nereus, and his wife Doris. Among the more famous Nereids were Amphitrite (who was the wife of Poseidon, although some say that she may have been one of the Oceanids), Galateia (the lover of the shepherd Acis) and Thetis (the mother of Achilles).

Nereus *Greece*
A sea god, son of the god Pontos, the sea, and the goddess Gaia, the earth. He was older than the god Poseidon, the ruler of the oceans, and was known as "The Old Man of the Sea". Nereus had the gift of prophecy and could change shape at will. He married the Oceanid (sea nymph) Doris and was the father of fifty sea nymphs known as the Nereids.

Nerthus *Germanic regions*
Meaning "Mother Earth", Nerthus was an early Germanic earth and fertility goddess worshipped by a number of tribes in Denmark. According to the Roman historian Tacitus, the effigy of Nerthus was kept in a sacred grove in a wagon that was covered with a cloth and touched only by her priest. Whenever he sensed the goddess's presence he would conduct the wagon, which was drawn by cows, through the countryside.

The visitation of Nerthus would bring a rare period of peace among the warring tribes. Wherever she came the people would hold joyful celebrations for several days. After her tour she was returned to her sanctuary and her wagon, vestments and perhaps her effigy were cleansed in a hidden lake by slaves. These slaves were then drowned immediately afterwards so that no outsiders would ever learn what the wagon contained.

Nessus *Greece*
A Centaur who brought about the death of the hero Herakles. Nessus abducted Herakles' new wife, Deianeira, and tried to rape her, but the hero shot him with his bow from half a mile away and Nessus ejaculated on the ground. As he lay dying, Nessus told Deianeira that if she mixed his blood and semen with olive oil she would have a potion which would ensure that her adulterous husband was never unfaithful again. Deianeira gathered the ingredients and kept them in a jar.

Later, when Herakles fell in love with a princess, Iole, Deianeira smeared one of his shirts with Nessus' potion and sent it to her husband, who was away celebrating a victory in battle. But when Herakles donned the shirt his body was immediately ravaged by the potion, which was in fact a lethal, corrosive poison. Herakles died in agony but at once became a god. Grief-stricken, Deianeira killed herself.

Nestor *Greece*
A king of Pylos in the southern Peloponnese. The elderly Nestor was

the oldest of the Greek leaders to take part in the Trojan War. He was treated with great respect by his compatriots, to whom he would recount long tales of his younger days and offer advice that was often, but not always, reliable. After the defeat of Troy he reached home safely and lived for many years longer.

Ngaan *Africa*
One of the first two gods to exist (the other being Mboom), according to the Kuba people of Zaïre. In the beginning Ngaan and Mboom, created the world. Each reigned over half their creation, which was covered in water and was dark. However, after an argument they departed from the world. Ngaan sank beneath the waters and Mboom went into the heavens, where he continued the process of creation.

Ngandjala-Ngandjala *Australia*
One of a race of tricksters that are found in the Aboriginal mythology of the western Kimberleys.

Similar to the Wurulu-Wurulu, the Ngandjala-Ngandjala are said to roam the bush in search of mischief such as ruining the harvest or destroying cave paintings made by ancestral heroes. However, some believe that the beings may at times be helpful, for example by cooking edible fruit in order to ripen it. In the rainy season the Ngandjala-Ngandjala are sometimes visible in the clouds, and the mist rising after a downpour indicates the location of the camp fires where they cook fruit.

The Ngandjala-Ngandjala are prey to the activities of the trickster, Unguramu. He steals edible roots from the fires of the Ngandjala-Ngandjala, who grab hold of his tail and pull it until he relents and tells them where he has put the stolen food.

Nightingale the Brigand, from a traditional tile design.

Nightingale the Brigand *Slav regions*
A monster of Russian folk mythology. Nightingale, a half-bird, half-human creature lived in a tree and waylaid travellers on the road to Kiev. His serpent-like hiss, beast-like howl and piercing whistle conjured up a screaming wind to flatten trees and plants, and kill humans. The monster was later killed by the folk epic hero Ilya Mromets.

Nihonshoki, **The** *Japan*
The *Chronicle of Japan*, the title of a work compiled by scholars and completed in AD720. The *Nihonshoki* is an important source of Japanese myth, but less reliable than the *Kojiki*, which was composed at about the same time.

The *Nihonshoki* is written mainly in Chinese script and the text is heavily influenced by Chinese and Korean mythical and historical traditions and dynastic chronicles.

Nikkal *Middle East*
The moon goddess, in Ugaritic (Canaanite) mythology. Nikkal is the consort of Yarikh, the moon god.

Ngaan: *see* Mboom

Ngandjala-Ngandjala: *see* Argula; *Mimi*; Namorodo; TRICKSTER; Wurlu-Wurulu

Nightingale the Brigand: *see* Muromets, Ilya

Nihonshoki, **The:** *see* Kojiki, The

Nikkal: *see* SUN, MOON AND STARS

Niobe

Niobe *Greece*

A queen of Thebes, the wife of King Amphion and daughter of Tantalus and Dione. Niobe bore seven daughters and seven sons (the Niobids) and was immensely proud of them. On the feast day of the Titan Leto, the mother of the divine twins Artemis and Apollo, Niobe rashly boasted that her own children were more of a blessing than Leto's. The Titan was furious at this and sent her twins to punish Niobe. The Niobids fell under a relentless hail of arrows, Artemis killing all the girls and Apollo all the boys (although in some accounts one son and one daughter survived).

Niobe was overcome with grief and remorse. The god Zeus, father of Artemis and Apollo, pitied her and turned her into a marble statue which wept unending tears.

Niobid *Greece*

One of the children of Niobe and Amphion.

Njord *Germanic regions*

A Scandinavian god of the sea and ships, the husband of the mountain goddess Skadi and the father of Freyr and Freyja. In one verse fragment, the marriage of Njord and Skadi failed because Njord was unhappy away from the sea and Skadi could not bear to be far from the mountains.

Nkongolo *Africa*

A tyrant king who features in the mythology of the central African savannah region. Nkongolo, the Rainbow King, was coloured red. He had sex with his two sisters, Bulanda and Mabela, and was also much given to drunkenness and cruelty: he cut off the ears, nose, hands or breasts of those subjects who displeased him. He was an enthusiastic builder, ordering the construction, among other things, of a huge tower by which he tried to reach the sky and regain immortality, which humanity had lost when the heavens and earth became separated. Unfortunately, the enterprise failed when the tower collapsed, killing many people.

The most common myth about Nkongolo concerns his rivalry with Mbidi Kiluwe, a visiting prince "from the east", and Mbidi's son, Kalala Ilunga. When Mbidi came hunting in the land of Nkongolo, the king did his best to please his guest, even lending him his two sisters. They became pregnant, Mabela bearing twins and Bulanda a son, Kalala Ilunga. Mbidi and Nkongolo argued over the son, each claiming him as his own, and Mbidi left in dudgeon. Nkongolo placed Kalala Ilunga in the care of a famous diviner, Majibu, and he grew up to be the fastest runner and best dancer in the land. Nkongolo grew jealous of his prowess and decided to kill him. He had a concealed pit full of sharp stakes made in the dancing ground and invited Kalala to a dancing competition. As the dancing began Kalala's drummer warned him in drum language of impending danger and Kalala fled, leaping over the heads of the people and escaping by boat across the Lualaba river to the land of his real father, Mbidi Kiluwe.

Nkongolo sent search parties across the river, but the waters rose and drowned them. He tried to build a causeway but failed. Finally he built a huge tower from which to look into the land on the other bank of the river. He ordered Majibu and another man to climb the tower and call Kalala back, but once Majibu reached the top he used his magic power to leap over the river and join Kalala. The tower then collapsed, killing many of the followers of Nkongolo.

Mbidi gave Kalala an army with which to fight Nkongolo, who fled in fear with his sisters to the caves of Kaii mountain. But the sisters let it be known where they were, and Kalala and his men found Nkongolo basking in the sun one morning by a cave. They seized him and cut off his head, which they buried in a termite mound, turning the ground about it red. They buried his body under a river. It is said that Nkongolo's spirit lives on in the form of a great serpent which sometimes appears in the sky in the form of a rainbow.

Nommo *Africa*

A creator spirit, according to the Dogon people of Mali. The myth says that in the beginning, there was a heavenly being called Amma, an egg which was the seed of the universe. Amma vibrated seven times before bursting open to reveal the first Nommo or creator spirit. This was followed by a female twin and then four more Nommo pairs.

The Nommos then created and organized the sky and earth, the succession of day and night, the seasons and human society.

Norn *Germanic regions*

A Scandinavian female divinity of fate. There were sometimes said to be three Norns, although their number varied, and it was unclear whether they belonged to the race of giants or gods. Like the Fates of Greco-Roman myth, they determined the destiny of humans and deities, visiting royal courts to decide the fate of princes as soon as they were born. The Norns were linked with a spring called the Well of Fate which was said to be located under Yggdrasil, the World Tree.

Nü Gua, from a painting of the early 20th century.

Nü Gua *China*

A great creator goddess. Nü Gua figures in some of the oldest Chinese creation myths. Her origin is obscure, but her name (like that of the god Fu Xi, with whom she is often associated in myth) is derived from words for gourds or melon, fruits which occur widely in the creation and fertility myths of other peoples. Nü Gua and Fu Xi may have begun as quite separate deities, but under the Han dynasty (202BC–AD220) they were often presented as husband and wife, with human heads and interlaced serpents' tails.

Myths about Nü Gua and Fu Xi describe the creation of humans and their early struggles involving ancient warfare and disasters, especially floods. Nü Gua was especially esteemed as the creator and protector of humanity. She descended from heaven after the earth and heavens had become separated and hills, rivers, plants and animals had

Nommo: *see* Amma; CREATION

Norn: *see* Fates, The; Yggdrasil

Nü Gua: *see* Fu Xi; Gong Gong; Gourd Children, The

Nuadhu Airgedlámh

appeared. Lonely on earth, she formed a number of small beings in her own image from mud: the first people. Pleased with her creation, she decided to speed up the process. She dipped a vine in muddy water and shook it so that drops flew everywhere. Every drop became a new human and the world was soon populated. When the first humans grew old and died, she taught people how to procreate and raise children.

Nuadhu Airgedlámh *Celtic regions*
"Nuadhu Silver-Hand", a king of the Tuatha Dé Danann, the divine race who were the fifth people to invade Ireland, according to the *Book of Invasions*. Nuadhu led the Tuatha Dé Danann to victory against the Fir Bholg at the first battle of Magh Tuiredh, but lost an arm in the battle. He was therefore obliged to abdicate, as only an unblemished man could be king. Bres ("The Beautiful"), whose father had been king of the Fomorians – enemies of the Tuatha Dé Danann – replaced him.

Bres was repressive and inhospitable and the land became infertile. The poet Coirbre satirized him so mercilessly that he broke out in facial boils and had to abdicate. To avenge his overthrow, he gathered an army of Fomorians against the Tuatha Dé Danann.

The physician Dian Cécht fashioned a silver arm to replace the one Nuadhu had lost in battle. Dian Cécht's son Miach later turned this into a real limb, and Nuadhu was restored to the kingship. However, he subsequently chose to abdicate in favour of Lugh, a stranger gifted in all the arts. Led by Lugh, the Tuatha Dé Danann defeated the Fomorians at the second battle of Magh Tuiredh. Nuadhu was killed in this battle by the Fomorian king, Balar of the Evil Eye.

Nudd *Celtic regions*
A royal figure in Welsh mythology. Nudd is etymologically related to the British god Nodens or Nodons, the focus of an important healing shrine at Lydney in Gloucestershire. Other shrines link Nodens with the Roman Mars, widely revered by the Celts as a protector deity.

Nudd's name is also etymologically identical to the Irish Nuadhu, and also appears in the alliterative by-form Lludd with the title "Llaw Eireint", "Silver-Hand", an exact equivalent of Nuadhu's title, Airgedlámh. Lludd Llaw Eireint is said to have ruled Britain, which was saved from invaders through the intervention of his brother Llefelys: this episode parallels the assistance given to Nuadhu against the Fomorians by Lugh.

In Geoffrey of Monmouth's *History of the Kings of Britain* (1136), Nudd/Lludd was the mythical King Lud of Britain, after whom Ludgate in London and the city of London itself were, wrongly, said to have been named.

Nuliajuk *Arctic regions*
One of the Inuit names for the Sea Spirit, the most important spirit in Inuit mythology.

Nun *Egypt*
The dark primeval ocean of chaos which existed before the first gods, in one account of creation. The chaotic energy within the waters of the Nun held the potential of all life forms. It also contained the spirit of the creator, but it had no place in which it could become embodied. Time and creation began when the first land rose from the Nun. The creator was able to come into existence on this primeval mound, which he did in the form of a bird (a falcon, heron or wagtail).

In another account, a primeval lotus grew out of the Nun and opened to reveal the infant deity.

The primeval waters of chaos were also embodied as a god, Nun, and a goddess, Naunet. They formed part of the eight primal divinities; the Ogdoad.

Nut *Egypt*

The sky goddess, the daughter of Shu and Tefenet and sister of Geb, the earth god. According to the most detailed version of the Egyptian creation myth, Nut and Geb had intercourse but embraced so tightly that Nut had no room to bear their children, Isis, Osiris, Nephthys and Seth. Aided by the eight deities of the Ogdoad, Shu parted the couple, lifting Nut high above Geb.

Nut, the sky, was at times portrayed as a naked woman arching over Geb, the earth, and sometimes as a star-covered cow. She was said to swallow the sun every evening. Sometimes it was said that she wanted to devour her own offspring: then she was depicted as a sow, which will also eat its farrow.

Nyame *Africa*

The mother goddess who created the universe, identified by the Akan people of Ghana with the moon.

Nyikang *Africa*

The mythical ancestor of the Shilluk kings and nation. Nyikang, the son of a divine male being and a female crocodile, left his homeland with his followers after a quarrel with his half-brother. He defeated the sun in battle and parted the waters of the White Nile to enable his people to cross over. He founded the Shilluk nation in the southern Sudan and was their first king. All kings since then, the Shilluk believe, have been incarnations of Nyikang.

Nymph *Greece*

A "Young woman" (*nymphe* in Greek) usually said to be of divine or semi-divine parentage. They came in many forms, including sea nymphs (for examle the Nereids and Oceanids) and freshwater nymphs (known as naiads); wood nymphs (called dryads) and nymphs of individual trees (known as hamadryads); and finally innumerable nymphs associated with local features. They were often portrayed as beautiful young women, who often fell in love with mortal men.

Nyx *Greece*

"Night", the darkness of the earth, one of the primal deities which arose from

Nyx (left) and Eos (right) disappear while Helios rises from the sea. From a Greek terracotta vase.

Chaos at the beginning of creation. According to Hesiod, Nyx and Erebos (the darkness of the underworld) had intercourse to produce Aither (the Ether, or bright upper air) and Hemera ("Day"). In the Orphic creation myth Nyx was the daughter and consort of Phanes, the creator god, and gave birth to the deities Gaia and Uranos.

Nut: *see*
Ennead, The; Geb; Isis; Nephthys; Ogdoad, The; Osiris; Seth; Shu (1)

Nyame: *see*
SUN, MOON AND STARS

Nymph: *see*
Nereid; Oceanid; Orpheus

Nyx: *see*
Chaos; Orphism

Nut, from a coffin painting dating from the 8th–11th century BC.

*Odin, from a 12th-
century tapestry.*

Oceanid *Greece*

One of the three thousand sea nymphs who were the daughters of the Titan Okeanos (or Oceanus) and Tethys. The Oceanids were deities who tended all the waters of the world. Among the more famous of them were Amphitrite (the wife of Poseidon, although she may have been a Nereid), Calypso (a lover of Odysseus), Clymene (the wife of Helios, the sun god), Doris (the wife of Nereus, the Old Man of the Sea), Metis (the first wife of Zeus) and Perseis (the mother of Aeëtes, Circe and Pasiphaë).

Oceanus *Greece*

A latinized spelling of the name Okeanos, the deity embodying the great river Ocean which was believed in myth to surround the earth.

Odin *Germanic regions*

The ruler of Asgard, home of the gods, as well as being the supreme deity of the Scandinavian pantheon. His antecedent was the ancient Germanic god Wodan. Both gods were associated with battle, magic, inspiration, the underworld realm and the dead.

Odin was the upholder of kings and the protector of brave young heroes, to whom he gave magic weapons, such as Sigmund's sword Gram, and other assistance. However, he would destroy his heroes when he felt the time was right. When the hero Sigmund was old, Odin decided that it was time for him to die. The god appeared before him in battle and caused Gram to break in two. Disarmed, Sigmund fell under his opponent's blows.

Odin was a shape-shifter, manifesting himself, for example, as a hooded old one-eyed man, a snake and an eagle. He was generally accompanied by wolves and ravens and rode on a magic eight-legged horse, Sleipnir.

Odin was said to summon kings and fallen heroes to Valhalla, the Hall of the Slain, in Asgard. In Viking literature the dead warriors are described as entering Valhalla with great pomp, accompanied by the Valkyries, fearsome goddess-warriors whom Odin sent to determine the course of battles and to select those who would die. In Valhalla the fallen would indulge in feasting and combat, and be ever ready to defend Asgard. The god's warrior devotees, the Berserks (which probably means "Bear Shirt"), wore bear or wolf pelts in battle and were renowned for falling into ecstatic battle-frenzies that made them totally impervious to pain.

The ecstasy associated with Odin made him a god of inspiration, revered by poets and orators. One myth recounts how the dwarfs made the gods a magic mead of inspiration from the blood of a giant mixed with honey. It was stolen by another giant, Suttung, and hidden in a mountain. Odin turned into a snake and slid into the mountain, where he tricked Suttung's daughter into giving him the mead to drink. But he did not swallow it and flew back to Asgard with it, in the form of an eagle.

He was a god of wealth, represented by the divine gold ring Draupnir, from which dropped eight new gold rings every nine nights. Odin also presided over magic and was the possessor of the secret of the runes, mystical symbols used in divination. Prisoners of war were sacrificed to him, and it was said that the course of the battle could be divined from the death movements of the victim. Odin himself was able to travel to the realm of the dead.

Odin was killed at the apocalyptic battle of Ragnarok by the monstrous wolf Fenrir.

Odysseus *Greece*

A king of Ithaca, an important figure in Homer's *Iliad* and the central figure of the *Odyssey*, which is named after him. Odysseus, whom the Romans called Ulysses or Ulixes, was the son of Laertes and Anticlea, the king and queen of Ithaca. But, some accounts made him the illegitimate son of Sisyphus, a famous trickster, from whom Odysseus was said to have inherited the

trickery and guile for which he was reknowned. He featured in much Greek tragedy as a cunning and pragmatic politician, and philosophers contrasted his complex, calculating and often deceitful nature with the directness and nobility of the great hero Achilles.

Odysseus first employed his cunning when he was a suitor for the hand of Helen, the beautiful daughter of King Tyndareos of Sparta. Odysseus advised Tyndareos that, to prevent a riot among Helen's unsuccessful suitors, he should make them swear to uphold the honour of the man eventually chosen as her husband. Tyndareos agreed and selected Menelaus for his daughter's hand. As suggested, Odysseus and the other princes undertook to defend Menelaus if his honour was slighted. As a reward for his counsel, Tyndareos then secured Odysseus the hand of his niece Penelope in marriage.

When Helen eloped with the Trojan prince Paris, all her former suitors came to Menelaus' aid and organized a military expedition against Troy under Agamemnon, Menelaus' brother. Odysseus, however, was reluctant to fight and pretended to be mad and plough the seashore. But the warrior Palamedes exposed the pretence forcing Odysseus to admit his sanity. As a result, Odysseus schemed to bring about Palamedes' death. At Troy he planted gold under Palamedes' tent claiming it was his payment as a Trojan spy. Palamedes was found guilty of treason and stoned to death by his comrades. Later in the siege of Troy, Odysseus designed the famous hollow wooden horse in which the Greek warriors hid and gained entry to the city.

After the fall of Troy the returning Greek fleet was scattered by storms, and Odysseus' ships became separated from

Odin: *see*
Balder; Draupnir; Fenrir; Frigg; Loki; Ragnarok; Valkyrie; Wodan

Odysseus: *see*
Achilles; Aeolus; Agamemnon; Ajax (1); ARGONAUTS, THE VOYAGE OF THE; Athene; Circe; Cyclops; Helen; Oceanid; Palamedes; Paris; Poseidon; Sisyphus; Teiresias; TROJAN WAR, THE HEROES OF THE

The sirens trying to lure Odysseus and his crew. From a red-figure stamnos *(short-necked jar) of the 5th century BC.*

the main body. Thus began the wanderings recounted in the Odyssey. After the storms Odysseus and his crew came to the city of the Cicones, which they sacked. Another storm drove them into a region of sorcery and monsters. They landed first on the island of the Lotus Eaters, whose inhabitants gave some of the crew lotus flowers to eat, wiping out their memories and making them so lethargic that they had to be carried back to their ships.

The next land was inhabited by the Cyclopes, the monstrous one-eyed shepherds. One of them, Polyphemus, took Odysseus and some of his crew captive in his cave and began to eat them. Odysseus got the monster drunk and told him his name was "Nobody". As Polyphemus lay in a drunken stupor, the hero and a few others drove a hot wooden stake into his eye, causing him to scream. Other Cyclopes came to see what was the matter, but on hearing Polyphemus groan "Nobody is hurting me!" they assumed nothing was wrong and left. When the blinded Cyclops rose the next morning, he unsealed the cave to let out his sheep and the Greeks escaped by holding on to the undersides of the animals. Ployphemus' son, the sea god Poseidon, cursed Odysseus to

wander the seas for ten years, for blinding his father.

Next, Odysseus came to the island of Aeolus, the lord of the winds, who gave him a sack containing unfavourable winds. He had sailed on to within sight of Ithaca when a crewman opened the sack while Odysseus was sleeping, releasing the winds, which then blew the voyagers onward to the land of the Laestrygonians. These giant cannibals sank all the ships but one, and ate their crews. Odysseus, in the one remaining ship, then landed on the island of the sorceress Circe. Half of the crew went to her palace, where she turned them into pigs and locked them in a sty. Aided by the god Hermes and a magic plant, Odysseus became immune to Circe's spells and compelled her to release his men. The Greeks stayed for a year with Circe, who advised Odysseus to consult the blind prophet Teiresias. Teiresias told him to go to the underworld and make an offering to Poseidon. In the underworld Odysseus met great former heroes, including his old colleagues Achilles and Ajax.

From the underworld Odysseus sailed past the islands of the Sirens, monsters with birds' bodies and women's heads. Their singing was irresistible and lured sailors onto rocks. Odysseus wanted to hear their song, so, following Circe's advice, he ordered his men to plug their ears with wax and strap him to the mast. The crewmen rowed safely past, deaf to their captain's bewitched demands to steer towards the beautiful voices.

The ship successfully negotiated the sea monsters Scylla and Charybdis and came to Thrinakia, the island of Helios, the sun, where it was becalmed. Ignoring Circe's advice, the starving crew killed some of Helios' cattle to eat. Helios, outraged, destroyed the ship and

The poet Homer, author of the Odyssey *and the* Iliad, *based on a bust.*

all its crew except for Odysseus. He was washed up on the island of the beautiful Oceanid (sea nymph) Calypso, who kept him as an unwilling lover for eight years, but Odysseus longed for home. She finally released him after the intervention of the goddess Athene, and Odysseus sailed on a raft to the luxurious land of the Phaeacians. Their king, named Alcinous, sent Odysseus home to Ithaca in a magical ship full of marvellous gifts.

Before announcing himself when they arrived home, Odysseus found Penelope, who had never believed him dead, surrounded by unwanted suitors. In disguise he discovered that his family and people were still faithful, then killed the suitors with the aid of his son Telemachus and was happily reunited with Penelope after twenty years.

Teiresias foretold that Odysseus' death would come from the sea. In some accounts Telegonus, who was the son of Odysseus and Circe, came to Ithaca and accidentally killed his father.

Odyssey, The *Greece*
A great verse epic attributed to the blind poet Homer (lived *c.*750BC). It recounts the wanderings and many adventures of Odysseus, the king of Ithaca, following the Trojan War.

Oedipus *Greece*
A king of Thebes, particularly famous for sexual transgression in Greek myth. According to one account of his story, King Laius and Queen Jocasta of Thebes learned from the Delphic oracle that their child would kill his father and marry his mother. So when Jocasta gave birth to a son, Laius pierced and bound its feet and exposed the baby on a hillside. However, a shepherd found the child and took him to Corinth, where he was adopted by King Polybus and Queen Merope. They named the boy Oedipus ("Swollen Foot").

Years later, during a feast, a stranger claimed that Polybus was not Oedipus' father. Annoyed by the charge, Oedipus went to Delphi, where the oracle told

Oedipus and the Sphinx, from a kylix *(shallow drinking cup) of* c.47BC.

Odyssey, **The:** *see*
Iliad, The

Oedipus: *see*
Antigone; Sphinx (1);
Teiresias

him that he would kill his father and marry his mother. He fled Corinth, believing Polybus and Merope were his real parents. On the road to Thebes he killed a stranger who insulted him; unknown to Oedipus, this was his father. He vanquished the Sphinx, a monster which devoured anyone unable to answer her riddle, for which the Thebans hailed him as their saviour and offered him the vacant throne and the hand of Queen Jocasta. Thebes prospered under Oedipus and he and Jocasta had four children; Antigone, Ismene, Polyneices and Eteocles.

Some years later Thebes was hit by drought, disease and famine. Creon, Jocasta's brother, went to Delphi and was told that the plagues would end only when Laius' killer had been expelled. The prophet Teiresias declared that Oedipus was the guilty man. Then a messenger from Corinth – the shepherd who had handed him as a baby to Polybus and Merope – came to tell Oedipus that Polybus had died and that he should return to Corinth to become king. Oedipus refused to go to Merope because of the old oracle, but the shepherd told him that she was not his real mother. The terrible truth dawned: Laius and Jocasta were his real parents, and it was Laius whom Oedipus had killed on the road to Thebes. Jocasta hanged herself in distress and Oedipus blinded himself with her brooch and went into exile with his daughters Antigone and Ismene. He died at Colonus near Athens.

Oenghus *Celtic regions*

An Irish deity, one of the Tuatha Dé Danann, often said to be the god of love. Oenghus was the son of the Daghdha and Boann. His modern description as god of love derived principally from the

assistance he lent to lovers, especially Diarmaid and Gráinne. Another myth recounts how Oenghus himself fell in love with a beautiful swan-maiden called Caer. Every two years she changed into a swan on the feast of Samhain (1 November). One year Oenghus took the form of a swan and flew off with her to his palace, Brugh na Bóinne (the prehistoric tombs of Newgrange, County Meath).

Oenghus bore the title Mac Óc (meaning "Young Son") and was probably identical in origin to the old British and Gaulish deity Maponus.

Ogdoad, The *Egypt*

A group of eight primal deities personifying the forces of chaos. The Ogdoad (from the Greek *okto*, eight) was made up of four couples, each pair an embodiment of an aspect of the primal world: Nun and Naunet (god and goddess of the primeval waters); Amon and Amaunet (of unseen forces); Heh and Hehet (of infinity); and Kek and Keket (of darkness).

Seven of the eight Ogdoad pictured around the sun god Ra-Harakhty, from a c.1350BC papyrus.

The deities of the Ogdoad were sometimes represented as frogs and serpents, which lived in the primordial slime, or as eight baboons hailing the dawn. The principal cult town of the Ogdoad was Khemenu (meaning "Town of Eight", known as Hermopolis to the Greeks, and now called el-Ashmunein). This was said to be where the sun first rose on a mythical "Island of Fire" after hatching from a cosmic egg that had been formed by the Ogdoad.

Ogetsu-no-hime *Japan*
The food goddess. In one account, the god Susano was hungry and ordered Ogetsu-no-hime to give him some food. The goddess obeyed, but drew the food out of her bodily orifices. Susano, deeply insulted, killed her. From her corpse sprang the crops which form the basis of the Japanese diet: rice (from her eyes), millet (from her ears); red beans (from her nose); wheat (from her genitals) and soy beans (from her anus).

Oghma *Celtic regions*
An Irish divine warrior, the son of the Daghda and one of the Tuatha Dé Danann. Oghma was famous for his strength, eloquence and poetic gifts and was credited with the invention of Ogham, the early Irish alphabet, which consisted of lines and notches. He was probably identical to the Gaulish Ogmios, who, in turn, was identified with the semi-divine Greco-Roman hero Hercules (Greek Herakles).

Ogmios *Celtic regions*
A Gaulish god identified with the Roman hero Hercules (Greek Herakles), except that he was an old man and revered as the god of eloquence. Ogmios was probably the same as the Irish god Oghma.

Oileus *Greece*
A king of Locris and a grandson of the god Poseidon. Oileus was an Argonaut and the father of the lesser Ajax, a hero of the Trojan War.

Oisín *Celtic regions*
A warrior and poet, the son of the hero Finn and Sadhbh, a woman of the Otherworld who sometimes took the form of a deer. Oisín ("Fawn") was raised by his mother in the wilderness and later found by Finn. He became one of the greatest warriors of the Fian, Finn's followers.

Oisín was put under a spell by the goddess Niamh, and went with her to her father's kingdom, the Otherworld or Tír na Nóg ("Land of Youth"). He dwelt there for a long time, but eventually became homesick for Ireland. Niamh allowed him to visit his homeland on horseback, on condition that he never set foot on Irish soil. Oisín returned to Ireland only to discover that the world he knew had long gone, and he had been in Tír na Nóg for three centuries without ageing. Soon afterward he fell off his horse, touched the ground, and at once aged three hundred years. Before Oisín died, he was visited by St Patrick, to whom he recounted all the tales of the Fian for posterity.

Ojin *Japan*
A ruler of Japan (died *c.*AD394), later deified as Hachiman, the god of war.

Okeanos *Greece*
A Titan, the son of Gaia and Uranos, who personified Ocean, a great river which, in Greek cosmology, surrounded the world. Okeanos married his sister Tethys, who bore the sea nymphs known as the Oceanids. (*See illustration on page 156.*)

Ogetsu-no-hime: *see* Inari

Oghma: *see* Daghdha, The; Herakles

Ogmios: *see* Herakles; Oghma

Oileus: *see* Ajax (2); ARGONAUTS, THE VOYAGE OF THE; Poseidon; TROJAN WAR, THE HEROES OF THE

Oisín: *see* Finn; Otherworld, The

Okeanos: *see* Elysium; Hades; Hephaistos; HERAKLES, THE LABOURS OF; Nymph; Oceanid

Okeanos (see entry on previous page), from a 1st-century AD mosaic.

The Izumo god Okuninushi, based on a porcelain figure.

Okuninushi *Japan*

"Great Lord of the Land", the chief god of Izumo in southern Honshu island and the central character in the important cycle of myths set in that region. Okuninushi, also called Daikokusama, was the descendant of the god Susano and his wife Kusa-nada-hime. Many of the myths about him centre on his rivalry with his eighty brothers.

The brothers were rivals for the hand of the beautiful princess Ya-gami-hime of Inabi. On their way to woo her, they met a rabbit with no fur lying in agony by the road. They told it to bathe in salt water to restore its fur, but this made the rabbit's pain worse. Okuninushi, who was serving as the brothers' squire, asked the creature how he had lost his fur. The rabbit explained that he had tricked some crocodiles into forming a bridge for him to cross from an island to the mainland, but just before he reached the end he had admitted the trick. The last crocodile had caught him and skinned him alive. Okuninushi told the rabbit, who was really a god in disguise, to bathe in a river, then cover his body with a certain pollen. This restored the rabbit's white fur. As a reward the animal ensured that Okuninushi won the hand of the princess.

Okuninushi's marriage to the princess prompted a series of attacks by his jealous brothers, in the course of which Okuninushi was killed twice, but was restored to life by the gods each time. Finally, Okuninushi defeated his brothers with the assistance of the storm god Susano, whose daughter, Suseri-hime, he married as his second wife.

All these quarrels reduced Izumo to anarchy and the sun goddess Amaterasu informed Okuninushi that he must surrender the region. Okuninushi conceded only on condition that a place be reserved for him among the major deities worshipped in Izumo. The goddess agreed and sent her grandson Honinigi to earth bearing three sacred talismans of her sovereignty: a Divine Mirror; beads; and a famous sword later known as Kusanagi ("Grass Mower"). Replicas of these talismans are still presented to each new emperor at his enthronement. Okuninushi is regarded as the protector of the imperial family and his shrine at Izumo-taisha is the most important Shinto place of worship after that of Amaterasu at Ise.

Olwen *Celtic regions*

The daughter of Ysbaddaden, a chieftain of the giants, and the heroine

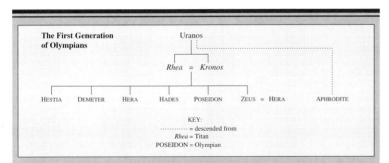

The First Generation of Olympians

Uranos

Rhea = Kronos

HESTIA　DEMETER　HERA　HADES　POSEIDON　ZEUS = HERA　APHRODITE

KEY:
············· = descended from
Rhea = Titan
POSEIDON = Olympian

OLYMPIANS, THE *Greece*

The highest mountain in Greece, Mount Olympus, was said to be the residence of Zeus and the other twelve principal deities of the Greek pantheon, who were therefore known as the Olympians. Their names were as follows:

OLYMPIANS, THE: *see* Hades; and individual names

Name	Parentage	Main functions
Aphrodite	Uranos	Goddess of love and sexuality
Apollo	Zeus and Leto	God of light and the arts
Ares	Zeus and Hera	God of war
Artemis	Zeus and Leto	Goddess of hunting and childbirth
Athene	Zeus and Metis	Goddess of wisdom
Demeter	Kronos and Rhea	Goddess of fertility and crops
Dionysos	Zeus and Persephone and Semele	God of wine and ecstasy
Hephaistos	Hera	God of craftsmanship; divine smith
Hera	Kronos and Rhea	Goddess of marriage; queen of Zeus
Hermes	Zeus and Maia	God of communication; divine messenger
Hestia	Kronos and Rhea	Goddess of the hearth
Poseidon	Kronos and Rhea	Ruler of the seas
Zeus	Kronos and Rhea	Supreme deity; ruler of the heavens

of a Welsh story which is part of the *Mabinogion*. The warrior Culhwch, Arthur's nephew, wanted to wed Olwen and was set a number of difficult tasks by Ysbaddaden before he would grant his consent. With the assistance of some men with extraordinary gifts, such as Arthur and Mabon, Culhwch succeeded and won the hand of Olwen. His most important task was to capture a magic boar, called Twrch Trwyth, and retrieve a wondrous comb and shears kept

between its ears. The hunt ranged over southern Wales, Cornwall and Ireland.

Olympia *Greece*

A city in the Peloponnese which was the site of the greatest Greek religious festival, held every four years (an Olympiad) in honour of the god Zeus, the chief of the Olympian gods (hence the city's name). At the end of every Olympiad all wars ceased for the July festival and the best athletes of the

Olympia: *see* Herakles, OLYMPIANS, THE; PELOPS,THE CURSE OF THE HOUSE OF, Zeus

Omam: *see*
HUMANITY, THE ORIGIN OF

Ometeotl: *see*
Five Suns, The;
Huitzilopochtli; Quetzalcoatl;
Tezcatlipoca; Xipe Totec

Oni: *see*
Emma-ho; Jigoku

Orestes: *see*
Aegisthus; Agamemnon;
Athene; Clytemnestra;
PELOPS, THE CURSE OF
THE HOUSE OF; Tyndareos

A reconstruction of the temple of Zeus at Olympia, with a statue of the god, seated in the centre.

Greek world converged on Olympia to participate in the great games. The foundation of the games, traditionally said to have begun in the 8th century BC, was sometimes attributed to mythical figures such as the hero Herakles or King Pelops. The games were abolished in AD393 by the Christian emperor Theodosius, presumably because of their pagan associations.

The temple of Zeus at Olympia contained an ivory and gold statue of the god, which stood 42 feet (13 metres) high. Sculpted by the great Pheidias, it was completed *c*.430BC, and was one of the seven wonders of the ancient world.

OLYMPIANS, THE *Greece*
See panel on previous page

Olympus, Mount *Greece*
A mountain in northeastern Greece, said to be the home of the gods.

Omam *South America*
The supreme creator deity, to one of the four main groups of the Yanomami people of southern Venezuela. Out fishing one day, Omam caught a woman in the river with no vagina, only a hole the size of a hummingbird's anus. Using the teeth of a piranha he created sexual organs and then had intercourse with her. She bore him many children who were the ancestors of the Yanomami.

Ometeotl *Central America*
The first deity to exist, according to Aztec creation mythology. Ometeotl ("Two-God") was a self-created deity which was both male and female. Its male manifestation was Ometecuhtli; its female, Omecihuatl. This primal couple governed the highest level of heaven, Omeyocan (which means "Place of Duality"), and coupled to produce the four great deities Huitzilopochtli, Quetzalcoatl, Tezcatlipoca and Xipe Totec. These four were joined by Tlaloc and his consort Chalchiuhtlicue.

Ometecuhtli and Omecihuatl were also believed to send the souls of unborn childen to earth.

Oni *Japan*
One of a group of demons believed to inhabit the earth and Jigoku, the Japanese hell. Oni are usually invisible, although some are able to adopt the form of a human or an animal. They are responsible for all kinds of misfortune, such as famine and disease, and may take possession of a person or steal his or her soul.

Orestes *Greece*
A king of Argos (or Mycenae) and Sparta, the son of Agamemnon and Clytemnestra. After Agamemnon had been murdered by Clytemnestra and her lover Aegisthus, the boy Orestes escaped from Argos with the aid either of his nurse or of his sister Elektra. He was raised at the court of his uncle, King Strophius of Phocis, and became the best friend of Strophius' son Pylades. After nine years Orestes consulted the oracle at Delphi about how to avenge his

Orestes killing Aegisthus, from a red-figure vase of the early 5th century BC.

father's death and was told to return to Argos to slay the murderers.

Orestes and Pylades went to Argos and contacted Elektra, who helped them gain entry to the royal palace in the guise of travellers seeking hospitality. Unrecognized by Clytemnestra, he claimed to have heard that Orestes was dead. Clytemnestra joyfully called for her husband, who had feared his return. Aegisthus came, unarmed, and Orestes killed him on the spot before cutting off his mother's head with one blow.

One version of the myth says that for committing matricide Orestes was forced to wander all over Greece. Eventually, however, after consulting the Delphic oracle, he went to Athens to face trial by the Areopagus, the name given to the court of Athenian elders. Orestes was exonerated of his crime with the casting vote of the goddess Athene, who argued that the murder of Agamemnon was a graver crime than that of Clytemnestra.

Orestes returned home to become king of Argos and later, after the death of his grandfather Tyndareos, he also became king of Sparta. Additionally, he conquered a large part of Arcadia in the central Peloponnese. Orestes married Hermione, the daughter of Menelaus, his uncle, and Helen. Pylades married Elektra. Orestes was said to have died in old age from a snake bite.

Orion *Greece*

A giant hunter, the son of the god Poseidon and of Euryale, the daughter of King Minos and Queen Pasiphaë of Crete. According to one of the numerous accounts of his fate, Orion cleared the island of Chios of wild beasts in return for the hand of Merope, the daughter of Oenopion, the island's king. After Oenopion reneged on his promise, Orion raped Merope in a drunken rage. In revenge, Oenopion put out his eyes. Orion waded through the sea – he was so tall the water only came up to his chest – and over land toward the home of the god Helios, the sun, who restored his sight. The hunter then had an affair with Helios' sister, the dawn goddess Eos.

Eos and Orion went together to Delos, where the goddess Artemis invited Orion to go hunting with her. The god Apollo was afraid that his chaste sister, like Eos, might fall for the huge hunter, so he told the goddess Gaia, the earth, that Orion had boasted he could kill every beast in the world. So Gaia sent a monstrous scorpion to kill Orion, who swam off to seek the protection of Eos on Delos. Apollo convinced Artemis that the swimming figure in the distance was a brigand who had raped one of her followers. The goddess shot Orion in the head and killed him. On discovering his true identity, she set him among the stars as the constellation that bears his name, pursued for ever by the scorpion (the constellation Scorpio).

Orion: *see* Apollo; Artemis; Eos; Gaia; Helios; Hephaistos; Minos; Poseidon

Orpheus singing, from a krater *(mixing bowl) of the 5th century BC.*

Orpheus *Greece*

The greatest mortal musician, son of King Oeagrus of Thrace and Calliope, the Muse of epic poetry. His paternity was also ascribed to the god Apollo.

Orpheus became famous for his singing and playing of the lyre, with which he could enchant nature itself. He was said to have charmed the waves when he sailed with Jason and the Argonauts. He also drowned out the voices of the Sirens when the *Argo* sailed close to their island, where they lured sailors on to the rocks with their haunting singing.

He married Eurydice, a dryad (tree nymph) or naiad (water nymph), and was overcome with grief when she died from a snake bite. He took his lyre and entered the underworld, the land of the dead, where his laments for Eurydice were so beautiful that Cerberus, the monstrous guard dog of the underworld, was charmed and let him pass. Hades and Persephone, the king and queen of the dead, were also greatly moved. They released Eurydice from death and allowed her to follow Orpheus back to earth, on condition that he did not look at her before reaching the entrance of the underworld. But as he neared the light of the world, Orpheus could no longer resist and turned to see his beloved. She disappeared at once, returning to the underworld forever.

Orpheus' sorrow was boundless. He refused all advances from other women, preferring only to lament his loss in song. Some Thracian women became so angry at his lack of interest in them that they tore him to pieces in a frenzy. Even then Orpheus' head and lyre brought forth their beautiful music. A temple, constructed above his head, became the site of a famous oracle.

Orpheus was the traditional founder of a mystic cult, named Orphism.

Orphism *Greece*

A mystery religion supposed to have been founded by the musician Orpheus after his return from the underworld. Its adherents, the Orphics, were concerned with the immortality of the soul, seeing death as welcome because it liberated the soul from the impure body. They always wore white and avoided contact with dead flesh, be it human or animal. They were vegetarians and opposed to animal sacrifice.

The Orphic creation myth is more philosophical and abstract than the one more widely known in Hesiod's *Theogony*. In the beginning Chronos (meaning "Time") was accompanied by Adrasteia ("Necessity"). From Chronos sprang Aither ("Bright Upper Air"), Erebos ("Underworld Darkness") and Chaos ("Yawning Void"). Chronos fashioned an egg in Aither and from the egg hatched Phanes (literally "Light"), the creator of everything, a deity both male and female with four eyes and golden wings. He had many names, including Eros ("Desire"). Phanes had a daughter, Nyx ("Night"), whom he married. Their offspring were the goddess Gaia, the earth, and Uranos, the sky. The myth hereafter is similar to the Hesiodic account. However, the Orphics believed that during his supremacy, Zeus created everything anew, swallowing Phanes and coupling with the goddess Persephone, queen of the underworld, to produce Dionysos-Zagreus.

Osiris *Egypt*

A great god and the first king, the son of the earth god Geb and the sky goddess Nut and the twin brother of Isis. As the eldest child of Geb and Nut, Osiris became the first ruler (pharaoh) on earth. He was a good and wise sovereign, revered as the god who taught humanity the secrets of farming and civilization. But his rule came under threat from chaotic powers, chiefly in the form of his brother, the god Seth, who ultimately brought about his death.

There are numerous accounts of the death of Osiris, a central episode in Egyptian myth. In one version, Seth grew jealous of his brother and plotted to take his throne. He ordered a beautiful painted chest to be made and declared that it would be given to whoever fitted inside it. Osiris tried it and found it a perfect fit, but Seth at once closed the chest and sealed it with lead. It was dropped in the Nile and drifted out to sea. Seth became king in his brother's place.

The mummification of Osiris by Anubis, from a Roman papyrus.

Most accounts relate how Isis, the devoted widow of her brother Osiris, retrieved the corpse and used her magic powers to revive it for long enough to conceive Horus, who later defeated Seth and recovered his father's throne. Anubis embalmed the body of Osiris and created the first mummy. But Seth later found the body and tore it to pieces. Each piece was buried at a different place throughout Egypt.

After death Osiris became ruler of Duat, the underworld. In early times he was the lord of a demonic kingdom. Later, however, he was seen as the just judge of the dead, one who welcomed virtuous souls to paradise.

Osiris was said to cause the annual growth of crops. The cutting and threshing of the harvest was compared to the killing of the god and the dismemberment of his body.

Other World, The *Slav regions*

A magical and fantastic land of Slavic folk tales. The Other World, or "Thrice Tenth Kingdom", lies beyond this world and is variously located above the earth or beneath it, or under the sea, or on the other side of a dense forest bounded by a flaming river. It is often the destination of a hero on a quest, who may have to climb a steep mountain or penetrate deep caves to reach it. The way to the Other World may be guarded by terrifying monsters, dragons and other perils. The land was said to be fabulously wealthy, with palaces that glittered with gold and silver. The object of the hero's journey was usually made of gold, for example golden apples or a golden bird.

One theory behind the heroic quest to the Other World and back is that it reflects the ancient Slav belief in shamanistic trance-induced journeys,

Osiris: *see*
Anubis; Ennead, The; Horus; Isis; Seth

Other World, The: *see*
ANCESTORS; COSMOLOGY; Otherworld. The

through which a shaman was said to acquire both wisdom and power.

Otherworld, The *Celtic regions*
A fabulous enchanted land of pleasure, wisdom and plenty. In this magical land, time stands still, and disease, old age and death are unknown. The Otherworld features in both Irish and Welsh myths and is referred to by various names, such as Tír na Nóg (the Irish for "Land of Youth"). It is a land of happiness, peace and revelry, where food and drink are dispensed from never-emptying magic cauldrons. However, it is also a land fraught with perils for uninvited visitors from the visible world. One Old Welsh poem, "The Spoils of Annwn", describes how Arthur and three boatloads of his followers travelled to Annwn, the Otherworld, to steal the magic cauldron of the king of Annwn. The mission was nearly disastrous, as only seven men returned safely. This story may have been the origin of the Arthurian quest for the Holy Grail.

The Otherworld may be beyond the sea, beneath the ground, or within one of the numerous topographical features that in Ireland were once believed to be *sídhe* or fairy dwellings, such as a hill or ancient burial chamber. It was reached through lakes or caves or through encounters with one of its inhabitants, who included gods and goddesses, spirits, heroes and ancestors.

The feast of Samhain (31 October–1 November) was said to be a time when the boundaries between this world and the Otherworld became fluid and Otherworld spirits walked abroad.

Ovinnik *Slav regions*
"Barn-being", a spirit found in Slavic folk mythology, believed to dwell in threshing barns. The *ovinnik* lurked in dark corners and resembled a scruffy black cat with eyes like hot embers. He was regarded as highly mischievous and was often blamed for barn fires.

Paao *Oceania*
A Hawaiian god believed to have begun the rites associated with Makihiki, the festival of the god Lono. Paao was said to have arrived in the Hawaiian islands from an unseen land over the sea. He founded a new religion and overthrew the existing dynasty of chiefs.

Pacariqtambo *South America*
"Place of Origin", the place from which the ancestors of the Incas were said to have emerged from the ground. Three brothers and three sisters came out of the ground through three caves at Pacariqtambo, close to the old Inca capital of Cuzco in Peru. One brother, Manco Capac, was the mythical founder of Cuzco and the Inca imperial dynasty.

Pachacamac *South America*
A pre-Inca creator god of the earth who was revered as the supreme deity by the peoples of the central coastal region of Peru. His importance was such that after the Inca rise to power his shrine at the city of Pachacamac (south of Lima, the Peruvian capital) continued to operate alongside that of Inti, the Inca sun god.

The worshippers of Pachacamac made offerings of gold and sacrifices (both human and animal), in return for which the god made prophetic utterances through his priests.

Padmasambhava *Tibet and Mongolia*
An Indian mystic and *tantrika* (practitioner of the occult) who brought Buddhism to Tibet at the invitation of the Tibetan king Khri Srong-lde'u-btsan in AD762. Many myths arose about him: for example, it was said that he was not born but appeared miraculously as an eight-year-old within the heart of a lotus flower. Raised by the king of Oddiyana, Padmasambhava was condemned to a life of penitence and asceticism after killing a royal minister. He could communicate with supernatural beings and attained great spiritual power. A cousin of the Buddha initiated him into the Buddhist way.

While he was staying in Tibet, Padmasambhava enlisted the aid of local spirits to counter the demons who were hindering work on the king's new temple. With the aid of these spirits the great temple of bSam-yas ("The

The tantrika *Padmasambhava in
wrathful guise, riding a tiger.*

Inconceivable") was soon built. When
Padmasambhava left Tibet, he promised
to return in spirit once a month to bless
those who had invoked his name.
Worshipped by Tibetan Buddhists as
"the second Buddha", he is said to have
lived for more than a thousand years.

Pah *North America*
The god of the moon, according to
Pawnee mythology. In the beginning,
the supreme creator spirit Tirawa gave
part of his power and a position in the
skies to each heavenly body. Shakuru,
the Sun, was sent to the east and Pah
headed for the west, from where he rises
at night to shed light in the darkness.

Palamedes *Greece*
A warrior prince, the son of Nauplius
the younger, king of Nauplia. While the
Greeks were organizing their expedition
against Troy, Odysseus was reluctant to
fight. So, he pretended to be mad, but

Palamedes forced him to admit his
sanity (*see* Odysseus). Odysseus
avenged this humiliation by claiming
that Palamedes was a Trojan spy. As a
result, Palamedes was arrested, found
guilty of treason and stoned to death.

Pale Fox *Africa*
A trickster and culture hero in the
mythology of the Dogon people of Mali.
According to the Dogon creation myth,
the creator god Amma made the fox
bring both order and disorder into the
world. Pale Fox stole seeds from Amma
and planted them in the earth, which
was Pale Fox's mother. However, this
was an act of incest, and as a result the
soil became dry and had to be purified.
So Amma gave people seed that had not
been stolen and they sowed it in the
ground. This is how the practice of
agriculture became established.

After this Pale Fox became an outcast
from human society and lived in the
wilderness. Wherever he went people
followed and planted new fields with
seeds. In this way human civilization
spread through the world. The paw
marks left by Pale Fox in sand are used
for divination: they are said to be his
way of communicating with the world.

Pan *Greece*
The god of woodlands and pastures.
Pan, whom the Romans identified with
Faunus or Silvanus, was of uncertain
parentage, but Hermes or Zeus was
often said to be his father. He was born
with the hindquarters of a goat and
horns on his head, and was raised by
nymphs. He was very lustful and
enjoyed cavorting with the nymphs,
who were frequently subjected to his
unwanted attentions. Among those he
pursued was Syrinx. It was said that
before he could catch her, she turned

The Greek god Pan, from a mosaic pavement.

into a bed of reeds, from which he made the first *syrinx* or Pan pipes.

Some said that Pan caused unidentified noises which startled humans and beasts in the countryside. He came to be seen as a god who spread alarm, hence the word "panic".

In one account, Pan coupled with Aphrodite, who bore their child Priapus, a rustic fertility god.

Pan Gu *China*

A primal creator god who features in the most important Chinese creation myth. According to this account, which had acquired its present form by AD300, Pan Gu was the offspring of the Yin and Yang, the two fundamental forces of the universe. He came into existence within a great cosmic egg, where he grew for 18,000 years, until the egg hatched. The dark heavy parts of the egg sank to become the earth, while the light translucent parts rose to become the skies. Pan Gu grew taller and pushed the earth and sky farther apart by ten feet (three metres) a day until finally, after another 18,000 years, they became fixed in their present positions. Exhausted, Pan Gu lay down and died. Wind and

cloud sprang from his breath, thunder from his voice, the sun from his left eye, the moon from his right eye, the stars from his hair and whiskers, rain and dew from his sweat. All other natural features arose from the parts of his body.

The cult of Pan Gu still persists in certain parts of southern China. (*See illustration on page 45.*)

Panathenaia, The *Greece*

A great annual festival in honour of the goddess Athene, the most important religious event in the calendar of Athens. At the climax of the festival, sacrifices were made to the goddess and a new robe (*peplos*) was presented to her statue in the Parthenon on the Acropolis. The public re-enactment of myth was an important feature of the Panathenaia.

Pandora *Greece*

The name given to the first woman, created by the Olympian gods to counter the aid given to men by the Titan Prometheus. After Prometheus had stolen fire from the forge of the smith god Hephaistos, Zeus asked Hephaistos to fashion the first woman out of soil. Athene then brought this new creation, Pandora, to life and adorned her with finery. Aphrodite gave her beauty and Hermes taught her the art of deceit.

Pandora was given a jar or chest (the so-called "Pandora's Box") and sent as a wife for Epimetheus, the brother of Prometheus. Ignoring his brother's warning never to accept a gift from the gods, Epimetheus took Pandora into the society of men. Curious to see inside the jar she unstopped it, and in doing so released its contents: all the evils to beset humanity, including toil, sickness and conflict. Hope alone remained in the jar. The myth of Pandora, who was created after men and the cause of many

Pan Gu: *see* CREATION; SUN, MOON AND STARS

Panathenaia: *see* Athene; *Iliad*, The; *Odyssey*, The

Pandora: *see* Aphrodite; Athene; Deucalion; Epimetheus; Hermes; Prometheus; Zeus

Hephaistos forming Pandora, from a vase of the 5th century BC.

Pani

ills, served to justify the inferior position of women in Greek society.

Pandora and Epimetheus were the parents of Pyrrha, who became the wife of Deucalion, and with whom she survived the great flood sent by Zeus.

Pani *Oceania*

A Maori goddess, the husband of the god Rongo-maui and mother of the first yams on earth.

Papa *Oceania*

The Maori creator goddess of the earth, the consort of the sky god Rangi and mother of the great gods of the Maori pantheon. Later, when her son Tane, the god of trees, was looking for a mate, he approached his mother first. She refused his advances and advised him to create a wife from the sand of Hawaiki island. This creature, Hine-hau-one ("Earth-created Maiden"), was the first human.

Paris *Greece*

A Trojan prince, the son of King Priam and Queen Hecuba of Troy. While she was pregnant with Paris, Hecuba dreamed that she would bear a firebrand that would destroy the city of Troy. The baby Paris was therefore abandoned at birth on Mount Ida. However, he was suckled by a bear and found by a shepherd, who raised him as his son. Later, as a handsome young man, he defeated his royal brothers in a boxing match and his identity was revealed by his prophetess sister, Cassandra.

Paris set in motion the events which culminated in the Trojan War when he attended the wedding on Mount Ida of the hero Peleus and the Nereid (sea nymph) Thetis, who later became the parents of the hero Achilles. One goddess, Eris ("Strife"), was not invited to the wedding, and in revenge she sent to the wedding feast a golden apple addressed simply "For The Fairest". However, the three great goddesses Aphrodite, Athene and Hera were guests at the nuptials and each of them claimed that the apple was for her.

To settle the dispute, Zeus asked Paris to choose the fairest goddess. Athene promised the Trojan wisdom and

Paris (far left) receiving the three contending goddesses, led by Hermes.

military prowess if he chose her; Hera promised royal power; and Aphrodite promised the most beautiful woman in the world. Paris chose Aphrodite, and in doing so earned Troy the unending enmity of Athene and Hera.

Paris' reward from Aphrodite was Helen, the beautiful wife of King Menelaus of Sparta who was reputedly the fairest woman in all Greece. Paris visited Sparta and Helen fell in love with him. While Menelaus was absent in Crete the pair eloped back to Troy. Menelaus and the hero Odysseus later visited Troy to request her return, but Paris, despite the misgivings of Hector, refused. All the leading princes of Greece, who had once sworn to uphold the honour of Menelaus, formed a military coalition under his brother Agamemnon, and sailed for Troy.

During the ensuing Greek siege of Troy, Paris faced Menelaus in single combat and was defeated, but before Menelaus could drag him from the field Aphrodite transported him to Helen's chamber. Later, Paris killed the Greek champion, Achilles, not in close combat but by shooting him in the heel (his only vulnerable spot), with a bow and arrow, which was considered a more cowardly weapon than a sword. Paris was mortally wounded by the Greek archer Philoctetes with a poisoned arrow that had once belonged to the hero Herakles.

Parthalón *Celtic regions*
The leader of the second people to invade Ireland, in the *Book of Invasions*. Parthalón, said to be a mythical descendant of Noah's son Japheth, arrived in Ireland nearly three hundred years after the Biblical Flood with a retinue of four leaders and five thousand followers. They led a settled existence, clearing and making habitable four plains in place of the previous one, rearing cattle, brewing ale, practising crafts and establishing legal surety.

The enemies of Parthalón were the monstrous Fomorians, a race descended from Noah's son Ham. In the end Parthalón's people were annihilated, not by the Fomorians, but by plague. Only one man survived, Tuan mac Sdairn.

Pauahtun *Central America*
A Maya god who appeared in four different aspects, each of which was said to support a corner of the heavens. Pauahtun (who was also referred to as "God N") was portrayed as a lecher and a drunkard, frequently sporting a tortoise shell or a conch. Pauahtun was also associated with the underworld land of the dead, thunder and mountains and was probably identifiable with the figures known as Bacabs.

Pegasus *Greece*
A winged horse, the offspring of the god Poseidon and the Gorgon Medusa. When the hero Perseus cut off Medusa's head, Pegasus sprang from her blood. According to one account Perseus then flew on Pegasus to rescue the beautiful

Pegasus, the magical winged horse of Greek myth.

Parthalón: *see*
Invasions, The *Book of*

Pauahtun: *see*
Bacab

Pegasus: *see*
Andromeda; Athene; Bellerophon; Chimera; Gorgons, The; Medusa; Perseus; Poseidon

Pelasgus

princess Andromeda from a sea dragon. However, it was more usually said that Pegasus had remained wild until the Corinthian prince Bellerophon tamed him after performing rites in honour of Athene and Poseidon.

Bellerophon later rode on Pegasus to kill the Chimera, a monster that infested the land of Lycia. However, when Bellerophon subsequently tried to fly on Pegasus to the peak of Mount Olympus, the home of the gods and goddesses, Zeus was angered by his presumption and sent a gadfly to sting his mount on the backside. Pegasus reared and threw Bellerophon to earth, crippling him for life. In some accounts, Pegasus himself was welcomed to Mount Olympus.

Pelasgus *Greece*

The first man, according to one account of creation. Pelasgus is said to have risen from the soil of Arcadia in the central Peloponnese. He founded the race of Pelasgians, who were an ancient non-Greek people who still inhabited some villages as late as *c*.450BC.

Peleus *Greece*

A king of Phthia in eastern Greece, the son of King Aeacus and Queen Endeis of Aegina. Peleus took part in the voyage of the Argonauts and in Meleager's hunt for the Calydonian boar. However, he was chiefly famous as the husband of the Nereid (sea nymph) Thetis and the father of the hero Achilles. After death, Peleus was granted immortality and went to live with Thetis in the sea.

Pelias *Greece*

A king of Iolcus in northern Greece, the son of the god Poseidon and a mortal, Tyro, and the uncle of the hero Jason. Pelias overthrew his half-brother, King Aeson, and usurped the Iolcan throne. In an attempt to get Aeson's son, Jason, out of the way he sent him on a mission to retrieve the Golden Fleece of Colchis.

Jason returned to find that Pelias had put Aeson to death. But Medea, Jason's sorceress wife, revived Aeson and instigated the murder of Pelias. She convinced Pelias and his daughters that if they cut him up and cooked his body he would become a young man again. According to one account, his most beautiful daughter, Alcestis, loved her father too much to contemplate harming him, regardless of the motive. Two daughters, Evadne and Amphinome, carried out the deed, only to discover that Medea had tricked them into brutally murdering their father.

PELOPS, THE CURSE OF THE HOUSE OF *Greece*
See panel on page 170

Penates, The *Rome*

The household gods of the larder or storehouse (in Latin *penus*). The Penates, who usually operated in pairs, were said to look after the sustenance of the family. Their images were offered food before meals and their altars were maintained near that of the hearth goddess Vesta. In Rome there was a shrine in honour of the Penates of the Roman state.

Penelope *Greece*

The daughter of King Icarius of Sparta and the Naiad (water nymph) Periboea. The wife of the hero Odysseus, Penelope was esteemed by the ancient Greeks as the paragon of wifely devotion and fidelity because of her loyalty to her husband throughout his twenty-year absence at the Trojan War. (*See illustration on opposite page.*)

Penelope (see entry on previous page)
grieving for Odysseus, based on a
Roman copy of a Greek statue.

following ecstatically in the wake of an "Eastern Stranger" claiming to bring the new cult of Dionysos. The stranger (in fact Dionysos in disguise) was captured on Pentheus' orders, but he easily escaped. He persuaded Pentheus to go into the hills and spy on the orgiastic revels of the Bacchants (female followers of Bacchus/Dionysos). But Pentheus was spotted by the women, who in their Dionysiac frenzy mistook him for a lion and tore him to pieces, led by his mother Agave.

Periboriwa *South America*

The Moon Spirit, in one Yanomami origin myth. Periboriwa's blood, it is said, spilled all over the earth, each drop turning into a human being as it hit the ground. Because they are born of blood, the Yanomami regard themselves as an especially fierce and warlike people. They believe that the less aggressive races of people were the offspring of one of Periboriwa's descendants.

Persephone *Greece*

A fertility goddess and queen of the underworld. Persephone (Proserpina to the Romans) was the daughter of Zeus and his sister, the fertility goddess Demeter, and was often referred to simply as Kore (meaning "Maiden"). One day, Persephone was in a field picking flowers with the Oceanids (sea nymphs). Suddenly, on a rare visit to the living world, the god Hades, ruler of the underworld, abducted her in his chariot and returned with her to his kingdom. Zeus had agreed for him to marry Persephone and make her his queen.

Furious at the kidnap of her daughter, Demeter left Mount Olympus and searched everywhere for Persephone. In the end she stopped the crops from growing, threatening humanity with

Penthesilea *Greece*

A queen of the Amazons, the daughter of the war god Ares and the Amazon queen Otrere. Penthesilea and her comrades fought on the side of Troy during the Trojan War. During the conflict she came face to face with the Greek hero Achilles and fell under his blows. However, as she died she and the hero fell in love.

Pentheus *Greece*

A king of Thebes, the son of Echion, one of the Spartoi or "Sown Men", and of Agave, the daughter of Cadmus, the first king of Thebes. Pentheus figures in a celebrated myth which concerns the growing worship of the god Dionysos. He learned that all the women of Thebes had left the city and gone into the hills,

Penthesilea: *see*
Achilles; Amazon

Pentheus: *see*
Dionysos

Periboriwa: *see*
Omam

Persephone: *see*
Demeter; Hades; Hermes;
ZEUS, THE CONSORTS OF

Persephone with Hades
in the Underworld, from
a red-figure vase.

THE CURSE OF THE HOUSE OF PELOPS *Greece*

A curse that inflicted many of the descendents of King Pelops, a powerful monarch of much of the Peloponnese, which was said to have been named after him (literally "Isle of Pelops"). Pelops was the son of King Tantalus of Lydia who was himself the victim of a famous curse, and Pelops' descendents, known as the Pelopids, were involved in the most notorious and bloody family feud to be found in Greek mythology.

Pelops was one of several suitors of Hippodameia, the daughter of King Oenomaus of Pisa in Elis. In order to find her a suitable husband, Hippodameia was required to accompany each suitor in a chariot race against Oenomaus. If victorious the suitor would win her hand. Despite the fact that he gave his opponents a head start, Oenomaus' own horses were a gift of the gods and he easily beat the suitors each time, whereupon he killed them with his spear.

According to one account, Pelops promised Oenomaus's charioteer Myrtilus (a son of the god Hermes), that he could spend a night with Hippodameia if he betrayed the king. Myrtilus replaced his master's axle pins with wax ones. During the race against Pelops, Oenomaus was closing on his rival when his chariot collapsed and he was killed in the tangled wreckage. As Oenomaus died he cursed Myrtilus to die at the hands of Pelops.

As was his right Pelops married Hippodameia. During a chariot ride on the wedding night, Myrtilus claimed his reward from Pelops, who responded by hurling him into the sea. As he drowned, Myrtilus cursed Pelops and his descendants.

Pelops became king of Pisa and later of all Elis, Arcadia and other areas of the Peloponnese. He died with a reputation for piety, wisdom and wealth. The foundation of the Olympic Games at Olympia in Elis was sometimes attributed to him. He was said, in some sources, to have atoned for killing Myrtilus by building a temple to Hermes.

The curse on Pelops fell less heavily on him than on his children. Two of his sons, Atreus and Thyestes, vied for the throne of Argos (or Mycenae). Atreus was successful, and in revenge Thyestes seduced Atreus' wife Aërope. Atreus put Aërope to death and invited his brother to a feast, at which he served him up some of his own children. When Thyestes discovered what he had eaten, he fled in horror and vowed revenge.

The oracle at Delphi told Thyestes to have a son by his own daughter. He assumed a disguise and raped his daughter Pelopia. He fled at once, losing his sword as he did so. Shortly afterwards, Atreus fell in love with Pelopia and married her. When she bore Thyestes' son, Aegisthus, Atreus assumed the child was his and raised him in his own palace.

Seven years later, Atreus sent his sons Agamemnon and Menelaus to fetch Thyestes back to Argos. He was flung into prison and Atreus ordered the boy Aegisthus to kill him as he slept. Thyestes woke just in time and recognized his own sword in the boy's hand. He realized that this was his son, who had received the sword from his mother. He sent Aegisthus to fetch Pelopia, who stabbed herself as soon as he told her that he, Thyestes, had raped her and fathered her child. On Thyestes' orders Aegisthus then assassinated Atreus and Thyestes became king of Argos.

With the aid of King Tyndareos of Sparta, Agamemnon later expelled Thyestes (who died in exile on Cythera) and regained the throne of Argos. Menelaus then succeeded Tyndareos at Sparta. Agamemnon and Menelaus were both betrayed by their wives, Clytemnestra and Helen. Helen eloped with Paris of Troy, an event which sparked off the Trojan War.

During her husband's absence at the war, Clytemnestra became the lover of Aegisthus and conspired with him to assassinate Agamemnon on his return from Troy. She and Aegisthus were subsequently killed by Orestes, who was her son by Agamemnon.

The curse of Myrtilus finally ended when the elders of Athens, persuaded by the goddess Athene, exonerated Orestes of the crime of matricide, on the grounds that in having killed Clytemnestra he had avenged the even greater crime of parricide.

famine unless Persephone returned. Zeus eventually gave way and sent the god Hermes to escort Persephone from the underworld. Before she left, Hades induced her to eat some pomegranate seeds. Demeter welcomed her daughter joyfully, but warned her that if she had consumed the food of the underworld she must return to Hades for ever. Persephone remembered the pomegranate seeds, but Zeus declared a compromise: Persephone would spend two-thirds of the year with her mother and the remaining third with Hades.

Persephone and Demeter were the focus of the Eleusinian Mysteries, a famous cult based at Eleusis near Athens. Unusually, the cult was open to all: men, women and even slaves were among its initiates, who were attracted by the promise of a special afterlife in the underworld.

Perses *Greece*

The son of the hero Perseus and Andromeda. Perses was raised by his grandparents, King Cepheus and Queen Cassiopeia of Ethiopia (Joppa in Palestine). He became a great conqueror in the region and was said to have given his name to Persia.

Perseus *Greece*

A great hero, the son of the god Zeus and his mortal lover Danaë, the daughter of King Acrisius of Argos. An oracle warned Acrisius that a son of Danaë would kill him, so he locked her in a bronze tower or dungeon. However, the god Zeus entered her room in the form of a shower of gold and had intercourse with her. Their child was Perseus, whom Danaë concealed for four years. Discovering the truth, Acrisius locked his daughter and grandson in a chest and hurled it into the sea. They were saved

Perseus escaping with Medusa's head in his bag. From a water-jar of the 5th century BC.

by a fisherman, Dictys, whose brother, Polydectes, ruled the isle of Seriphos.

Perseus then lived and grew to manhood on Seriphos. Polydectes fell in love with Danaë, but she refused his advances. To be rid of Perseus, who was her protector, Polydectes sent him on a seemingly impossible mission: to bring back the head of the Gorgon Medusa, a monster whose stare turned living creatures instantly to stone. With Perseus gone, Polydectes locked Danaë in a chamber and refused her food until she agreed to marry him.

Perseus was aided on his mission by the god Hermes and goddess Athene. Three monstrous hags, the Graeae, directed him to their sisters, the Gorgons, but told him to go first to certain nymphs who would give him winged sandals, a "cap of darkness" (a cloak to render him invisible) and a leather bag in which to carry the head. Hermes gave the hero a curved sword and he proceeded to Medusa's lair. In order to avoid looking on her directly Perseus watched her reflection in his shield (or, some say, Athene guided his hand while he looked away). He struck off her head and put it in the bag.

On his way back to Seriphos in triumph, Perseus rescued the beautiful princess Andromeda from a dragon and

Perses: *see* Perseus

Perseus: *see* Medusa; Perses; ZEUS, THE CONSORTS OF

married her. On arriving home, the hero revealed Medusa's head to Polydectes and his supporters, turning them to stone. He rescued Danaë and went with her back to Argos. Acrisius, who remembered the old oracle, fled to Larissa in Thessaly. One day Perseus attended games in the same city and accidentally struck Acrisius with a discus, fulfilling the prophecy. Perseus became king of Argos but, because he was the murderer of its former monarch, chose instead to rule Tiryns. He did so for many years, founding many cities. He and Andromeda had several children.

Perun *Slav regions*
The ancient eastern Slavic god of thunder, lightning and warfare. His statue stood in shrines at Kiev, the first city of Russia (modern Ukraine) and Novgorod, the second city. In the late 10th century AD, Perun began to replace Rod, who represented light, fertility and creation, among aristocratic worshippers.

Traces of the cult of Perun havebeen detected among the western Slavics. The god's name in Polish, Piorun, is also the word for thunder.

Phaedra *Greece*
A queen of Athens, the daughter of King Minos and Queen Pasiphaë of Crete, the sister of Ariadne, and the second wife of the hero Theseus. Hippolytus, the son of Theseus and his Amazon wife Antiope, followed the goddess Artemis and preferred hunting to amour. He thereby offended the love goddess Aphrodite, who in revenge made Phaedra fall in love with him. She tried to hide her passion for her stepson, but her nurse revealed it and he fled in revulsion. Phaedra committed suicide but left a note in which she accused Hippolytus of raping her. Theseus discovered this note

and invoked a curse on Hippolytus. When his son rode along the seashore in his chariot, a sea dragon suddenly sprang from the waves causing his horses to bolt, and drag him to his death.

Phaethon *Greece*
The son of the sun god Helios and the Oceanid (sea nymph) Clymene. When Helios promised to grant his son any request, Phaethon (also spelled Phaeton) asked to drive his father's chariot of the sun for a day. Helios reluctantly agreed, knowing that this was a foolhardy venture: Phaethon could not control his father's horses and ran amok in the sky. At one point he drove the sun chariot so close to the ground that the people there were scorched black (and this was why some nations had dark skins). Before he could do any more harm, Zeus killed him with a thunderbolt.

Phineus *Greece*
A Thracian king and also a prophet. According to one account, Phineus blinded his two sons after their stepmother Idaea falsely accused them of attempting to seduce her. In punishment Zeus offered him death or loss of sight and Phineus chose the latter. His decision to live in darkness offended the sun god Helios, who sent the Harpies, monsters with the faces of hags and the claws and bodies of birds, to plague him. They did so by constantly snatching his food or defecating on it. Phineus nearly died of starvation, but was rescued by two of the Argonauts, Calais and Zetes.

Phlegethon *Greece*
"River of Fire", one of the five rivers of the underworld, also known as the Puriphlegethon. The river was said to consist of liquid fire.

Pityocamptes *Greece*
"Pine Bender", a brigand who lived on the road to Corinth. Pityocamptes, or Sinis, waylaid travellers and strapped them between two bent-over pine trees. He would then release the trees, tearing his victim apart. He was killed in the same way by the hero Theseus.

Pleiades, The *Greece*
The seven daughters of the Oceanid (sea nymph) Pleione and the Titan Atlas. According to one account, the Pleiades (the singular of which is Pleiad) were pursued by the giant hunter Orion until Zeus turned them all into stars to save them. The Pleiad, Maia, was the mother of the god Hermes.

Pollux *Rome*
The name by which the hero Polydeuces was known to the Romans.

Polybus *Greece*
A king of Corinth, husband of Merope and adoptive father of Oedipus.

Polydeuces *Greece*
A hero, the son of Queen Leda of Sparta and the god Zeus. Polydeuces (called Pollux by the Romans) and his brother Castor were known as the Dioscuri, which means "Sons of Zeus".

Polyneices *Greece*
A king of Thebes, the son of Oedipus and Jocasta and the brother of Antigone, Eteocles and Ismene. Polyneices and his brother Eteocles inherited Oedipus' throne as joint rulers but quarrelled soon after and Eteocles, supported by Jocasta's brother Creon, seized the throne for himself. Polyneices fled to Argos and, with the aid of seven warriors known as the Seven Against Thebes, returned to attack Eteocles.

Creon routed the Argives, but his nephews Polyneices and Eteocles killed each other in single combat.

Creon assumed the Theban throne and ordered a magnificent funeral for Eteocles. He declared that Polyneices had been a traitor and that anyone who sought to carry out any burial rite would be put to death. Antigone gave her beloved brother's corpse a token funeral and as a result was arrested. She was imprisoned in a cave where she committed suicide.

Polyphemus *Greece*
A Cyclops, the son of the sea god Poseidon and the sea nymph Thoösa. Polyphemus was a shepherd on an island (possibly Sicily). He fell in love with a beautiful sea nymph, Galateia., However, she loved Acis, a handsome young shepherd. When Polyphemus crushed Acis to death beneath a boulder, Galateia turned her dead lover into a stream. In another account of this tale (one which excludes Acis), Polyphemus wooed the nymph and eventually won her heart.

Another story about Polyphemus tells how he took the hero Odysseus and his

Blinding Polyphemus, from a black-figure kylix (cup), 6th century BC.

Pityocamptes: *see*
Theseus

Pleiades, The: *see*
Atlas; Maia; Orion; SUN, MOON AND STARS; TITAN

Pollux: *see*
Dioscuri, The

Polybus: *see*
Oedipus

Polydeuces: *see*
Dioscuri, The; Leda; ZEUS, THE CONSORTS OF

Polyneices: *see*
Antigone; Creon; Oedipus; Seven Against Thebes, The

Polyphemus: *see*
Odysseus; Poseidon

men captive, and began to eat them, but then Odysseus got him drunk, blinded him with a red hot stake and escaped.

Pontos *Greece*

"The Sea", a primal deity embodying the waters. Pontos sprang from the goddess Gaia, the earth, and coupled with her to produce the sea deities Nereus and, according to one account, Phorcys and Ceto.

Poseidon *Greece*

The god of the sea, the son of Kronos and Rhea and brother of Demeter, Hades, Hera, Hestia and Zeus. Like his brother Zeus, who assigned to him the rule of the oceans, Poseidon was a god of awesome power and violence, which was manifested in thunderstorms and earthquakes. In ancient art he closely resembled Zeus, except that Poseidon wielded not a thunderbolt but a trident, a three-pronged fork.

Poseidon married Amphitrite, a sea nymph, and she bore their son Triton, a merman-like creature. The sea god was renowned for adultery, for example with the goddess Gaia, the earth; she bore

Poseidon, from a red-figure wine cup dating from the 6th century BC.

him a monstrous daughter, Charybdis, and a giant son, Antaeus. Another of his lovers was the Gorgon Medusa, with whom the god (in the form of a horse or bird) had intercourse in a temple of the goddess Athene. For this sacrilege Athene turned Medusa into a snake-haired monster. (Poseidon often appears as Athene's rival in myth, most notably in the account of their contest for the protectorship of Athens, which Athene won.) Amphitrite tolerated most of Poseidon's infidelities, but when he fell for the nymph Scylla she turned her into a hideous sea monster.

Poseidon's emblems were the trident, the horse (which in one account he invented) and the bull. He was known to the Romans as Neptune.

Priam *Greece*

A king of Troy in northwestern Asia Minor (modern Turkey), the son of King Laomedon and Queen Strymo. Under King Priam's wise rule, Troy became powerful and prosperous. He married Hecuba, a princess of Phrygia, who bore many children, including Paris, Hector and Cassandra. Following Hecuba's dream that her child would destroy Troy, Priam had the baby Paris exposed on a mountain. But he survived and later

Priam imploring Achilles to surrender Hector's body, from a Greek vase.

eloped with Helen, the queen of Sparta, thereby causing the Trojan War, which ended in the death of Priam and his sons, and the destruction of Troy. During the war, Priam's Greek enemies treated him with more dignity and respect (he was by then very old) than they did other Trojans, particularly when he entered the Greek camp in order to plead for the corpse of his son Hector, who had been slain by the hero Achilles. However, after the fall of the city he was slain on the altar of Zeus by Neoptolemus, the son of Achilles.

Priapus *Greece*

A rustic fertility god, the protector of orchards and gardens. Priapus was the son of the love goddess Aphrodite, but his father was variously said to be Dionysos, Hermes, Pan or Zeus. He was a comic and obscene figure, usually portrayed as an ugly, squat old man with an enormous erection giving us the English word "priapic".

Procrustes *Greece*

"The Stretcher", an innkeeper who killed travellers on the road between Athens and Eleusis. Procrustes made all those who came his way lie down on a bed; if they were too short for it he would rack them to the right length; if they were too tall he would chop them down to size. The hero Theseus killed him by cutting off his head.

Prometheus *Greece*

A Titan, the divine protector of the human race. Prometheus ("Forethought") was either the son of the Titans Iapetus and Themis, or of Iapetus and the Oceanid (sea nymph) Clymene. He did not oppose Zeus and the Olympians during their battle against Kronos and the Titans, but he resented the defeat of

Prometheus having fashioned the first man, from a bas relief in Naples, Italy.

his race. He decided to spite Zeus by promoting the interests of men, created as equals in the time of Kronos but treated as inferior by Zeus, according to Hesiod's *Theogony*. (In an altervnative account, Prometheus himself created the first man, Phaenon, from clay).

Zeus and men met to decide how to divide up their food. The men prepared a sacrificial beast, and Prometheus told them to pour fat over the bones, so that they glistened temptingly. Zeus saw the tasty-looking bones and, as Prometheus had predicted, decided that they must always be given to the gods.

However, he soon discovered that Prometheus had tricked him into leaving men the succulent meat. As punishment, Zeus deprived mankind of fire. But Prometheus stole a flame from the god Hephaistos and, with it hidden in a stalk of fennel, took it to men. Prometheus also taught men how to use fire in skills such as metalworking

Having created the first woman, Pandora, to unleash evils on humanity, Zeus turned on Prometheus: he had him bound to a rock and sent an eagle to peck out his liver. When the bird had done so, the organ grew back at once, but the eagle plucked it out again. This agonizing torment was repeated for thousands of years until, according to one account, Prometheus was finally released by the hero Herakles.

Proteus: *see*
Okeanos; Poseidon

Ptah: *see*
Amon; Atum; Khnum

The god Ptah, based on
a Late Period bronze
statuette.

Purukupali; *see*
DEATH, THE ORIGIN OF;
Dreamtime; Mudungkala

Pwll: *see*
Epona; *Mabinogion*, The;
Manawydan; Otherworld, The

Pyrrha: *see*
Deucalion; Epimetheus;
FLOOD MYTHS; Pandora;
Zeus

Prose Edda, The *Germanic regions*
A collection of old Scandinavian myths
gathered *c*.AD1230 by the Icelandic poet
Snorri Sturluson.

Proteus *Greece*
A sea god, the son of the Titans Okeanos
and Tethys. Proteus possessed the gift of
prophecy, but disliked being asked
questions and would take any form to
avoid his questioners.

Ptah *Egypt*
A great creator god, revered as the
divine craftsman. He was said to have
made gods and humans from precious
metals. He created deities by thinking of
them in his heart and speaking aloud
their names.

Pulang Gana *Southeast Asia*
The earth spirit of the Iban, one of the
Dayak (non-Muslim) peoples of
Borneo. It is said that long ago, people
tried to clear a patch of jungle for the
first rice farm, but could not do so
because Pulang Gana kept reviving all
the cut trees. The spirit allowed them to
grow rice if they offered him beads, jars
and shells.

***Puranas*, The** *India*
A group of Hindu religious texts, which
were composed *c*.AD250–*c*.AD1700. The
group forms the greatest source of
Indian myth. There are eighteen "Great"
Puranas and many "Minor" *Puranas*.

Purukupali *Australia*
The ancestral figure responsible for
human mortality, according to the Tiwi
people of Melville and Bathurst islands.
Purukupali was one of the first people,
the son of Mudungkala, a blind old
ancestral heroine of the Dreamtime.
Purukupali married and his wife had a

son. They lived in the same camp as the
Moon Man, Tjapara, a bachelor who
desired Purukupali's wife. He went into
the forest with her one day, leaving her
son under the shade of a tree. But while
they were gone, the shade moved and
the child died in the scorching heat.

This made Purukupali angry and he
announced that from that time on all
people would die. Tjapara promised to
bring the son back to life. They fought
over the body but eventually Purukupali
seized it and walked into the sea.
Tjapara turned into the moon: the
features of the moon are the scars that he
sustained from his fight.

Pwll *Celtic regions*
A lord of Dyfed in Wales and the
protagonist of the First Branch of the
Mabinogion. Pwll went hunting and
attempted to steal the kill of Arawn, the
king of the Otherworld (Annwn).
Furious at Pwll's behaviour, Arawn
declared eternal enmity unless both men
exchanged identities and realms for one
year, after which Pwll must slay
Arawn's enemy, Hafgan. Pwll agreed
and went to Annwn in the form of
Arawn, leaving the latter to rule Dyfed.
A year later Pwll completed his side of
the bargain and met up with Arawn. The
two hailed each other as friends and left
for their own lands. After this Pwll was
often referred to as "Lord of Annwn".

Another myth recounts how Pwll won
the hand of Rhiannon, a supernatural
woman. She and Pwll were the parents
of the hero Pryderi.

Pyrrha *Greece*
The daughter of Epimetheus and
Pandora and wife of Deucalion. She and
her husband were the only two survivors
of a great flood sent by the god Zeus to
destroy the human race.

Qudshu *Egypt*

A goddess of good health and consort of the fertility god Min. Of Syrian origin, Qudshu seen at times as a form of the goddess Hathor. She is depicted naked, holding lotus flowers and snakes, standing on the back of a lion.

Quetzalcoatl *Central America*

One of the most important Aztec deities, although he has his origins in pre-Aztec cultures. For example, Quetzalcoatl (meaning both "Feathered Serpent" and "Precious Twin") was revered by the Toltecs (9th–12th centuries AD), who worshipped him as the god of the morning and evening star. The Aztecs adopted Quetzalcoatl as the patron of priests, learning and crafts and the inventor of the calendar. He appeared in numerous other guises, such as the god of twins and, especially, as the god of the wind, Ehecatl. As a great creator god, he played an important part in the myth of the Five Suns (he presided over the second Sun or world era). With his twin brother, the dog-headed god Xolotl, Quetzalcoatl descended to the under-world land of the dead to steal

bones from which the human race was recreated, after having been destroyed in the four cosmic upheavals.

The mythical doings of the god Quetzalcoatl became confused with those of a historical Toltec priest-king called Topiltzin-Quetzalcoatl. It was said that Quetzalcoatl disliked the blood sacrifices demanded by Tezcatlipoca and the two gods argued. In the end Quetzalcoatl was expelled from Tula, the Toltec capital, in AD987. He reached the Gulf of Mexico and immolated himself, to be reborn as the planet Venus. According to another account, the god sailed away on a raft, but it was predicted that he would come back one day. This prophecy was exploited by the conquistador Hernán Cortés, who was believed to be Quetzalcoatl returning when he landed in Mexico in AD1519.

Quirinus *Rome*

A god of war, in origin possibly the Sabine equivalent of Mars. After his deification, Romulus came to be identified with Quirinus. The Quirinal, one of the seven hills of Rome, was named after him.

Qudshu: *see* Hathor

Quetzalcoatl: *see* Ehecatl; Five Suns, The; Tezcatlipoca; Tlaloc

Quirinus: *see* Mars; Romulus

Quetzalcoatl, from the 16th-century Codex Telleriano-Remensis.

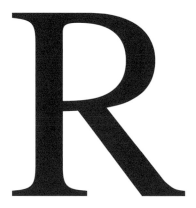

Ra *Egypt*

The creator sun god and supreme deity of Egypt. As the solar god, Ra took numerous forms. The morning sun was a child, or else Khephry, the scarab. The noonday sun was Ra-Harakhty ("Ra, Horus of the Horizon"), a human figure with a falcon's head surmounted by a sun disc. In most accounts of the sun's rule on earth he is called by this name, which represents a fusion of Ra and the ancient god Harakhty, a manifestation of Horus. The evening sun was Atum or Ra-Atum, depicted in human form wearing the royal crown of Egypt. The night sun had no precise name but his image (in human form with a ram's head) bore the caption "Flesh (of Ra)".

The sun was said to be born each dawn from Nut, the sky goddess. He was mature at noon and old in the evening. At night he passed through the underworld land of the dead on his barque, and the god Seth and the myriad spirits of the blessed dead would help defend him against the constant attacks of Apep, the serpent of chaos. The sun would be reborn again at dawn.

According to one account, Ra (also called Ra-Harakhty) once lived on earth as the ruler of gods and humanity. However, he grew weary and Nut, the sky goddess, carried him into the heavens, where he created the stars and the celestial paradise. Each day Ra travelled across the sky but at night he entered the underworld, depriving the world of light. So he created the moon and made Thoth, the moon god, his deputy. Finally, he appointed the god Osiris to rule humanity. But one day he would grow weary and the world would dissolve back into chaos, and the creation cycle would begin anew.

Rabbits

See HARES AND RABBITS

Radha *India*

One of the *gopis*, the young women of the tribe of cowherds among whom the god Krishna was raised. Radha was Krishna's favourite *gopi*, and the pair's passionate relationship (it is not clear whether Radha ever became one of Krishna's many wives) is considered symbolic of the intimacy between the god and his worshippers.

Radha and Krishna, from a Kangra painting of the 17th century.

Radiance *Tibet and Mongolia*

The white light which, together with its counterpart Black Misery (black light), was the first thing to exist, in pre-Buddhist creation mythology. Later a huge cosmic egg appeared from which Black Misery produced the evils of the world. Radiance, though, brought forth blessings, such as happiness, long life, prosperity and many benevolent deities.

Radish *China*

A popular hero of Chinese Buddhist mythology. Radish, a disciple of the Buddha, went on a long journey. Before he left he gave his mother, Lady Leek Stem, money to give to mendicant monks, but she kept it for herself and lied to Radish when he returned. When she died she therefore went to hell and, whilst there, was inflicted with great torments. Radish had by now attained the enlightened status of saint (*arhat*) and had adopted a new name, Mulian. He learned through enlightenment that his mother was in hell and went there to rescue her. However, only the Buddha could release her. Mulian visited the Buddha, who freed Lady Leek Stem as a black dog. Mulian eventually found the dog and, after he had passed a week in fervent piety, his mother became human again. Thereafter she did good works and acquired many blessings.

Ragnarok *Germanic regions*

"The Twilight of the Gods", the apocalyptic battle between the gods and their enemies which resulted in the destruction of the old divine order, according to Scandinavian myth. In one account, the trickster Loki broke free from the fetters in which the gods had put him and mustered an army of giants to attack Asgard, the gods' home. His followers destroyed Bifrost, the bridge leading to Asgard, and the giant army arrived in a ship.

The monstrous wolf Fenrir, son of Loki, broke free and devoured Odin, who was the chief of the gods. Odin's son Vidar then tore Fenrir apart. The god Thor killed the World Serpent which lurked in the waters surrounding the world, but was overcome by its venom and died. Loki faced his old enemy Heimdall, the sentry of Asgard, and the pair slew each other. Then Surt, the fire giant, set the world aflame. The heavens collapsed and the earth was overwhelmed by the seas.

The old world vanished, but a new one appeared, green and beautiful, with a new sun. From the surviving children of the old deities, such as Vidar, sprang a new generation of gods. A human couple, who had survived the calamity by hiding in the branches of Yggrasil, the World Tree, repopulated the earth.

Rama *India*

A divine warrior hero, the seventh avatar (incarnation) of Vishnu and, like Krishna, an important figure in his own right. According to the epic the

Radiance: *see*
Black Misery

Radish: *see*
Buddha; UNDERWORLDS;
Yama (2)

Ragnarok: *see*
Asgard; Fenrir; Heimdall;
Loki; Odin; Thor; Yggdrasil

Rama: *see*
Hanuman; Krishna; VISHNU,
THE AVATARS OF

Rama, the divine warrior hero of Hindu myth and son of Dasharatha.

Ramayana, there was once a childless king called Dasharatha, the ruler of the holy city of Ayodhya. He performed a sacrifice in order to be granted male offspring. At the gods' request, Vishnu became incarnate as Dasharatha's four sons, in order to destroy Ravana, the demon ruler of the island kingdom of Lanka. The greatest of these four sons were Rama and Bharata. Their brothers Lakshmana and Shatrughna became their respective loyal aides.

A great sage, Vishvamitra, enlisted the help of Rama on a mission against the Rakshasas, a race of demons. He was successful and the sage took Rama and Lakshmana to the court of King Janaka of Videha. Part of Rama's purpose while there was to marry Sita, Janaka's beautiful daughter, who had sprung from a furrow ploughed by Janaka. King Dasharatha chose Rama as his heir, but Rama was exiled for fourteen years and left with Sita and Lakshmana. During this time, Bharata was persuaded to rule in Rama's place as his regent. A female Rakshasa, Shurpanakha, tried to seduce Rama and Lakshmana, but the latter drove her off. In revenge she induced her brother, the evil King Ravana, to kidnap Sita and carry her off to Lanka. Rama and Lakshmana at once launched a search for Sita. With the devoted support of the monkey Hanuman, they destroyed Ravana's kingdom and his army of Rakshasas, and Sita was recovered. Rama fought and killed the demon king.

Rama greeted Sita coldly, convinced that she must have been unfaithful during her captivity. She underwent an ordeal by fire and the gods appeared to Rama to tell him he was an incarnation of Vishnu. The god of fire presented Sita, unhurt and exonerated, and the two were happily reunited. Dasharatha appeared and blessed his sons, telling Rama to return to Ayodhya and assume the kingship.

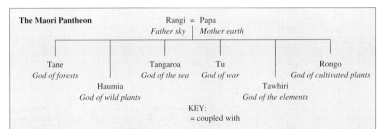

The Maori Pantheon

Rangi = Papa
Father sky | Mother earth

Tane
God of forests

Tangaroa
God of the sea

Tu
God of war

Rongo
God of cultivated plants

Haumia
God of wild plants

Tawhiri
God of the elements

KEY:
= coupled with

Ramayana, The *India*

One of the two great Sanskrit verse epics (along with the *Mahabharata*). The *Ramayana*, composed between *c*.200BC–*c*.AD200, focuses on the life and heroism of the god Rama and included much other mythological material.

Rangda *Southeast Asia*

A fierce sorceress queen of Balinese mythology. Rangda ("Widow"), who is depicted as near-naked with long hair and nails, is the leader of a band of evil witches. Her immortal opponent is the spirit king Barong, the opponent of evil. The combat between Rangda and Barong, acted out in Balinese dance, always ends in Barong vanquishing Rangda. Rangda may have originated in a legendary 11th-century evil queen of Bali, Mahendradatta.

Rangi and Papa *Oceania*

The primal creator deities of the Maori pantheon. Rangi, the sky god, and Papa, the earth goddess, embraced so tightly in the primordial void that none of their six children could escape after they had been born. Tu, the god of war, proposed killing their parents, but Tane, the god of forests, said it was better to force them apart. Each god in turn tried to separate the deities but only Tane succeeded. Then Rangi and Papa assumed the positions they have kept to this day (*see family tree above*).

Rapithwin *Middle East*

The ancient Persian god of the summer and warmth. Rapithwin ruled the land all year until the onset of the demon of winter, when he withdrew beneath the earth to keep the underground waters warm. He returned when winter, and its demon, departed.

Rata *Oceania*

A hero who features in Maori and other outer Polynesian mythologies. His father, known as Wahieroa, was killed by monstrous lizards who served his enemy, Puna. Rata embarked on a search for his body. He eventually found the head inside Matuku, a great shark, and recovered the remainder of the body from Puna's lizard monsters. But on the way home Rata himself was cut to pieces by the lizards.

Raven *North America*

A culture hero and trickster, prominent in the Native American and Inuit mythology of Alaska and the American and Canadian northwest coast. Raven was born by magical means, the offspring of a woman who swallowed a feather or, in other accounts, a stone.

Some peoples, such as the Tlingit of southern Alaska, envisage two Ravens, one a trickster and the other a culture hero. Usually, however, the character has both tricksterish and creator qualities, as in the Tsimshian story of

Raven (left) shown with the sun disc between his ears, from a native American headdress.

how Raven stole the heavenly bodies from a greedy chief and hurled them into the sky.

The Raven Father is the principal creator figure of the Alaskan Inuit. In the "first times" of the world he descended from the sky and created dry land, then a man, then numerous types of animal and plant, then a woman as man's companion. Then he taught them various skills, such as how to raise children, make fire and keep animals.

Remus *Rome*
A founder of the city of Rome, with his brother, Romulus.

Renenutet *Egypt*
A snake goddess of the harvest, especially associated with granaries and fields. Renenutet also presided over the weaning of infants.

Rhadamanthys *Greece*
The son of Europa and Zeus and brother to Minos and Sarpedon. In one tradition, after death he and his brothers became underworld judges of the dead.

Rhea *Greece*
A Titan, the daughter of the goddess Gaia and the god Uranos and the mother of Demeter, Hades, Hera, Hestia, Poseidon and Zeus. Rhea married her brother Kronos, the chief of the gods, who had overthrown their father. Gaia prophesied that Kronos would also be overthrown by one of his offspring, so he devoured each of his children as they were born. But Rhea saved her youngest child, Zeus, by concealing him the moment he was born and presenting Kronos with a rock wrapped up in swaddling clothes, which he swallowed. Zeus later fulfilled Gaia's prophecy.

Rhea was sometimes identified with the Near Eastern goddess Cybele, the Great Mother.

Rhiannon *Celtic regions*
A princess, the daughter of the king of the Otherworld. Rhiannon appears in the *Mabinogion* as the wife of the hero Pwll, lord of Dyfed. She was associated with horses and is probably identifiable with the Celtic horse goddess Epona.

The Celtic princess Rhiannon. This picture is redrawn from a relief.

For example, she first appeared to Pwyll on a magic white mare which no horse could ever catch. Later, she was falsely charged with devouring her son Pryderi, and forced to carry Pwyll's guests from the horse block into his palace in punishment. She was released from this when Pryderi, who had been kidnapped, reappeared several years later.

Rhpisunt *North America*

A woman, the daughter of a chief, who according to a northwestern myth, married the son of a bear. She was out picking berries when she encountered two young men, who led her to the house of the bear people. Bear coats hung everywhere, for bears had human form but always wore bear coats when they went out. She married the bear chief's son and bore twin cubs.

Later, Rhpisunt's brothers came across the bear's den and when they left, she and her cubs went with them. Back at her home, her cubs took off their coats to reveal two handsome boys, who became great hunters. Rhpisunt grew old and died and the twins returned to the bear people. But Rhpisunt's people always had good hunting when they reminded the bears of their kinship.

Rice Mother *Southeast Asia*

A female protector spirit of rice. Each Balinese family fashions a "Rice Mother" from sheaves of rice. This effigy is hung close to the rice paddy to ensure a good crop. When the harvest is over, the family places it in the rice granary to mind the crop.

Roal *South America*

The creator deity of the Q'ero community of the Andes near Cuzco, the ancient Inca capital. Before the sun existed, a mighty race of humans lived

in the world. Roal offered to give them his own power, but they declared that they did not need it.

So, deciding to punish them for this insult, Roal created the sun, which dried up their bodies and made them blind. They hid from the sun and only occasionally emerged at sundown or on the night of a full moon.

The mountain spirits (Apus) created a woman, Collari, and a man, Inkari: the progenitors of a new race of people.

Rod *Slav regions*

A principally eastern Slavic god of light, fertility and creation. His cult, which occupied a similar status to Svantovit's among the western Slavics was closely associated with that of dead ancestors and of the Rozhanitsy, mother and daughter deities whose festival marked the completion of the harvest. By *c.*AD1000 the cult of Rod had been supplanted among the aristocracy by that of the thunder god Perun.

ROME, THE KINGS OF

See panel on next page

Romulus *Rome*

The joint founder and legendary first king of Rome, which was said to have been founded in 753BC and named after him. King Numitor of Alba Longa, a

Romulus and Remus suckling from the she-wolf, based on a bronze statue of between the 6th and 5th centuries BC.

Rhpisunt: *see* ANIMALS

Rice Mother: *see* Inari; Pulang Gana

Roal: *see* Viracocha

Rod: *see* Perun

Romulus: *see* Aeneas; Ascanius; Mars; ROME, THE KINGS OF; Vesta

The Rice Mother, from a 19th-century northern Balinese figure.

ROME, THE KINGS OF:
see
Romulus

Based on a Roman coin showing the second legendary king of Rome, Numa (on the left).

Rona (1): see
SUN, MOON AND STARS

ROME, THE KINGS OF

There were said to have been seven kings of Rome between the traditional date of the city's foundation (753BC) and the establishment of the republic (510BC). The names of these legendary kings were as follows:

King	Traditional dates of reign (all BC)	Deeds
Romulus	753–715	Founder of the city
Numa Pompilius	715–673	Founded important religious institutions
Tullius Hostilius	673–642	Celebrated soldier
Ancus Marcius	642–616	Built first Tiber bridge
Tarquin the Elder	616–579	Built first stone walls; began temple of Jupiter and Minerva; annexed territory
Servius Tullius	579–534	Constitutional reform
Tarquin the Proud	534–510	Annexed territory; despot

descendant of the hero Aeneas, was overthrown by his brother Amulius, who ordered Numitor's only child, Rhea Silvia, to become a Vestal virgin. One day, in a sacred grove, the god Mars raped her as she slept. When she bore twins, Romulus and Remus, Amulius commanded that they be abandoned in the river Tiber. Cast adrift in a basket, they were saved by a she-wolf and adopted by a shepherd, Faustulus.

Eventually, Faustulus explained the truth about their origins. Romulus killed Amulius and restored his grandfather Numitor to the throne. The twins decided to found a new city where the she-wolf had found them. They argued over the exact spot and Romulus, acting on a sign from the gods, began to mark out a boundary ditch on the Palatine Hill. Remus jumped over it to show how ineffective it was as a defence. Considering this an act of sacrilege, Romulus killed him, becoming the sole ruler of the new settlement, Rome.

Romulus drew many men to the city by declaring it a safe-haven for runaways. However, there were no women, so Romulus invited the chiefs of the surrounding Sabine tribes to a festival, during which his men abducted all the unmarried Sabine women. A war ensued between the Romans and the Sabines which ended after the Sabine women appealed for peace to their fathers and new husbands.

The two peoples were united and Romulus ruled jointly with Titus Tatius, the Sabine monarch, until the latter's death shortly after the war. Romulus ruled alone, the first king of Rome, for a further thirty-three years.

Rona (1) *Oceania*

A god who fights with the moon, according to Maori mythology. The fight began when the moon kidnapped Rona's wife. As the moon grows battle-weary, it wanes. Rona and the moon then take time to recover their strength, which is when the moon waxes. When the moon is full, the fight recommences.

Rona (2) *Oceania*

A rapacious female cannibal in the mythology of Tahiti. Rona, who was known as "Long Teeth", had a beautiful daughter called Hina, who fell in love with a man called Monoi. However, Rona captured Monoi and devoured him. Hina turned to No'a-huruhuru, the "Hairy Chief", for help and with his aid Rona was killed.

Rongo *Oceania*

The Maori god of peace and cultivated plants, one of the six offspring of the primal deities Rangi and Papa. In his manifestation as Rongo-maui he is said to have brought the first yams (sweet potatoes) to earth from heaven. He is the deity known in Hawaii as Lono.

Rukmini *India*

An incarnation of the goddess Lakshmi, one of the wives of Krishna, and the mother of his son Pradyumna.

Rusalka Slav regions

A female spirit which lived in lakes and rivers and appeared as a beautiful young woman dressed in leaves. In southern Russia and Ukraine, *rusalka* were once commonly said to be manifestations of the souls of dead infants or drowned maidens. Their appearance and beautiful singing lured men to a watery grave, and during Rusalnaia week (the seventh after Easter) the *rusalka* were said to go into fields and forests and attack from behind, tickling their victims to death. They particularly disliked women and tried to steal the souls of unwary girls or punish women who did chores in Rusalnaia week.

Rongo: *see*
Lono; Rangi and Papa.

A redrawing of a Maori stone figure, thought to be Rongo.

Rukmini: *see*
Krishna

Rusalka: see
Kikimora; Vila

SACRED MOUNTAINS, THE

See map on opposite page

Sakka *India*

The king of the gods in Tavatimsa (a lower realm of the Hindu heavens) and one of the incarnations of the god Indra. According to Buddhist mythology, Sakka acted to propagate the Buddha's teachings during the Buddha's past incarnations.

Sarpedon *Greece*

A warrior king, the son of Europa and Zeus and the brother of Minos and Rhadamanthys. He and his brothers ruled Crete jointly until all three of them fell in love with the same beautiful youth, Miletus. Sarpedon was the one to win his love, and as a result caused Minos to expel them, as well as Rhadamanthys.

In a full and eventful career, Sarpedon assisted in the foundation of the kingdom of Lycia in southwestern Asia Minor. He married and had a son, Evander, later king of Lycia. Finally, when he died he became a judge of the dead in the underworld.

Sati *India*

A goddess, the daughter of Daksha and the first wife of Shiva. According to one account, when Shiva was excluded from a horse sacrifice arranged by her father, Sati was so overcome with shame that she burned herself to death. She was reincarnated as Parvati or Uma, the god's second wife.

Satyr *Greece*

One of the mythical male followers of the god Dionysos (the Roman Bacchus). Satyrs were part man and part goat with

Satyrs drinking, from a wine cooler of the 5th century BC.

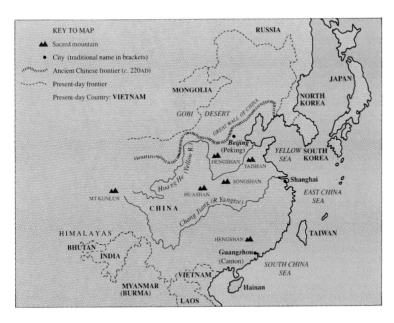

Scáthach: *see*
Cú Chulainn; Fer Diadh

Sciron: *see*
Theseus

Scylla and Charybdis: *see*
Odysseus

Sea Spirit, The: *see*
Air Spirit, The; Bladder
Festival, The; Moon Spirit,
The

The five most sacred mountains of China; Hengshan (northern and southern peaks), Huashan, Kunlun, Songshan and Taishan. The mountains have been thought of as active deities, responsive to prayers and sacrifices.

long, horse-like tails, and were usually depicted naked with an erection. They were interested almost exclusively in the joys of wine, revelry and sex, and often persued maenads or bacchants.

Scáthach *Celtic regions*
A warrior-sorceress who fostered many Irish heroes and taught them the skills of warfare. Her most famous pupils were the Ulster hero Cú Chulainn and his foster-brother Fer Diadh.

Sciron *Greece*
A brigand who waylaid travellers near Megara in the Corinthian isthmus. Sciron asked those he encountered to wash his feet, but as soon as they bent

down he would kick them off a cliff into the sea to be devoured by a giant turtle. Theseus hurled him over the same cliff.

Scylla and Charybdis *Greece*
A pair of female sea monsters, located in the Straits of Messina, between Sicily and mainland Italy. Charybdis, the daughter of the god Poseidon and the goddess Gaia, became a giant whirlpool, which sucked in water three times a day with force enough to swallow a ship.

Scylla was originally a beautiful sea nymph. In one account, Poseidon fell in love with her, so Amphitrite, his jealous wife, put magic herbs into the pool where she bathed, turning Scylla into a six-headed monster. Its home was a cave opposite Charybdis. It often snatched sailors off their ships to eat them.

Sea Spirit, The *Arctic regions*
The most important of the three principal spirits in the belief of the Inuit of Canada and Greenland, the others

A sea spirit, based on a wood carving found in the Solomon Islands.

being the Air Spirit and the Moon Spirit. The Sea Spirit, who is called Sedna and Nuliajuk among other names, presides over all the creatures eaten by humans. She takes the form of a woman and lives at the bottom of the sea, sending forth the creatures to be hunted for food.

According to one Canadian Inuit myth, the Sea Spirit was originally a girl whose father forced her to marry a dog. When this marriage failed, she married a stormy petrel, but her father retrieved her. However, the petrel found them and caused a storm which nearly upset their kayak. The terrified father tried to throw the girl to the seabird, but she clung to the side of the boat, so he hacked off her fingers. She sank to the sea-bed and became the Sea Spirit. Her severed fingers became seals and walruses. There she was rejoined by her father and the dog.

Sekhmet *Egypt*

The lioness goddess. In contrast to the other important feline goddess, Bastet, Sekhmet ("The Powerful") was a terrifying deity and often the agent of divine retribution. For example, she was sent by the god Ra to punish the rebellious human race but had to be restrained from wiping out humanity entirely. Infectious disease was believed to be the goddess's messenger, and criminals were occasionally sacrificed in her honour. Sekhmet was depicted in human form with the head of a lioness.

Selene *Greece*

The goddess of the moon, the daughter of the Titans Hyperion and Thea. She is most notable as the lover of Endymion, a king of Elis in the Peloponnese, by whom she had fifty sons. In one story, Selene did not want Endymion to age and die. She put him into a magic sleep so that he remained young for ever.

Selqet *Egypt*

The scorpion goddess who presided over childbirth and whose task it was to watch over mummified bodies during burial. She was one of the deities who protected the goddess Isis from her hostile brother Seth as she nursed the infant Horus. Selqet was depicted as a woman with a scorpion on her head, or as a scorpion with the head of a woman.

Semara *Southeast Asia*

The Balinese god of love. According to the Balinese creation myth, Semara resides in the Floating Sky, the second of six heavens that lie above the earth.

Semele *Greece*

A princess of Thebes, the daughter of King Cadmus and Queen Harmonia. The god Zeus became the lover of Semele in the guise of a handsome

The lion-goddess Sekhmet.

mortal, thereby arousing the jealousy of his wife Hera. So the goddess disguised herself as an old woman and told Semele that her lover was none other than Zeus, and that to prove it, all she had to do was to ask him to show himself in all his glory.

Semele therefore persuaded Zeus to promise her a favour. After he had agreed, she requested to see him in his full majesty. The god was reluctant, but his promise bound him to do as she wished. Finally, he appeared in his entire divine magnificence, riding in his celestial chariot accompanied by a brilliant display of thunderbolts and lightning. However, as he (and of course the cunning Hera) had foreseen, this sight was too much for any mortal, and Semele was burned to a cinder. From her ashes Zeus retrieved their unborn child, the god Dionysos.

Separate Heavenly Deities, The
Japan
A group of five primal deities who were the first gods to exist. They were: Amanominakanushi-no-kami (meaning "The Lord of the Centre of Heaven"), who was the oldest; Takamimusubi and Kamimusubi; and two lesser divinities, Umashiashikabihikoji-no-kami and Amanotokotachi-no-kami.

Seth *Egypt*
The god personifying the forces of disorder and sterility, the son of the sky goddess Nut and the earth god Geb, and the brother of Osiris, Isis and Nepthys. Osiris became the first king on earth, but Seth was jealous, so brought about his brother's death and took the throne. He was later challenged by the god Horus, son of Osiris and Isis, and their struggle for the kingship is a central episode of Egyptian mythology. In the end the gods

Seth, standing in front of the sun god whilst spearing Apep. From a papyrus of the 11th century BC.

who arbitrated in their conflict decided in favour of Horus, and Seth had to accept their judgment. In compensation he went to live in the divine sky realm as the god of storms with two foreign goddesses, Anath and Astarte, as new wives. His first wife, Nephthys, had left him after the death of Osiris. Many myths present the followers of Seth perpetually struggling against those of Horus, the god who symbolized order.

Seth was often represented as a hybrid animal, part pig and part wild ass. His earthly domain was the barren desert and most animals of the desert were associated with him. Oxen and asses were also linked to Seth, because they threshed barley and thus trod on the body of Osiris, who was believed to be manifested in the crops. For this reason, it was said, Horus condemned these beasts to suffer constant beatings.

As the strongest of the gods, Seth fulfilled the positive role of defending the sun god on his nightly journey through the underworld. During this journey the sun's barque was attacked by Apep, the serpent of chaos. Seth was often depicted in ancient art in the act of spearing Apep.

Separate heavenly deities, The: *see*
IZANAGI AND IZANAMI

Seth: *see*
Anath; Astarte; Apep; Ennead, The; Geb; Horus; Isis; Nephthys; Nut; Osiris; Ra

Setna Khaemwese *Egypt*

A prince, the son of the pharaoh Ramesses II (*c.*1279BC–1213BC). He was a high priest of the god Ptah and was responsible for the restoration of some of the ancient monuments of Giza. This probably accounts for his later reputation as a practitioner of magic. The mythical Setna was the focus of stories about the rivalry between the priest-magicians of Egypt and those of Nubia to the south, in which the Egyptians were victorious.

Seven Against Thebes, The *Greece*

Seven warriors who took part in the civil war between Polyneices and Eteocles, the sons of Oedipus. After Oedipus left Thebes to go into exile, Polyneices and Eteocles, who (in one account) had expelled him, inherited his throne as joint rulers. Each agreed to rule alternately for one year at a time, but after the first year Eteocles refused to give up the throne for his brother's turn. Polyneices fled to Argos and assembled seven contingents of troops, each under one of the following commanders: King Adrastus of Argos; Amphiaraus; Capaneus; Hippomedon; Parthenopaeus; Tydeus; and Polyneices himself.

During the ensuing siege of Thebes, each contingent assailed one of the city's seven gates. The expedition was a failure, as Oedipus had cursed both his sons. They killed each other in single combat and the Seven were annihilated, except Adrastus who escaped back to Argos on his swift horse.

Seven Sages, The *India*

Seven men of great wisdom and spiritual power who appear frequently in Indian myth. The Seven Sages are: Atri; Bharadvaja; Gautama; Jamadagni; Kashyapa; Vasistha; and Vishvamitra.

Seven Sisters, The *Australia*

Seven wandering ancestral heroines of the Dreamtime, also referred to by their Aboriginal name of Kungarankalpa. The complete route of the sisters has been pieced together from stories told about them by different Aboriginal clans living along its course. The sisters fled southward from the centre of Australia to escape from a lecherous man called Nyiru. Various features of the landscape mark the course of the chase: for example, a low cliff was the windbreak that they built when they camped one night.

On reaching the southern coast (near modern Port Augusta), the seven sisters went into the sea and then leaped into the sky. Once in the sky they became the constellation Kurialya (The Pleiades).

Shachar *Middle East*

The Ugaritic (Canaanite) deity of dawn. Together with its sibling Shalim (meaning "Dusk"), Shachar is the offspring of the supreme god El and the fertility goddesses Anath and Astarte.

Shalakapurusha *India*

One of a series of spiritual and temporal leaders, prominent in the Jain account of the history of the universe. In this, the universe passes for ever through alternate periods of ascent or decline (the present epoch is said to be one of decline). Sixty-three Shalakapurushas appear in each period. They consist of twenty-four Tirthamkaras ("Saviours"), twelve universal Emperors, and nine triads of heroes. Each triad is made up of a Baladeva, a Vasudeva and a Prativasudeva. The Baladeva is always described as the elder brother of the Vasudeva and the Prativasudeva is their evil opponent. The Vasudeva-Baladeva relationship is clearly derived from the

Hindu mythology of Krishna and his elder brother Balarama: illustrations of the two sets of brothers bear a close resemblance to each other.

Shango *Africa*

A divine ancestral king of the Yoruba people of western Africa. Shango, one of the most important Yoruba deities, was famed for his martial prowess and as a magician. His oppressive rule led to his overthrow, after which he is said to have hanged himself on a tree. Then he ascended to heaven and became the god of rain and thunder. Representations of him show him wielding a twin-headed axe, the symbol of thunder. His wife, Oja, was a lake which after Shango's death became the river Niger.

Shapash *Middle East*

The Ugaritic (Canaanite) name for the goddess of the sun.

Shashti *India*

A goddess of childbirth and protector of newborn children. Her name means "sixth", because she is venerated on the sixth day after childbirth. This is said to mark the end of the most dangerous time for both mother and baby.

Shiva *India*

One of the *trimurti*, the Hindu trinity of Brahma, Shiva and Vishnu, and among the most complex of all Indian deities. He originated as the early Vedic god Rudra ("Ruddy" or "Howler"), a malign storm god, who was later addressed as Shiva (meaning "Auspicious") in order to propitiate him.

Shiva is a destroyer and angry avenger, but also a benign herdsman of souls. With similar ambivalence, he is associated with asceticism and yoga (he meditates on Mount Kailasa) but also

Shiva riding the bull Nandin, from a 19th-century painting.

with the erotic. Shiva is worshipped in the form of a linga or sacred phallus. According to one myth, Vishnu and Brahma were disputing who was the greatest when Shiva appeared in the form of a fiery column, the linga. Brahma took the form of a goose and flew to find the top, while Vishnu became a boar and sought the bottom. Both failed and were forced to concede to Shiva's authority.

Both ascetic and erotic aspects are found in a myth that relates how Shiva smeared himself in ashes and visited a forest where many sages lived a life of asceticism. The sages feared he would seduce their wives and cursed the god to lose his penis. Shiva was castrated, but with his own complicity. The world then grew dark and cold and the sages lost their virility until they had placated Shiva by erecting a linga.

Shiva is depicted with a pale or ashen

Shapash: *see*
SUN, MOON AND STARS

Shashti: *see*
Devi

Shiva: *see*
Brahma; Churning of the ocean, The; Daksha; Ganesha; Ganga; Nataraja; Sati; Skanda; Vishnu

The Hindu goddess Shri, or Lakshmi.

face and a blue neck caused when, in a protector role, he consumed the poison which sprang from the churning of the ocean (the poison threatened to destroy humanity). Another instance of the god as protector is the myth of how he broke the fall of the goddess Ganga, the Ganges, when she descended from heaven to cleanse the world with her waters. Other attributes of Shiva are a necklace of skulls, coiled locks like those of an ascetic, and in the middle of his forehead, a third eye (*shakra*) of enlightenment and destruction. He is also Nataraja, "Lord of the Dance", the source of all movement in the cosmos.

Shiva's wife appears variously as Sati, the daughter of the creator god Daksha, and Uma or Parvati, the daughter of the mountain Himalaya. His marriage brings an element of domesticity into the god's austere life, and he is often portrayed in a family group with Parvati and their children, Skanda and Ganesha.

Shri *India*
The goddess of prosperity (*shri*), also called Lakshmi ("good fortune"). According to some accounts, Shri arose from the ocean when it was churned by the gods (Devas) and demons (Asuras). Shri found herself immediately attracted to Vishnu, who, as the god who presided over the churning, had first claim on the beautiful goddess. The pair were frequently associated, although earlier myths sometimes linked her with the god Indra. As the consort of Vishnu, Shri came to represent the perfect Hindu wife because she was loyal and submissive to her husband.

Shu (1) *Egypt*
The god of air, the offspring of the creator deity Ra-Atum and brother of Tefenet, the goddess of moisture. Shu

and Tefenet coupled to produce the sky goddess Nut and the earth god Geb.

Shu (2) *China*
The emperor of the Northern Sea, according to the creation myth which relates to the death of the emperor Hun Dun (or "Chaos").

Sida *Oceania*
A wandering culture hero of Papua, also known as Sido, Soido, Sosom, Souw and other variations. Sida features in the mythology of the communities which live along the rivers Fly and Purari of southern Papua and in the mountainous interior. Like the ancestral heroes of the Aboriginal Australians, this figure travelled through the world, leaving various features of the landscape to mark the places where he passed. For example, a small lake denotes the spot where he urinated. Each community knows the incidents that took place in its own territory. In most places the myths are part of a secret male cult and become known only to initiates.

The hero is represented as possessing a very long penis and he was shamed on account of his desire for sex. According to the Daribi, Souw's penis tried to enter a young woman, but she cried out and it withdrew. Souw was furious at being humiliated in this way and gave humanity, war, death and witchcraft. But then he wandered into the highlands and deposited hairs that became dogs and pigs, which were useful domestic animals. Elsewhere he is said to have given people their first vegetables and stocks of fish.

Sigmund *Germanic regions*
A hero, the son of Volsung and so a descendant of the god Odin. One night, Odin appeared in the midst of the

warriors' hall in the guise of a one-eyed old man and plunged a magnificent sword into the tree trunk supporting the roof. Whoever removed the sword, he declared, would possess it. Then the figure vanished. In turn, all the warriors tried to pull out the sword, but only Sigmund succeeded.

With this divine sword, Gram, Sigmund became famous for many heroic exploits. When Sigmund was old, Odin decided that it was time for him to die. A one-eyed old man appeared before him in battle and caused Gram to break in two. Disarmed, Sigmund fell under his opponent's blows. His widow, Hjordis, kept the fragments of Gram for their son Sigurd.

Sigurd *Germanic regions*

A great hero of Scandinavian myth, the son of Sigmund and Hjordis and a descendant of the god Odin. Sigurd, known as "The Volsung" after his grandfather Volsung, was raised at the court of his stepfather Hjalprek, where Regin, a clever but malign smith, fostered him and taught him many skills. Aided by an old man (the god Odin in disguise), the hero chose a wonderful horse, Grani, descended from Sleipnir, Odin's eight-legged steed.

Regin told Sigurd of a great horde of treasure guarded by his brother Fafnir the dragon. He forged two swords for the warrior, but these were too weak, so Regin forged a weapon of unsurpassed sharpness from the pieces of the magic sword Gram, which the god Odin had once given to Sigurd's father Sigmund.

The smith advised Sigurd to dig a pit, hide in it, and stab Fafnir as he crawled over it. But Odin, disguised as an old man, warned Sigurd that Regin wanted the horde for himself and expected Sigurd to drown in Fafnir's blood. To

Sigurd (right) roasting Fafnir's heart, from a 12th-century wood-carving.

Sigurd: *see* Odin; Sigmund; Valkyrie; Volsung

survive, he must dig a number of pits to catch the blood. So Sigurd complied and killed Fafnir. Later, when the hero was roasting Fafnir's heart, he poked it to see if it was cooked and burned his finger. He sucked the finger and when Fafnir's blood touched his tongue he could understand the speech of birds. He overheard them saying that Regin intended to kill him. He decapitated the evil smith and rode off with the treasure.

However, the hoard contained a gold ring, upon which the dwarf Andvari (from whom the treasure had originally been stolen) had laid a curse that promised death to its possessor. This curse later fell on Sigurd. He was loved by a Valkyrie, Brynhild, whom he promised to marry but whom Odin had imprisoned in an enchanted sleep within a ring of flame. However, another warrior, Gunnar, wanted to marry her and so Sigurd, who had lost his memory, impersonated Gunnar to cross the ring of fire (this was an initiation ceremony). Brynhild married Gunnar but later discovered the trick and had Sigurd assassinated before immolating herself.

Sigyn *Germanic regions*

A goddess, the wife of the trickster Loki. After he had caused the death of Balder, the gods trapped him and bound him across three rocks with serpents dripping venom into his face. Sigyn faithfully sat with a bowl to catch the drops of poison until the day that Loki broke from his bonds and fought the gods at Ragnarok.

Siosire *Egypt*

A royal magician-priest, the son of Setna Khaemwese. In one myth, a Nubian chief came to the Egyptian court with a letter which Siosire read out. It related how an Egyptian magician called Horus son of Paneshe had once defeated a Nubian sorcerer in a contest of magic and banished him for 1500 years. The Nubian then declared that he was the sorcerer and had returned to seek revenge. Siosire in turn declared that he was Horus son of Paneshe, returned from the land of the dead to confront him. The Nubian was again vanquished and Siosire-Horus returned to the underworld.

Siren *Greece*

One of a group of three (sometimes two) female monsters usually depicted with the bodies of birds and the heads of women. The Sirens lived on an island identifed with Sicily. It was said that their song was so irresistibly beautiful that any mariner who heard it would immediately sail toward the creatures – only to be shipwrecked. In another account, those who fell under the Sirens' seductive spell would land on the shore, where they would sit and listen until they wasted away and died. After the hero Odysseus sailed past safely, the defeated Sirens are said to have leaped into the sea and drowned.

A siren, with the head of a girl and the body of a bird.

Sisyphus *Greece*

The founder and first king of Corinth, noted for his cunning. Before he died he told his wife Merope (one of the Pleiades), to leave him unburied and accord him no funeral rites. After Sisyphus' shade had descended to the underworld, Merope did as he had instructed, much to the annoyance of the god Hades, the ruler of the underworld. Hades told Sisyphus to leave the underworld temporarily in order to ensure that Merope gave him a proper funeral. Sisyphus came back to life in Corinth and resumed his reign, defying the orders of Hades. When he finally died in advanced old age, Sisyphus was sentenced in the underworld to eternally having to push a rock up to the top of a hill, only to see it roll back down again to the bottom.

Sita *India*

The daughter of King Janaka of Videha and the wife of the god Rama. Sita, which means "Furrow", sprang from a furrow ploughed by Janaka.

Skanda between Shiva and Parvati, based on a bronze scultpure dating from the 2nd century AD.

Skadi: *see*
Freyja; Freyr; Njord

Skan: *see*
Wakan Tanka

Skanda: *see*
Ganga; Shiva

Sobek: *see*
Neith; Osiris; Seth

Sphinx (1): *see*
Echidne; Oedipus; Sphinx (2); Typhon

Sita, from a scroll painting, dating from the mid-19th century AD.

Skadi *Germanic regions*

A goddess of the mountains, the wife of Njord and mother of the goddess Freyja and the god Freyr. Skadi wore skis and hunted in the forests of the north. Her marriage to Njord, a sea god, was said to have broken down because she could not bear to be away from the mountains, while he could not bear to be away from the sea. In one myth, Skadi persuaded Skirnir to make the long and dangerous journey to the underworld land of the giants in order to woo the beautiful female giant Gerd on her son's behalf.

Skan *North America*

The Lakota god embodying the sky. Skan is the most powerful of the Superior Gods, four primal deities which are aspects of the supreme being Wakan Tanka.

Skanda *India*

The son of Shiva and Parvati. When Shiva and Parvati first had intercourse, the gods interrupted them for fear that Shiva's offspring might be too powerful. Shiva spilled his fiery semen, which was too hot to hold and was passed around the gods until it came to Ganga, the Ganges, where it was incubated. Skanda was born with six heads and was suckled by the Krittikas (the Pleiades), whence his alternative name of Karttikeya. He vanquished a demon called Taraka and saved the world from destruction, becoming the leader of the armies of the gods. When Parvati first saw him, milk flowed from her breasts, and she accepted him as her own son.

SNAKES AND SERPENTS

See panel on next page

Sobek *Egypt*

The crocodile god, the offspring of the mother goddess Neith. Sobek (or Sebek) presided over rivers and lakes and was a protector deity of the Egyptian pharaohs. However, in some areas he was far less benign and was associated with the god Seth, the enemy of the first pharaoh, Osiris.

Sphinx (1) *Greece*

"The Strangler", a monster with the head of a woman, the wings of a bird and the body of a lion. One of the monstrous offspring of Echidne and Typhon, the Sphinx was sent to plague Thebes after either the citizens or its

SNAKES AND SERPENTS

Among the most common creatures to feature in mythology, the snake or serpent has similar fundamental associations around the world. Snakes live within the earth and are almost universally perceived as symbols of fertility and the fecundity of the soil. Serpents or dragons – the two creatures are close relatives – were said to pull the chariot of the Greek earth and fertility goddess Demeter. The Aztec earth goddess Coatlicue ("Serpent Skirt") was said to have had two serpent heads. In Irish tradition snakes were said to emerge from their underground lairs on 1 February (Imbolc), the feast of the goddess Brighid, heralding the approach of spring. The form of the snake links it with the penis and with male generative powers (sometimes literally, as in the story of the Papuan culture hero Sida, whose long member is mistaken for a snake).

An Aztec sculpture of a double-headed rattlesnake.

The frequent combination of phallic serpent and female earth goddess may represent a symbolic act of intercourse designed to ensure the renewed growth and continuance of nature. This renewal is aptly and strikingly demonstrated by the snake itself when it discards its old skin to reveal a new one underneath.

The snake is a highly ambivalent animal. Although it is linked with the fruitfulness of nature it is often venomous and its home beneath the earth or in the ocean depths is traditionally seen as the seat of turbulent and potentially malign forces. The race of serpents, called the *nagas*, appear in Hindu myth usually (but not always) as the adversaries of the human race. In Egypt, the desert-dwelling serpent was a symbol of sterility and drought, associated with the god of disorder, Seth. The serpent in the Biblical Garden of Eden is probably the best known example of the snake as an agent of evil.

Snakes may be attributed cosmic dimensions. A great serpent is often believed to encircle the earth, either separating it from the forces of chaos or itself embodying those forces, like the World Serpent of Scandinavian myth, which lives in the sea around Midgard, the earth. The cosmic serpent is often said to manifest itself in the form of a rainbow, an image found in Africa, Australia and elsewhere.

king, Laius, showed disrespect for the gods. The monster would devour anyone, who, when challenged, could not answer her riddle: What animal has four legs, then two legs, then three legs? No one knew the answer, and the Sphinx was well fed on Theban flesh. Help came in the form of Oedipus, who gave the Sphinx the answer to the riddle: a man, who crawls on all fours as a baby, walks on two legs until old age, and then hobbles with a stick. On hearing the answer, the Sphinx threw herself to her death. "Sphinx" is often used to refer to similar hybrid creatures in other cultures.

Sphinx (2) *Egypt*

The name given to a hybrid creature with a human head, a lion's body and, in some accounts, a bird's wings. It symbolized the divine spirit vested in the person of the pharaoh, whom it protected. In representations of the sphinx the head may bear the features of a particular monarch, such as the 4th-Dynasty pharaoh Khephren (*c*.2600BC), whose portrait appears on the Great Sphinx of Giza.

Stentor *Greece*

A Greek herald during the Trojan War who was renowned for his astonishingly loud voice, hence the word "stentorian".

Stribog *Slav regions*

The ancient eastern Slavic god of the wind. Little is known about this deity, but vestiges of belief in powerful wind spirits survive in the Whirlwind monster of Russian folk myth, who carries off maidens, and Nightingale the Brigand, a monster who creates a howling wind that can flatten trees and kill humans.

Stymphalian Birds, The *Greece*

A flock of monstrous man-eating birds which infested Lake Stymphalos in Arcadia. The hero Herakles killed them as the sixth of his twelve labours.

Styx *Greece*

"Hateful", one of the five rivers of the underworld, land of the dead. According to some accounts the Styx was a branch of the great river Ocean which surrounded the earth. On its course through the underworld it was said to encircle the land of the dead nine times,

and the other underworld streams were its branches or tributaries. Styx was governed by a divinity of the same name. She was a daughter of Okeanos and Tethys.

Sualtamh *Celtic regions*

A warrior, the husband of Deichtine, sister of King Conchobar of Ulster, and father of the hero Cú Chulainn.

Sugriva *India*

A monkey king of India. Sugriva was overthrown by his brother Valin. One of his ministers, Hanuman, enlisted the help of the divine hero Rama, who slew Valin and restored Sugriva to his throne. Sugriva returned the favour by helping Rama defeat the demon king Ravana.

Sujata *Southeast Asia*

The heroine of a popular Buddhist myth of Thailand. Sujata, the daughter of a rich landowner, had a baby son and wished to make a thanks-offering of rice mixed with rich milk to the god of the bo or peepul tree (*ficus religiosa*). She approached someone sitting under the tree whom she assumed was the god. In fact it was the Buddha on the first of the forty-nine days of his enlightenment. The god was sustained throughout this time by the rice and milk that Sujata joyfully offered him.

SUN, MOON AND STARS
See panel on next page

Sun Wukong *China*

The Monkey King, the protagonist of the 14th-century novel *Journey to the West* by Wu Cheng'en. After causing mischief on earth, Sun Wukong was lured to heaven by the promise of a post in the celestial civil service. But the post was purely honorary, intended only to

Sphinx (2): *see*
Sphinx (1)

Stribog: *see*
Muromets, Ilya; Nightingale the Brigand

Stymphalian Birds, The: *see*
HERAKLES, THE LABOURS OF

Styx: *see*
Acheron; Cocytus; Hades; Lethe; Phlegethon; UNDERWORLDS

Sualtamh: *see*
Conchobar; Cú Chulainn

Sugriva: *see*
Hanuman; Rama

Sujata: *see*
Buddha

Sun Wukong: *see*
Buddha; Guanyin; Jade Emperor, The; Xi Wang Mu

Sun, Moon and Stars

SUN, MOON AND STARS

Its importance to the sustenance of all life often earns the sun the position of head of the pantheon and supreme creator. The sun is most often seen as a male god, as in ancient Egypt and among the Inca, but it may be female, as in Japan where it is manifested as the sun goddess Amaterasu.

The moon is generally female, with notable exceptions, such as the Egyptian god Thoth. An example of a supreme creator moon is Nyame, the mother goddess who created the universe, according to the mythology of the Akan people of Ghana. The moon is male in most of Oceania: in parts of New Guinea it is associated with nocturnal hunting, a male activity, while the sun is female, because women's work is carried out mainly in daylight.

The male moon figures in southern Africa, often as the consort of the planet Venus. The sun and moon are looked on as a married couple in other regions, while in the Americas they are often seen as a brother and sister who are incestuous lovers. They come together in the dark, and the female sun paints dark patches on her brother's cheek so she will know him later: this explains the features of the moon visible from earth. Other accounts of the lunar features include the Western idea that it is a face (the Man in the Moon) and the Chinese and Central American one that it is a hare, which Buddhist mythology claims was one of the Buddha's past incarnations.

The phases of the moon are also accounted for in various ways. In Maori myth, the (male) moon is constantly fighting a god called Rona, and wanes as the moon grows weary. At the new moon the two pause to restore their strength, and begin fighting again at the full moon.

The sun and moon are sometimes seen as the eyes of a great creator deity. The Egyptians envisaged the moon as the right eye of the god Horus and the sun as his left eye. Similarly, in Chinese myth the left eye of the cosmic giant Pan Gu became the sun and his right eye became the moon.

Certain heavenly constellations are personalized in myth, with strikingly similar perceptions occurring in different cultures. The Greeks conceived of the Pleiades as the seven daughters of Atlas and Pleione. In the Southern Hemisphere, the Pleiades are also widely seen as a group of sisters. Here, their appearance heralds the onset of the rains. The Greeks claimed that Ursa Major, the Great Bear, was a nymph, Callisto, who had been turned into a bear. Similarly, that part of Ursa Major which we call the Plough or Big Dipper is known to Native Americans as the Heavenly Bear.

The most significant individual star in most mythologies is Venus, the Morning Star. Venus is usually female, and in the Mediterranean and Near East is often identified with goddesses of love, sexuality and fertility, such as the Greek Aphrodite (Roman Venus), the Canaanite Athar and the Babylonian Ishtar and Inanna. Ishtar-Inanna formed part of a great heavenly triad of deities consisting of the sun, moon and the planet Venus. For the Aztecs, Venus was associated with death and resurrection, and was identified with the god Quetzalcoatl.

The moon spirit, Tarqeq, based on a mask.

allow the rulers of heaven to keep an eye on the mischievous monkey. Sun Wukong soon discovered the ploy and began to misbehave. In the end he was given the job of overseeing the garden of the heavenly empress Wang Mu Niang Niang, in which grew the peaches eaten by the gods and goddesses to replenish their immortality. The monkey devoured as many peaches as he could before slipping away to earth.

Angered by this, the entire celestial government soon sought Sun Wukong. Eventually he was caught by the Buddha, who locked him in a mountain for five hundred years until the merciful Bodhisattva Guanyin interceded on his behalf. He was freed on condition that he accompanied a Buddhist pilgrim (the narrator of the novel) on a journey to India to acquire Buddhist texts. After the journey Sun Wukong was deified and returned to heaven.

Superior Gods, The *North America*
Four primal deities (known as Sky, Rock, Earth and Sun) which were the first manifestations of Wakan Tanka, the Lakota supreme being.

Surabhi *India*
The divine cow of plenty, the mother of all cattle. Surabhi is said to be one of the treasures which arose from the churning of the ocean.

Surong Gunting *Southeast Asia*
A culture hero of the Iban people of Borneo. Surong Gunting travelled to see his grandfather, a spirit called Sengalong Burong. On the way he learned from the stars about the annual cycle of farming, and Sengalong taught him numerous rituals and bird omens for cultivation and headhunting. Surong was sent home after impregnating his

aunt, a grave transgression which could ruin the harvest. When he arrived home he passed on all his new knowledge.

Susano *Japan*
The god of storms and the divine embodiment of the forces of disorder. Susano was a fierce but not always malevolent deity who sprang from the primal father god Izanagi as he bathed in a stream. Izanagi divided the world among his three most powerful children; he gave Amaterasu the heavens, Tsuki-yomi the night and he assigned Susano the overlordship of the oceans. But Susano felt that he had done badly out of the division, became angry, and was banished by his father for his defiance.

Susano then became engaged in a long struggle with his sister Amaterasu, the sun goddess. His stubborn attempt to overthrow Amaterasu nearly brought catastrophe to the world precipitating

The storm god Susano, with Kusa-nada-hime behind him.

the "Divine Crisis" during which the terrified Amaterasu withdrew into a cave, depriving the world of sunlight and causing many calamities. In the end, however, she emerged from the cave to continue her reign and Susano was expelled from heaven. On earth he found himself in the land of Izumo in southern Honshu island. Near the river Hi he won his wife, Kusa-nada-hime, by rescuing her from the eight-headed dragon Yamato-no-Orochi. The god eventually took up residence in the underworld. Later Susano assisted his descendant Okuninushi in the of defeat his eighty jealous brothers.

Svantovit *Slav regions*
An ancient western Slavic god of great power. At his temple at Ankona on the Baltic island of Rügen (in modern Germany), a massive four-sided statue of Svantovit held a bull's horn which was filled with wine. The temple priest would examine the wine every year, and if the level had gone down greatly it was seen as a bad omen for the next harvest. If the horn remained nearly full the prospects were good. A white horse, kept in the temple, would be driven between two rows of spears to predict the future: the more spears the horse knocked over, the gloomier the forecast.

Svarog *Slav regions*
The supreme elemental deity of the ancient Slavics, the divine personification of the sky. Svarog's most famous shrine was at Rethra in the area of the Polabians ("People on the Elbe"), a western Slavic people living in what is now northeastern Germany. The temple contained a golden effigy of the god wearing a helmet resembling a bird with outstretched wings.

Svarog had two sons: Dazhbog, who was the sun god, and Svarozhich, who was the personification of fire.

Svarozhich *Slav regions*
Meaning "Son of Svarog", Svarozhich was the divine personification of fire, said to be the offspring of the sky god Svarog. The veneration of Fire (also called Ogon, "fire", a word related to the Sanskrit *agni* and Latin *ignis*) was the most marked expression of the ancient Slavic reverence for the forces of light.

Syrinx *Greece*
A nymph of Arcadia, one of the retinue of the goddess Artemis. The god Pan fell in love with Syrinx and tried to catch her, but she asked some river nymphs to turn her into a bed of reeds. Pan cut some of the reeds to make the first syrinx or pan-pipes.

Táin Bó Cuailnge, The *Celtic regions*
The *Cattle Raid of Cooley*, an Irish epic probably composed *c.*AD700 but known from manuscripts of the 12th–14th centuries. The *Táin*, the central work in the great cycle of Irish heroic myths from Ulster, focuses on the war between Queen Medhbh of Connacht and "The Men of Ireland", and their opponents King Conchobar of Ulster and "The Men of Ulster". The war is sparked by the theft, on Medhbh's orders, of the magnificent Brown Bull of Cooley in Ulster. The leading character in the story is the Ulster hero Cú Chulainn, Conchobar's champion.

Takamimusubi *Japan*
A powerful god, one of the five primal "Separate Heavenly Deities".

Talos *Greece*
A bronze giant made by the god Hephaistos for King Minos of Crete. Talos ran around the island's coastline looking out for foreign invasion. If he encountered intruders he would hurl rocks at them or make himself red hot and then hug his victims to death. When

the Argonauts attempted to land on Crete, the sorceress Medea killed Talos by sending him to sleep and then removing a plug in his ankle to drain his single vein, which ran from head to foot through his body.

Tane *Oceania*
The Maori god of trees and forests, one of the six offspring of the primal deities Rangi, the sky, and Papa, the earth. Tane succeeded in forcing apart his parents, who had been locked in a tight embrace, but in doing so incurred the jealousy of his siblings. Tawhiri, the god of the elements, blew down all Tane's trees and caused Tane's offspring, the fish, who until then had lived in the forests, to flee to the sea, the domain of the god Tangaroa. It is said that Tane, furious at the loss of his offspring, has been at loggerheads with Tangaroa ever since.

Tane wanted a wife and went first to his mother Papa. She rebuffed his advances and told him to create a female version of himself from the sand of Hawaiki island. This creation, Hine-hau-one ("Earth-created Maiden"), was the first human. She bore a daughter,

Tangaroa

A possible represen-
tation of Tangaroa, from
an ironwood carving.

Hine-titama, whom Tane also married. When Hine-titama found out that he was her father, she fled to the underworld in horror and became Hine-nui-te-po, the goddess of death. Since then all humans have been mortal.

Tangaroa *Oceania*
The Maori god of the sea, the son of Rangi and Papa. Unsurprisingly, the sea god was very important throughout Polynesia and was known by various forms of the same name, such as A'a in the Tubuai or Austral islands and Ta'aroa in Tahiti. Outside New Zealand, on the smaller islands, he was widely revered as the supreme creator deity.

According to Maori myth, most of the things in the sea were the creation of Tangaroa and those on land the creation of his brother Tane, the god of trees and forests. However, all fish were the progeny of Tane and lived in the forests until Tawhiri, the god of the elements, blew down the trees and drove them in panic into the sea. The loss of all the fish to his brother Tangaroa annoyed Tane. They have been in conflict ever since: Tane's trees furnish wood for canoes, with which men overcome the waves, while the ocean of Tangaroa tries to overwhelm the forests of the islands.

Tantalus *Greece*
A king of Lydia in western Asia Minor (modern Turkey), the son of the god Zeus and the Titan Pluto. According to one account, Tantalus asked the gods of Olympus to dine with him and then cooked his son Pelops in order to test their omniscience. To their anger, the deities knew at once what they had been served and restored Pelops to life. They condemned Tantalus to suffer perpetual thirst and hunger in the underworld, with food and water for ever just beyond

his grasp. In a different version of the myth, Tantalus earned his punishment when he stole ambrosia and nectar, the food of the Olympians.

Tantalus and his descendants (he was the father of Niobe and ancestor of the Pelopids) were renowned for suffering terrible curses.

Taranis *Celtic regions*
Meaning "The Thunderer", Taranis was the ancient Celtic god of thunder. He was associated with Jupiter of classical myth, but probably represented only the thunder aspect of the great Roman deity.

Tarpeia *Rome*
A famous traitor in the mythical early history of Rome. When the Romans were fighting the Sabines, Tarpeia, the daughter of a Roman commander, fell in love with the Sabine king Titus Tatius. In one account, she offered to let him into Rome if he gave her "what the Sabines wear on their left arms" – meaning their gold bracelets. With her aid the Sabines entered the city, but Titus Tatius regarded her treason with contempt. His warriors were ordered to hurl at her "what the Sabines wear on their left arms": their shields. Tarpeia was crushed to death under their weight. The Tarpeian Rock, from which traitors were thrown to their deaths, was said to have been named after her.

Tartaros *Greece*
A primal deity embodying the darkest regions of the underworld. According to Hesiod, Tartaros, Gaia, Eros, Erebos and Nyx were first to arise after Chaos came into being. However, Tartaros features little in myth as a deity. As a region Tartaros was described in early accounts as an even deeper land than the realm of Hades, but the name later came

to be used more or less as a synonym for the underworld, especially the part of it where the dead were punished.

Tarvaa *Tibet and Mongolia*

A famous shaman of Mongolian myth. Tarvaa lived in ancient times. When he was fifteen, he grew sick and fell unconscious. His family thought that he was dead and quickly put his body outside the house, where crows pecked out his eyes. Tarvaa's soul, upset that his family should be so hasty to consider him dead, travelled to the land of spirits. As he was not dead, the judge of the dead turned his soul away, but offered him any gift he wanted. Tarvaa chose to have eloquence and knowledge of the wonders of the spirit world. When his soul returned to his body, Tarvaa, who was by now blind, awoke and became a great wise shaman.

Taweret *Egypt*

A protector goddess of women and children. Taweret also assisted in the rebirth of the dead in the primal waters of the Nun. She was often depicted as a fearsome beast, part crocodile, part lion and part hippopotamus, with pendulous breasts. She was sometimes said to be the consort of the god Seth, who could also be manifested as a hippopotamus.

Tawhaki *Oceania*

A famous hero of Maori myth. Tawhaki and his brother Kariki were the sons of the semi-divine Hema and a sky goddess. After Hema was killed by monsters, Tawhaki journeyed to the place where his father died to avenge his death. On the journey the hero had numerous adventures which form the bulk of the myth cycle. In many of them the rather stupid and bumbling Kariki is compared unfavourably with his heroic

and noble brother. During their travels Tawhaki married and had a son, Wahieroa, whose son Rata is another celebrated hero of Polynesian myth.

Tawhiri *Oceania*

The Maori god of the elements, the son of the sky god Rangi and earth goddess Papa. The Maori creation myth recounts how Tawhiri, jealous of his brother Tane, god of forests, sent great storms that blew down all his trees. All the fish, who at that time dwelt in trees, sought refuge in the ocean and since then the two have been at loggerheads.

Tefenet *Egypt*

The primal goddess of moisture, the offspring of the creator deity Ra-Atum and the sister of the air god Shu. Tefenet and Shu coupled to produce the sky goddess Nut and the earth god Geb, who in turn were the parents of Osiris, Isis, Seth and Nepthys.

Teiresias *Greece*

A celebrated blind prophet of Thebes, also spelled Tiresias. According to one account, Teiresias came across two copulating snakes and hit the female with his stick. He immediately turned into a woman. Eight years later he encountered the same snakes and struck the male, at once becoming a man again.

Later, the god Zeus claimed that women had more pleasure during intercourse than men, but his wife Hera disagreed. They consulted Teiresias, the only person who could know the truth, and he declared that women had nine times the pleasure of men. Hera, who was furious at this answer, struck him blind. However, Zeus compensated Teiresias by granting him the gift of prophecy. The prophet was said to have lived for seven generations.

*Teshub, shown as both
warrior and storm god.*

Telepinu *Middle East*
The Hittite god of agriculture, the son of the weather god Teshub. According to one myth, Telepinu went into hiding and made the land, animals and people barren. When the gods found him he flew home on an eagle and fruitfulness was restored.

Tereus *Greece*
A Thracian king who, some say, was the son of the war god Ares. He lent military assistance to King Pandion of Athens and received the hand of his daughter Procne as a reward. Later, Tereus accompanied Pandion's other daughter, Philomela, from Athens to Thrace to visit Procne. Before they reached his city, he raped her and cut out her tongue so that she could not say what had happened. He then imprisoned her and told Procne that she was dead.

However, Philomela wove a tapestry which recounted everything and had it smuggled to Procne, who came to her at once and freed her. The two sisters took their revenge by killing Itys, the son of Tereus and Procne, and serving him up as a meal to his unwitting father. When Tereus had finished the meal Procne showed him his son's head. Tereus was horrified and pursued the sisters, but before he caught them they turned into birds. Philomela became the swallow and Procne the nightingale, which was said to utter the cry "Itys, Itys" in remorse for the son she had lost.

Teshub *Middle East*
The weather god of the Hittites. Teshub was one of the most important deities in the Hittite pantheon. In the beginning the ruler of heaven was Alalu, but he was deposed by the god Anu. The god Kumarbi in turn overthrew Anu and bit off his penis, but was impregnated by

Anu's sperm. He gave birth to three "terrible gods", probably three different aspects of Teshub.

It seems to be that Teshub overthrew Kumarbi (the sources are incomplete). Kumarbi then coupled with the Sea (who represented chaos). The coupling produced a giant son, Ullikummi, who forced Teshub to abdicate. So, Teshub went to the wise god Ea, who destroyed Ullikummi's strength. Once Ullikummi became weak, the struggle between Kumarbi and Teshub was renewed.

Tethys *Greece*
A Titan, the daughter of the goddess Gaia, the earth, and the god Uranos, the sky. Tethys married her brother Okeanos and became the mother of the sea nymphs known as the Oceanids.

Tezcatlipoca *Central America*
"The Lord of the Smoking Mirror", the greatest god of the Central American pantheon. Every other creator divinity was regarded as an aspect of Tezcatlipoca. According to the Aztec creation myth, the primal divinities Ometecuhtli and Omecihuatl coupled to produce the four great deities who were known as Tezcatlipoca, Huitzilopochtli, Quetzalcoatl and Xipe Totec, who are referred to as the Four Tezcatlipocas. Xipe Totec (the "Red Tezcatlipoca") ruled over the first Sun or world epoch.

The cult of Tezcatlipoca came to central Mexico *c.*AD1000 with the Toltecs and by the time of the Aztecs (*c.*AD1325) the god had accumulated the greatest number of manifestations and titles of any deity. Among his titles were Yoalli Ehecatl ("Night Wind"), Yaotl ("Warrior") and Titlacuan ("He of whom we are Slaves"). Tezcatlipoca was associated with darkness, war and death, and was said to confront warriors

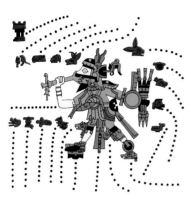

Tezcatlipoca, "The Lord of the Smoking Mirror", from a codex.

at crossroads at night. The Aztecs venerated him as the protector deity of magicians and royalty. He was thought of as an omnipresent, but invisible, god of the shadows, who possessed a magic mirror that enabled him to foretell the future and look into people's hearts. He brought bravery, riches and good fortune, but also death and misery.

Reflecting Tezcatlipoca's supreme position was his identification with the jaguar, which was revered as the king of beasts and lord of the night. Probably the most important of all his jaguar manifestations was the jaguar deity Tepeyollotli (which means "The Heart of the Mountain").

Thalia *Greece*
"Jollity", one of the three Graces, the daughters of the god Zeus and the sea nymph Eurynome.

Theia *Greece*
A Titan, the daughter of the goddess Gaia and the god Uranos. Theia married her brother Hyperion and from this union she became the mother of the divinities Helios (the Sun), Eos (the Dawn) and Selene (the Moon).

Themis *Greece*
A Titan, the daughter of the goddess Gaia and the god Uranos. According to some accounts, Themis ("Order") was the wife of the Titan Iapetus and the mother of Titans Atlas and Prometheus, and of Epimetheus and Menoetius. She became the second consort of the god Zeus and bore a number of important goddesses: Dike ("Justice"); Eirene ("Peace"); the Fates; and the Seasons.

Thens, The *Southeast Asia*
The lords of the sky according to certain creation myths, one of which, "The Thens and the Three Great Men", was popular in northern Thailand and Laos. The myth recounts how in the beginning the sky world and the earth were joined by a rattan bridge. The lords of the sky world were the Thens and the earth was ruled by the Three Great Men: Khun K'an, Khun K'et and Pu Lang Seung. One day, the Thens commanded the earth people to offer them a portion of their food as a token of respect. However, the people refused and the Thens overwhelmed the world with a flood. The Three Great Men built a house on a raft and sailed to the sky world to see the Then king.

Once they were there, the king sent the earth people to dwell with his relation, Grandfather Then Lo. But then the floodwaters below began to retreat and the earth people asked to go back to earth. The king gave them a buffalo and sent them home.

Three years later the buffalo died and three gourds grew from its nose. Pu Lang Seung drilled a hole in each gourd and people came out. First came a primitive slave people (the region's aboriginal population). Khun K'an then freed more people from the gourds and they poured out in great numbers.

Theogony, The

Some Thens later came from heaven to teach people various skills. The builder Then Teng taught people how to mark time and to plan cultivation. Pitsanukukan instructed people in metalworking and how to make tools, as well as to prepare food and weave. Sik'ant'apatewada showed people how to dance and sing, and how to make and play musical instruments. After he had returned to heaven the rattan bridge was destroyed, severing all contact between heaven and earth.

Theogony, **The** *Greece*

An account of the origin of the universe and its governing divinities by Hesiod, a writer of the 8th–century BC. The first important attempt to systematize the many prevailing Greek myths about the beginnings of the cosmos, it became the most widely accepted account. Hesiod relates the genealogy of the Olympian gods and goddesses of myth from Chaos (meaning "Yawning Void").

Theseus *Greece*

A king of Athens and one of the greatest Greek heroes. Theseus was the son of King Aegeus of Athens and Aethra, a princess of Troezen in the Peloponnese. The childless Aegeus visited King Pittheus of Troezen, who got his guest drunk and gave him Aethra as a concubine. Aethra became pregnant, and Aegeus told her that if the child was a boy he was to come to Athens as soon as he could lift a particular rock. Under this rock Aegeus had left a sword and sandals by means of which he would know his son.

The child was Theseus. As a young man he set out for the Athenian court with the tokens of recognition. By the time he reached Athens he was already famous, because on the way he had vanquished a series of notorious brigands, such as Pityocamptes, Sciron and Procrustes. Aegeus welcomed the valiant stranger, but the sorceress Medea, whom Aegeus had married in the intervening years, recognized the youth through her magic powers. Considering him a threat to· the succession of her son Medus, the sorceress persuaded the king that the newcomer planned to kill him. He gave her permission to poison the stranger's wine at a banquet. However, as Theseus was about to drink, Aegeus spotted the tokens of recognition and knocked the cup from his hand. He hailed his son and banished Medea and Medus.

At his father's request Theseus went to Marathon and killed a wild bull (father of the Minotaur of Crete) that was terrorizing the countryside. The hero then went to Crete and killed the Minotaur, but his triumphant return was tempered with tragedy. Aegeus had requested that when Theseus returned, he should hoist a white sail if all had gone well and a black one if the mission had been a disaster. Forgetting this instruction, Theseus returned with the black sail hoisted. Believing his son to be dead and stricken with grief, Aegeus threw himself into the sea.

Now king of Athens, Theseus fought alongside the hero Herakles in order to defeat the Amazon warriors, taking the Amazon Antiope as his prize. She gave birth to a son, Hippolytus, and was killed in battle against Theseus when the Amazons invaded Attica.

The Athenians revered Theseus as a just and fair king who established legal institutions and brought all Attica under Athenian rule. He is said to have retired to the island of Scyros and died there. His supposed bones were reburied in a temple in Athens in the 5th century BC.

Thetis *Greece*
A Nereid (sea nymph), one of the daughters of Nereus and Doris. Thetis married a mortal, King Peleus of Phthia. It was their wedding that was the occasion for the contest of beauty between Athene, Aphrodite and Hera which led to the Trojan War. Thetis was the mother of the hero Achilles.

Thor *Germanic regions*
The Scandinavian god of the sky and thunder, and the divine protector of the community. He was derived from the earlier Germanic sky· and thunder deity Donar, called Thunor ("Thunder") by the Anglo-Saxons. Thursday was named after him. Thor, said to have been the son of Fjorgyn (a name for the earth), was of immense stature, with a red beard, flaming eyes and a huge appetite. He was hearty and blunt and had a furious temper, which he often took out on the giants, enemies of the gods.

Thor's weapon was a great magic axe-hammer, which symbolized thunder and lightning. It had tremendous destructive power, shattering giants and mountains at a single blow. The hammer was also an instrument of life and healing: after Thor had devoured his own goats for supper he restored their bones to life with his hammer.

Thor was a highly popular deity, especially famous in western Norway and Iceland. He was venerated as the protector of farmers and of the councils and assemblies of the people. There are many stories of his adventures, and the highly predictable fate of the giants and monsters who crossed his path was often recounted with robust humour. One myth tells how Thor went fishing with the giant Hymir for the World Serpent, a dragon that lived in the sea surrounding the earth. Using an ox head

Thor shown fishing for the World Serpent, from a stone relief.

as bait, Thor hooked the monster, which put up a fierce struggle. As the serpent's monstrous head appeared above the waves, Thor prepared to bludgeon it with his hammer, but Hymir was so alarmed that he cut the god's line and the monster escaped. Thor was so incensed with the giant that he hurled him into the sea. Thor finally killed the World Serpent at the apocalyptic battle of Ragnarok, but in doing so he was poisoned by its venom and died.

Thoth *Egypt*
The god of the moon. In one account, the sun god Ra created the moon as a light for the night sky and placed it under Thoth's supervision. Thoth was associated with the occult and secret knowledge and was said to have written the first book of magic. He also invented hieroglyphic writing and was venerated as the patron of scribes. The god was ususally depicted as a baboon, an ibis or a human with the head of an ibis. He was identified with the Greek Hermes.

Three Epochs of Creation, The
Southeast Asia
The Dayak (non-Muslim) peoples of southern and western Borneo recount how the universe came into existence in

Thetis: *see*
Achilles; Nereid; Paris; Peleus; Troy

Thor: *see*
DRAGON; Hymir; Jupiter; Loki; Ragnarok; Thrym

Thoth: *see*
Ra; Hermes

Three Epochs of Creation, The: *see*
CREATION

Thoth, the Egyptian god of the moon and the patron of scribes.

three stages. In the beginning, everything was within the mouth of the coiled Watersnake. The first epoch of creation started when two mountains arose: Gold Mountain, which was the home of the lord of the lower cosmos, and Jewel Mountain, the home of the lord of the upper cosmos. These two mountains clashed together several times, and each clash produced part of the universe: the clouds and skies; the mountains and cliffs; the sun and moon; the Celestial Hawk and the great fish Ila-Ilai Langit; the creatures Rowang Riwo with the golden spittle and Didis Mahendera with the jewel eyes. The first epoch of creation came to an end when the golden headdress of the god Mahatala appeared.

In the second epoch rivers emerged and land and hills were created by the divine maiden Jata. In the final epoch the Tree of Life arose, uniting the upper and lower worlds.

Thrym *Germanic regions*

A giant who stole the hammer of the god Thor, according to Scandinavian myth. Thrym insisted on the hand of the great goddess Freyja before he would return the hammer. Thor disguised himself as Freyja, and went to Jotunheim, the home of the giants. A wedding feast was prepared and when the hammer was laid in the lap of the "bride" (a traditional act of blessing in pagan Scandinavia), Thor seized it, annihilated Thrym and the other giants present, and returned to Asgard, home of the gods.

Thunderbird *North America*

A great eagle-like creature which in many Native American traditions embodies the spirit of thunder and the elemental forces of creation and destruction. Lightning is said to flash

A traditional depiction of the North American Thunderbird, redrawn.

from the animal's eyes or beak and thunder is the sound of its beating wings. The Thunderbird is believed to have awesome creative and destructive power, and anything struck by lightning is said to possess special spirit force.

In the northwestern coastal region, the Thunderbird is a great sky god that preys on whales, which it can carry off in its talons. The Lakota of the Plains see the creature (Wakinyan) as a manifestation of the supreme being Wakan Tanka and there is a cult based upon personal encounters with the beast. In the West there is said to be one Thunderbird in each of the four quarters of the world.

Tiamat *Middle East*

The goddess personifying the primal salt-water ocean, according to the Babylonian (Akkadian) creation myth. Tiamat coupled with Apsu, the sweet-water ocean, to produce many great gods, including Ea, who in turn fathered Marduk. Ea killed Apsu and, in revenge, Tiamat attacked Ea and the other younger gods using a horde of fierce monsters. The gods then chose Marduk as their champion. He slew Tiamat, then cut her in two: one half of her corpse became the sky, the other half the earth. Depictions of the slaying of Tiamat portray her as a dragon or similar monster, which represents the embodiment of the primordial chaos which must be overcome before the ordered cosmos can arise.

Tian *China*
"Heaven", the divine embodiment of the celestial regions. Tian was venerated under the Zhou dynasty (1050BC–221BC) before being replaced by the Jade Emperor, the ruler of heaven.

Tintiya *Southeast Asia*
The male supreme being of Balinese myth. In Balinese cosmology, Tintiya resides in the highest of the six heavens that lie above Mother Earth.

Tirawa *North America*
"Arch of Heaven", the supreme being of the Pawnee. In the beginning, in Pawnee myth, Tirawa created Shakuru (the Sun), Pah (the Moon), the Morning Star, the Evening Star, a Star of Death, and four stars to hold up the sky. He assigned to each heavenly body its place in the heavens and gave it a portion of his power.

Tishtrya *Greece*
The Persian god of rain. According to one account, Tishtrya took the form of a white horse to fight Apaosha, the demon of drought. After three days Apaosha was victorious and the earth became stricken with drought. Tishtrya appealed to the supreme god Ahura Mazdah for help. Ahura Mazdah gave him the strength to vanquish Apaosha, thereby ensuring the return of the rains.

TITAN *Greece*
See panel on next page

Tithonus *Greece*
A Trojan prince, the brother of King Priam of Troy. Eos, the goddess of dawn, became his lover (or wife) and asked the god Zeus to grant Tithonus eternal life. However, she forgot to ask for eternal youth as well. Eventually Eos became so disgusted by Tithonus' withered appearance that she imprisoned him in her palace.

Tiv'r *Oceania*
The ancestral culture hero of the people of the Trans-Fly area of Papua New Guinea. One day Tiv'r heard a faint roaring inside his wife's womb. He sent various birds to retrieve whatever was making the noise and one of them extracted the first bullroarer. The spirit of this object was known as Tokijenjeni, who was Tiv'r's son.

The bullroarer object is a length of wood which is spun around the head at the end of a line to produce a roaring sound that is believed to be the voice of the bullroarer spirit. Bullroarers are widely used in Melanesia during secret male initiation rituals.

Tiwaz *Germanic regions*
The ancient Germanic god of war and lawgiving, who was identified with the Roman god Mars. According to the Roman author Tacitus, a great god and "ruler of all" was worshipped in a sacred wood and all entering the wood had to be bound. This god may have been Tiwaz, who became the Scandinavian Tyr, the binder of the wolf Fenrir. Known to the Anglo-Saxons as Tiw or Tig, Tiwaz gave his name to Tuesday, in imitation of the Roman *Martis dies* (Mars day).

Tian: *see*
Jade Emperor, The

Tintiya: *see*
Agung, Mount; Antaboga;
Basuki; Batara Kala;
Bedawang; Semara

Tirawa: *see*
SUN, MOON AND STARS;
Wakan Tanka

Tishtrya: *see*
Ahura Mazdah; Apaosha

Tithonus: *see*
Eos

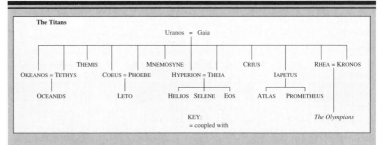

The Titans

Uranos = Gaia

THEMIS   MNEMOSYNE   CRIUS   RHEA = KRONOS
OKEANOS = TETHYS   COEUS = PHOEBE   HYPERION = THEIA   IAPETUS

OCEANIDS   LETO   HELIOS SELENE EOS   ATLAS PROMETHEUS

KEY: *The Olympians*
= coupled with

TITAN: *see*
Cyclops; Hekatoncheires,
The; Oceanid; OLYMPIANS,
THE; Zeus; and individual
names

TITAN *Greece*

One of a race of deities, the offspring of the earth goddess Gaia and the sky god Uranos. The first generation of Titans were six brothers (Coeus, Crius, Iapetus, Hyperion, Kronos and Okeanos) and six sisters (Mnemosyne, Phoebe, Rhea, Theia, Tethys and Themis). Their offspring were also called Titans, except Zeus and his siblings (the first Olympians) and the daughters of Okeanos and Tethys (called the Oceanids). The goddess Aphrodite was also a Titan, descended from Uranos alone.

In one account, Uranos hated the Titans and their brothers, known as the Cyclopes and the Hekatoncheires, and forced them back into their mother. Insulted, Gaia gave the youngest Titan, Kronos, a stone sickle with which he cut off his father's genitals the next time Uranos and Gaia had intercourse. Uranos' severed genitals struck the water and turned to white foam, from which sprang Aphrodite, the goddess of love.

The Titan Atlas. The illustration is redrawn from a coin.

Kronos, now supreme in heaven, freed his Titan siblings, but left the Cyclopes and Hekatoncheires. He married his sister Rhea. Fearing being overthrown like his father, he devoured each of his offspring as Rhea gave birth. But Rhea saved the youngest, Zeus, who was later to plot the downfall of his father. Metis, (an Oceanid), gave Kronos an emetic that made him vomit out Zeus' siblings who were Demeter, Hades, Hestia, Hera and Poseidon. They joined forces with the Cyclopes and Hekatoncheires (freed by Zeus) and fought Kronos and his supporters in a battle called the Titanomachy ("Battle of the Titans"). Not one female Titan, nor Okeanos, Prometheus nor the sun god Helios, joined the battle against Zeus, who was victorious. Kronos and his allies were confined in the underworld with the Hekatoncheires as jailers. Some say that Kronos later became ruler of Elysium.

Tjapara *Australia*
A man who became the moon, according to the Tiwi people of the Melville and Bathurst islands.

Tlaloc *Central America*
The Aztec lord of rain and chief fertility god. In origin Tlaloc was an ancient pre-Aztec rain deity. He had close affinities with the Maya rain god, Chac but it was under the Aztecs that his cult spread to the whole of Mexico. An ambivalent deity, Tlaloc brought the gentle rain that fertilized the soil but also devastating rainstorms. His divine assistants were called the Tlaloque and their sister, Chalchiuhtlicue, was Tlaloc's wife. The god presided over many lesser fertility deities, such as the maize gods Chicometeotl, Centeotl and the "Four Hundred Rabbits" (Centzon Totochtin).

Tlaloc was particularly associated with mountains, where rain clouds gathered and the sources of rivers were to be found. During his festival, young children were sacrificed on mountain tops. The Aztec heavenly paradise, Tlalocan, was named after him. Only Tlaloc's victims – such as those who had drowned or been struck by lightning – could enter Tlalocan.

Tonalpohualli *Central America*
The Aztec sacred calendar. It consisted of 260 days which were divided into twenty weeks of thirteen days, each week and day having a presiding deity. The calendar, which was used for religious purposes, ran alongside the regular solar calendar in cycle that lasted fifty-two years. At the end of this period a great ceremony called "New Fire" marked the recommencement of the cycle and the symbolic rebirth of the world. The Maya version of this calendar was known as Tzolkin.

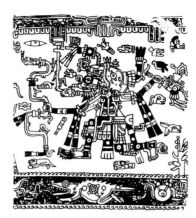

The Central American god known as Tlaloc, from a codex dating from the Late Classic period.

TRICKSTER
See panel on next page

Trimurti *India*
The divine triad of the great gods Brahma, Shiva and Vishnu. Brahma is seen as the originator of the cosmos, Vishnu as its preserver, and Shiva as its destroyer. Recent Hinduism has shown a tendency to prefer five gods: Shiva, Vishnu, Devi, Ganesha and Surya.

Trojan Horse, The *Greece*
A hollow giant model of a horse devised (in some accounts by the epic hero Odysseus) as a means of smuggling the Greek army into the besieged city of Troy. The horse was left outside the walls of Troy and the Greek fleet then pretended to depart. The Trojans brought it within the city walls and, under cover of darkness, the Greek warriors, who were concealed inside, emerged and opened the city gates for their comrades. The Greek victory and destruction of Troy swiftly ensued. (*See illustration on next page.*)

Tjapara: *see*
Purukupali

Tlaloc: *see*
Centeotl; Centzon Totochtin;
Chalchiuhtlicue;
Chicometeotl

Trimurti: *see*
Brahma; Devi; Ganesha;
Shiva; Vishnu

Trojan Horse, The: *see*
Odysseus; Troy

TRICKSTER

In most mythologies of the world there are figures known as tricksters, whose principal characteristics are cunning, quick-wittedness and a propensity for mischievous or humorous behaviour. These characters may be human in form (but mortal or divine), such as Hermes, Eshu, Maui and Loki, but they are very frequently anthropomorphized animals, such as rabbits (which are popular trickster figures), tortoises

Eshu shown in various forms, from a Yoruba shrine of the 19th century.

and spiders. The effects of their activities may be creative or destructive, or both. Tricksters (who are usually male) often fall victim to their own antics.

In North America the trickster is frequently the same as the culture hero. For example, the Raven trickster of the northwest coast employs his trickery to outwit the adversaries of humanity, and steal fire and the heavenly bodies for the benefit of the world. The Oceanic trickster Maui falls into much the same category.

Elsewhere the trickster may be more purely subversive or even dangerous, a bringer of chaos without having any compensating characteristics which benefit the human race and the cosmic order. The west African trickster Eshu and the Chinese Monkey King (also known as Sun Wukong) spread disorder indiscriminately among humans and the gods until they are brought to book. But the most notorious trickster in this respect is probably the Scandinavian god Loki. His mischief-making brings about not only his own death but also the destruction of the world.

TROJAN WAR, THE HEROES OF THE *Greece*
See panel on next page

Troy *Greece*

A city in northwestern Asia Minor besieged and destroyed by the Greeks under Agamemnon. The myths about the Trojan War and its aftermath were first recounted in a series of epic poems, of which the most celebrated were the *Iliad* and the *Odyssey*, attributed to the blind bard Homer, who lived *c*.750BC. The Greeks viewed the story of the war, in which most of the rulers of the various Greek states took part, as the history of the heroic deeds of their

The Trojan horse (see entry on previous page), here being built by Athene. The illustration is from a red-figure kylix (drinking cup), from the 5th century BC.

TROJAN WAR, THE HEROES OF THE

Many great heroes fought in the Trojan War. The chief warriors on each side were as follows:

TROJAN WAR, THE HEROES OF THE: *see* individual names

Greeks	Status	Characteristics
Achilles	Prince of Phthia	Greatest Greek warrior; slain by Paris
Agamemnon	King of Argos or Mycenae	Commander-in-chief; brother of Menelaus
Ajax (1)	Prince of Salamis	Next greatest warrior (after Achilles)
Ajax (2)	Prince of Locris	Swift runner and expert spear thrower
Calchas	Seer of Megara or Mycenae	Chief prophet of the Greeks
Diomedes	Prince of Argos	Refused to fight Glaucus owing to family ties
Menelaus	King of Sparta	Husband of Helen: her elopement caused the war
Nestor	King of Pylos	Elder statesman and raconteur
Odysseus	King of Ithaca	Chief Greek schemer; devised Trojan Horse

Trojans and allies

Aeneas	Prince of Troy	Son of Aphrodite; ancestor of the Romans
Glaucus	Prince of Lycia	Lycian commander; slain by Ajax (1)
Hector	Prince of Troy	Greatest Trojan warrior; slain by Achilles
Paris	Prince of Troy	Elopement with Helen caused the war
Priam	King of Troy	Father of Hector and Paris
Sarpedon	King of Lycia	Grandson of Zeus; slain by Patroclus

ancestors. The Romans adopted this tradition, claiming that many of the Trojan heroes ended up in Italy, where they founded numerous cities. The most famous of these was Aeneas, whose descendants founded Rome itself.

Archeological evidence has shown that the ancient city of Troy was indeed destroyed by fire and then abandoned *c.*1100BC, at the end of the Bronze Age: in the epic poems of Homer the warriors are described as using weapons both of bronze and iron. The town was also called Ilion (Latin *Ilium*), hence the title of Homer's *Iliad.*

Tsuki-yomi *Japan*

The moon god, and the son of the primal creator Izanagi and brother of the sun goddess Amaterasu and storm god Susano. According to the *Nihonshoki*, Tsuki-yomi killed the food goddess Ogetsu-no-hime in disgust after she served food produced from her bodily orifices. The moon god told his sister Amaterasu, and she was so angry that she swore never to lay eyes on him again. This is why the sun and moon live so far apart.

Tu *Oceania*

The Maori god of war, and the son of the earth goddess Papa and the sky god Rangi. According to the Maori creation myth, Tu was attacked by his brother Tawhiri, the god of the elements. However, none of Tu's other brothers came to help him, so Tu turned on them. He trapped fish and animals, the offspring of Tangaroa and Tane, and ate the wild plants and crops, the offspring of Haumia and Rongo. Tu acquired magical knowledge that enabled him to control all his brothers' progeny: the weather, animals, plants and material possessions.

Tuatha Dé Danann *Celtic regions*

The fifth race of invaders to rule Ireland, according to the *Book of Invasions*. The Tuatha Dé Danann ("People of the Goddess Danu"), or simply Tuatha Dé, were descended from followers of Nemhedh, the leader of the third race of invaders, who had gone into exile to "the northern islands of the world". During their exile, the Tuatha Dé had acquired a great knowledge of supernatural lore, and became skilled in all arts. The progeny of a mother goddess, Danu, they were regarded as possessing divine natures and some of the more famous Tuatha Dé have clear links with ancient Celtic divinities.

The Tuatha Dé under their king, Nuadhu, defeated the Fir Bholg (the fourth race of invaders) at the first battle of Magh Tuiredh and later vanquished the monstrous Fomorians at the second battle. They were defeated by a sixth race of invaders, the Milesians (the Celts). The kingdom was then divided, the Tuatha Dé Danann ruling the Otherworld below ground and the Milesians ruling the world above.

Twrch Trwyth *Celtic regions*

A giant magic boar, originally a king who was punished by God for his wickedness by being turned into a beast. According to the story of Olwen and Culhwch in the *Mabinogion*, the boar was hunted by Mabon, son of Modron and Arthur.

Tyr *Germanic regions*

A Scandinavian god, one of the Aesir or sky deities. Tyr, who evidently represented a later form of the ancient Germanic god Tiwaz, appears to have been a battle god. He figures in myth chiefly as the only god who would dare to bind the monstrous wolf Fenrir.

U

Ugarit *Middle East*

An ancient city in northwestern Syria which flourished *c.*1500BC–*c.*1200BC. Tablets discovered there have revealed much about the religion and mythology of the ancient Canaanites, often referred to as "Ugaritic" myth.

Ull *Germanic regions*

A Scandinavian god, the stepson of the god Thor. Ull, who was a great hunter, was depicted with skis or snowshoes and a bow. In one myth, the god Odin was banned from heaven for seducing a maiden unfairly and Ull was chosen to rule Asgard, home of the gods, instead. Odin returned after ten years and expelled Ull, who fled to Sweden.

Uluru *Australia*

The Aboriginal name for the great sandstone outcrop also known as Ayer's Rock. It was of great spiritual significance in traditional Aboriginal belief.

Umashiashikabihikoji-no-kami *Japan*

One of the five primordial gods known as the Separate Heavenly Deities.

UNDERWORLDS

See panel on next page

Uranos *Greece*

Uranos (taken from the Greek *ouranos* meaning "sky") is a primal deity who embodies the heavens and is the son of the earth goddess Gaia (he had no father). He coupled with Gaia to produce eighteen offspring, who were three Hekatoncheires; three Cyclops; and twelve Titans. He despised his mighty progeny and forced them back into Gaia's womb. Gaia, offended, gave her last-born, the Titan Kronos, a stone sickle with which he castrated Uranos the next time he and Gaia had intercourse. The severed genitals fell into the sea, and turned to white foam, from which sprang the love goddess Aphrodite. Blood from Uranos' wound spattered onto Gaia and spawned a race of giants and, some say, the Furies.

Utnapishtim *Middle East*

The survivor of a great deluge sent by the gods to destroy the human race. In the Akkadian epic of Gilgamesh, the god Enlil, displeased with humanity,

Ull: *see*
Odin; Thor

Uluru: *see*
Bell Bird Brothers

Umashiashikabihikoji-no-kami: *see*
Separate Heavenly Deities, The

Uranos: *see*
Aphrodite; Cyclops; Furies, The; Gaia; Hekatoncheires, The; Kronos; TITAN; Zeus

Utnapishtim: *see*
Atrahasis; Ea; Enlil; FLOOD MYTHS; Gilgamesh; Ziusudra

UNDERWORLDS

In the mythological traditions of many peoples a lower region is said to exist beneath this one. The "underworld", usually a place of darkness, is often envisaged as a land inhabited by the souls of the dead. It may be their permanent home or a place through which spirits may pass on their way to heaven or on their way to be reborn on earth. There is known to be a widespread belief in Africa that the souls of the dead spend a certain time in the underworld but are then reborn as mortals. In the lower region, Mictlan, found in Aztec belief, all but a few special cases must undergo many perils before ascending to one of the heavens.

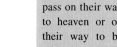

A soul being led into the Underworld from Egyptian myth, based on a fresco.

Elsewhere the dead are said to experience a process of judgment which determines whether a soul is sinful and if so what penalty it will suffer. The beliefs of the ancient Egyptians described how the heart of the deceased was weighed in the throne room of Osiris, lord of the underworld, against a feather of Maat, the goddess of justice and truth. If the heart was heavier (that is, owing to its burden of sin) the soul would be devoured by a monster. If not, the soul joined the blessed spirits.

Worlds beneath this one are not necessarily linked solely with the dead. The Celtic Otherworld, which was often located underground, was an echanted place existing in a parallel universe. In the myths of the Scandinavia, the home of the earth gods, Vanaheim, and the home of the race of giants, Jotunheim, were underground. According to the Chewong of Malaya, there are parallel worlds both below and above this one, the underside of each world being the sky of the world beneath.

decided to destroy them in a flood. Utnapishtim told Gilgamesh how, to survive the flood, he had built a cube-shaped boat. Later, as the waters receded, he sent a dove, a swallow and a raven to find land. Utnapishtim emerged from his boat to offer a sacrifice to the assembled gods. Taking the wise god Ea's advice, Enlil agreed not to destroy humanity, but simply to punish them when necessary. He then bestowed the gift of immortality on Utnapishtim.

Utu *Middle East*

The Sumerian sun god, equivalent to the Akkadian Shamash. Utu is the son of the moon god Nanna (Akkadian Sin) and the brother of Inanna (Akkadian Ishtar), the love goddess. These deities make up the great Babylonian divine triad.

Vajrapani *India*
"The Wielder of the Thunderbolt", a Bodhisattva who was venerated as the annihilator of evil.

Valkyrie *Germanic regions*
"Chooser of the Slain", a female divinity of destiny. The Valkyries selected which warriors would die in battle and accompanied the fallen to Valhalla, the feasting hall of the slain in Asgard, the home of the gods. Valkyries were also protective spirits, instructing young warriors in the art of war and watching over them in battle. They were generally described as female mounted warriors of noble character, although some sources have been known to portray them as bloodthirsty giants.

Vamana India
A divine dwarf, who became the fifth avatar (incarnation) of the god Vishnu. Vamana asked the demon Bali, who had conquered the world, for as much land as he could cover in three strides. Bali consented and the dwarf turned himself into a giant whose three strides took him from one end of the earth to the other.

Vampire *Slav regions*
One of the revenant undead found in Slavic folklore ("vampire" comes from

The Hindu god Vamana.

Vajrapani: *see* Bodhisattva

Valkyrie: *see* Odin

Vamana: *see* VISHNU, THE AVATARS OF

A 6th-century pendant, possibly of a Valkyrie.

Vanir, The

Vampire: *see*
AFTERLIFE

Vanir, The: *see*
Aesir, The; Asgard; Freyja;
Freyr; Njord; Skadi

Varaha: *see*
VISHNU, THE AVATARS
OF

Varuna: *see*
Indra; Uranos

Vedas, The: *see*
Mahabharata, The; *Puranas*,
The; *Ramayana*, The

Venus: *see*
Aphrodite

Vessantara: *see*
Buddha; Indra

the south Slavic word *vampir*). Categories of social undesirables, such as murderers, thieves, whores, heretics and witches, may become vampires, leaving their coffins at midnight to have sex with the living, or feed off their blood. A sharp stake of hawthorn or aspen might be driven through the corpse as a means of ensuring that the dead would rest in peace. Elsewhere, corpses might be beheaded, dismembered or mutilated. In Croatia, ankles and heels were maimed to prevent the dead from walking.

Vanir, The *Germanic regions*
The Scandinavian earth deities, one of two races of gods and goddesses (the other being the Aesir). Mainly associated with the depths of the earth and water, they were revered as the guarantors of the prosperity of land and the guardians of its rulers. Symbols of the Vanir included the boar and the ship. The chief divinities of the Vanir were Freyr and his sister Freyja, the children of the sea god Njord and the mountain goddess called Skadi.

The Vanir and Aesir were enemies at first but made peace and lived together in Asgard, the home of the gods in the sky. The Vanir also had their own residence, Vanaheim, under the earth.

Varaha *India*
A divine boar, the third avatar (incarnation) of the god Vishnu. Varaha appeared when the earth, envisaged as a beautiful woman, became immersed in the ocean. The boar lifted her out of the water with his tusks.

Varuna *India*
A Vedic god embodying sovereignty. He was the rival of the martial Indra, who appears to have ousted him from the position of chief of the Vedic gods.

Varuna was the guardian of cosmic order (*rta*) and symbolized the more passive aspects of sovereignty. Indra was a more active representative of the force upon which kingship is dependent.

Vayu *India and Middle East*
The Persian and Vedic god of the air and wind.

Vedas, The *India*
The earliest Indian religious texts. The *Vedas* (from *veda*, "Knowledge") were composed *c.*1000BC in Sanskrit, the ancient language of India, but were considered so sacred that they were transmitted only orally in exactly the same form for many centuries before they were written down. The oldest is the *Rig Veda*. The term Vedic is used to refer to the deities and myths which are alluded to in the *Vedas*.

Veles *Slav regions*
The ancient Slavic earth god, also called Volos. He was revered as the protector of herds and trade and also as the guardian of the dead. With the advent of Christianity, Veles became a saint, Vlas or Blasius.

Venus *Rome*
The goddess of love and sexuality. Originally a goddess of gardens and springtime fruitfulness, she came to be wholly identified with the Greek goddess Aphrodite.

Vessantara *India*
A prince, the last human incarnation of the Buddha before Siddhartha Gautama. Vessantara, the son of King Sanjaya, was astonishingly generous, but gave away so much that the people forced Sanjaya to exile him. The prince distributed all his possessions and

settled in a Himalayan valley with his family. Then an old brahman, Jujaka, asked for his children as servants and Vessantara happily obliged. He might have given his wife, too, but the god Sakka prevented it. Jujaka went to King Sanjaya, who, after paying him a ransom for Vessantara's children, felt remorse for exiling his son. He revoked his banishment and the family was happily reunited.

Vila Slav regions
One of a race of female spirits of the dead. The *vila* is described as for ever young and beautiful, with long, fair hair. The Bulgarians said that she and her companions represented the souls of young women who died unbaptized. The Poles claimed that the *vila* was condemned to float between heaven and earth because she had been frivolous in life. Prominent in southern Slavic folk myth, she was beneficial and loved to dance and sing. There are stories of *vila*s marrying mortal men.

Viracocha *South America*
The supreme Inca creator deity. He had no name but was referred to by various titles reflecting his status as the omnipresent primal god who bestowed life on all beings, earthly and divine. The most frequently used title was Ilya-Tiqsi Wiraqoca Pacayacaciq, ("Ancient Foundation, Lord, Teacher of the World") hence Viracocha (the usual hispanicized spelling).

Viracocha created the world and then populated it with giants. However, they disobeyed the creator, who wiped them out (in one account) with a great flood. He then created a new race of humans from clay and brought them all to life. He sent them into the earth, from which they were told to emerge through caves

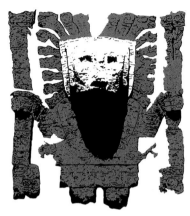

Viracocha, the Inca creator deity, based on a sculpture.

into their respective lands.

The world was still dark, so Viracocha commanded the sun, moon and stars to rise from Lake Titicaca. He bestowed tokens of royalty on Manco Capac, who became the first king of the Incas. Then Viracocha journeyed through the new world, shaping the landscape and teaching. In one account, when he reached the coast he sailed away to his divine domain, leaving the running of the world to his divine progeny such as Inti, Mama Kilya and Ilyap'a.

Vishnu *India*
A god of the of the *trimurti*, the Hindu divine triad of Brahma, Vishnu and Shiva. Vishnu is the preserver of the cosmos that emanates from Brahma and is reabsorbed by Shiva before emanating again from Brahma. In Hindu cosmology, between emanations Vishnu rests in the cosmic waters on the back of the snake Ananta ("The Infinite"). He is the world's protector: whenever it comes under threat, Vishnu appears in one of a number of avatars or incarnations in order to save it. Two of

Vesta: *see*
Hestia

Vila: *see*
Kikimora; Rusalka

Viracocha: *see*
CREATION; HUMANITY, THE ORIGIN OF; Ilyap'a; Inti; Mama Kilya; Manco Capac; Roal

Vishnu: *see*
Brahma; Shiva; Shri; VISHNU, THE AVATARS OF

VISHNU, THE AVATARS OF *India*

Vishnu manifested himself in various human and animal avatars or incarnations to save the world from evil. The number of avatars was eventually set at ten, although their identities may vary. The usual sequence is as follows:

Name	Form	Relevance
Matsya	Fish	Saved the first man, Manu, from the world deluge
Kurma	Tortoise	Supported Mt. Mandara during the churning of the ocean
Varaha	Boar	Raised the earth from the ocean on its tusks
Narasimha	Man-lion	Killed the demon Hiranyakashipu
Vamana	Dwarf	Vanquished the demon Bali
Parashurama	Human	Killed the hundred-armed demon Arjuna
Rama	Human	Killed the demon king Ravana
Krishna	Human	Killed the demon king Kamsa
Buddha	Human	Misled the sinful to ensure their punishment
Kalkin	Human	The avatar to come: a messianic figure

these incarnations, Rama and Krishna, are important deities in their own right.

In early myth, Vishnu is praised for measuring and pervading the universe in three strides, confirming it as a place for both gods and humans to dwell. He is identified with the cosmic pillar, the axis of the universe which supports the heavens and connects them to the earth.

The Hindu god Vishnu, from a 19th-century painting.

Vishnu's consort is Lakshmi or Shri, the beautiful goddess of good fortune. She is said to have arisen from the churning of the ocean, over which Vishnu presided.

VISHNU, THE AVATARS OF *India*
See panel above

Vishvamitra *India*
One of Hinduism's seven great sages.

Volsung *Germanic regions*
A warrior of Scandinavian myth, the son of Rerir and great-grandson of the god Odin. Volsung was the father of the warrior Sigmund and grandfather of Sigurd, known as "The Volsungs".

Vulcan *Rome*
An ancient Roman god of fire, as well as volcanoes and thunderbolts. Vulcan, who was probably an early form of the Roman Jupiter, came to be identifed with the Greek Hephaistos.

Wakan Tanka *North America*
"Great Mystery", the supreme divinity of the Lakota (Sioux) people. Wakan Tanka is conceived of as a remote creator who governs the universe through various deities which are all aspects of his being. These aspects are all addressed in prayer as "Father", while the transcendent Wakan Tanka is called "Grandfather". Wakan Tanka presides over important rituals involving the sacred pipe of the Lakota.

According to the Lakota creation myth, the first four gods were Inyan (Rock), Maka (Earth), Skan (Sky) and Wi (Sun). These deities, the Superior Gods, grew lonely and created other aspects of Wakan Tanka. First were the Associated Gods: Moon, Wind, Falling Star and Thunderbird. Then the Kindred Gods: Two-Legged (humans and their relatives, bears), Buffalo, Four-Winds and Whirlwind. Finally, the God-Like were more abstract beings related to the soul and sacred power: Nagi (Shade of the Dead), Nagila (Shade-Like), Niya (Breath of Life) and Sicun (Spirit Power). These sixteen deities are known as the Tob Tob (Four-Four).

WAKAN TANKA, THE ASPECTS OF
See panel on next page

Wandjina *Australia*
An ancestral spirit of the primordial Dreamtime, in the Aboriginal mythology of the Kimberley region. Each clan is said to possess a *wandjina*, associated with an animal, as its protective ancestor.

Watatsumi-no-kami *Japan*
The god of the sea, ruler of the oceans, sea creatures and numerous lesser divinities. His daughter Toyotama-hime married Hiko-hoho-demi ("Fireshade"). They were the grandparents of Jimmu-tenno, first emperor of Japan.

Wawilak Sisters, The *Australia*
Two ancestral heroines of the Dreamtime, according to the Aboriginal mythology of the Yolngu people of Arnhem Land. The Wawilak journeyed across the primordial landscape, shaping the environment and naming creatures and plants. The younger sister was pregnant and later gave birth to a boy, and the elder carried a baby boy in

Wakan Tanka: *see* WAKAN TANKA, THE ASPECTS OF, White Buffalo Woman

Wandjina: *see* Dreamtime; Widjingara

Watatsumi-no-kami: *see* Jimmu-tenno

Wawilak Sisters, The: *see* Dreamtime; Seven Sisters, The

The Aspects of Wakan Tanka

Wakan Tanka

Superior Gods	Associate Gods	Kindred Gods	God-like
Sun	Moon	Two-legged	Nagi
Sky	Wind	Buffalo	Nagila
Earth	Falling Star	Four-winds	Niya
Rock	Thunderbird	Whirlwind	Sicun

a cradle. The elder sister unwittingly allowed her menstrual blood to fall into a pool, angering the serpent Yurlunggur

The Wawilak sisters inside the serpent Yulunggur, from a bark painting.

who lived there. The serpent caused a great storm and flood. The sisters sang songs to appease him, but Yurlunggur swallowed the women and their sons, then reared up into the sky as a rainbow.

The deluge receded. Yurlunggur returned to earth at a spot which became the first initiation ground of the Yolngu and regurgitated the sisters and their sons. Two men came along and learned the sisters' songs, then carried out the first Yolngu rites of passage, initiating the boys into adulthood.

White Buffalo Woman *North America*
A mysterious and beautiful woman of the Buffalo people, in Lakota myth. She visited the Lakota and brought them the sacred pipe central to Lakota ritual.

Widjingara *Australia*
The first human to die, to the Worora of the western Kimberleys. Windjingara was killed by ancestral *wandjina* beings who, contrary to the marriage rules, had wanted to steal a woman betrothed to someone else.

Widjingara later became the native cat (Dasyurus), a nocturnal marsupial which scavenges on corpses.

Wisakedjak *North America*
The trickster figure of the Cree people, also known by the anglicized form "Whiskey Jack". In Cree mythology, the supreme being Gitchi Manitou asked

Wisakedjak to teach animals and people to live in harmony, but instead he sowed discord. Angry, Gitchi Manitou sent a great flood which only Wisakedjak and a few animals survived. The world and its inhabitants were created anew, but Wisakedjak kept few of his powers.

Wodan *Germanic regions*

The ancient Germanic god, Wodan, was the forerunner of the Scandinavian Odin. He brought good fortune in battle but finally sentenced his followers to defeat and death. Like the Roman Mercury, with whom he was identified, the god was a guide in the underworld. He also came to have associations with the sky and was symbolized by the eagle. Wodan was linked with runes, magic symbols used in divination, and was the inspiration of poets and heroes. Kings revered him as their divine ancestor. His wife was the goddess Frea.

Wodan was known to the Anglo-Saxons as Woden. He also gave his name to Wednesday.

Wolf *North America*

A creator figure in the mythology of the Shoshoni people of North America. In early times, Wolf and Coyote were the most important people, but Coyote always tried to defy Wolf. One day they discussed death. Wolf said that people could be brought back to life when they died by shooting an arrow under them, but Coyote argued that if that happened there would soon be no room on earth. So Wolf decided that Coyote's son would be the first to die. The grieving Coyote soon came to Wolf and asked for his son to be revived as Wolf had suggested. However, Wolf reminded him of his remark that when people die, they should remain dead. It has been that way ever since.

Woot *Africa*

An ancestral culture hero in the mythology of the Kuba people of Zaïre. In one Kuba creation myth, the god Mboom had nine children called Woot, and each assisted in creating the world. The first six formed the landscape and Woot the Sculptor created the first people from wooden balls. Death first came to the world when the eighth Woot killed the ninth Woot in a quarrel.

Another account describes how Mboom vomited human beings, including Woot. All the humans and animals lived harmoniously in one village and spoke the same language. But Woot was expelled for having sex with his sister Mweel, who bore a son. Woot then cursed the land, which grew dark and barren. Eventually the villagers persuaded Woot to lift his curse. He went into exile with his followers, shaping the landscape as he went and creating more animals, plants and tribes, each with its own tongue. Woot became the ancestor of the Kuba kings and nation.

Works and Days, The *Greece*

A poetic work by Hesiod (lived *c*.700BC). A major source of Greek myths, it is an agricultural treatise. In the first part Hesiod addresses his brother Perses on the benefits of a just life, illustrating many myths.

Wurulu-Wurulu *Germanic regions*

Trickster beings in the Aboriginal mythology of the western Kimberleys. Similar in their disruptive effect to the Ngandjala-Ngandjala, the Wurulu-Wurulu steal honey from wild bees' nests with bottle-brush flowers (*banksia*) tied to sticks. If a nest is found empty, it means that Wurulu-Wurulu have been there first.

Wodan: *see*
Frea; Mercury; Odin

Wolf: *see*
Coyote; DEATH, THE ORIGIN OF; CREATION; CULTURE HERO; Mboom

Works and Days, The: *see*
Theogony, The

Wurulu-Wurulu: *see* Argula; *Mimi*; Namorodo; Ngandjala-Ngandjala; TRICKSTER; Unguramu

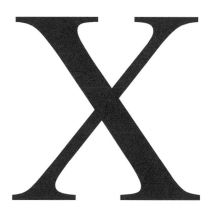

Xi Wang Mu, based on a porcelain figure.

Xbalanque and Hunahpu
Central America

The Hero twins whose story is told in the *Popul Vuh*, the sacred book of the Quiche Maya. The gods of Xibalba, the underworld, challenged the twins to play the Maya ball game. In the underworld they passed safely through many perils but then Hunahpu was decapitated by a bat. The game was about to begin, so his brother persuaded a turtle to act as his head. As soon as the gods became distracted, Xbalanque replaced his brother's head. The twins then impressed the gods by cutting

The hero twin Xbalanque, from a vase dating from c.8th century BC.

themselves up and reforming. The gods requested that this be done to them and the boys happily obliged – but left them dismembered. They re-emerged from the underworld as the sun and moon.

This myth reflected Maya belief that after death a Maya ruler should endeavour to outwit the underworld gods and then be reborn in the heavens.

Xi He *China*

The queen of heaven, in early Chinese mythology. Xi He was the wife of Di Jun, the lord of heaven, and mother of the Ten Suns. Every day Xi He escorted one of the suns around the sky from their home in the Fu Sang tree, a giant mulberry that grew beyond the eastern horizon. This continued every day for many years until the suns rebelled against their parents and appeared in the sky all at once. Yi the Archer saved earth from the burning heat by shooting all but one of the suns from the sky.

Xi Wang Mu *China*

"The Queen-Mother of the West", a powerful tyrant goddess who was said to live on the sacred Mount Kunlun, the abode of the celestial immortals, far to the west of the Chinese heartland. She was the wife of the Emperor of the East and originally a fearful deity. In later Chinese tradition Xi Wang Mu became the queen of heaven, wife of the Jade Emperor. In this equally powerful (but less forbidding) role, she was known as Wang Mu Niang Niang.

In both early and later traditions Xi Wang Mu was the keeper of the elixir of immortality. In her gardens grew the trees which bore the peaches of eternal life. These peaches ripened every six thousand years and were then eaten by the gods and goddesses in order to replenish their immortality.

The Aztec maize goddess, Xilonen, based on a volcanic stone statue.

Xibalba *Central America*
The Maya underworld. Xibalba ("Place of Terror") was said to consist of nine levels. It contained numerous "houses" in which the dead faced a range of perils, for example the House of Knives, House of Fire, House of Jaguars and House of Bats. The underworld was entered through caves or ponds and lakes. The Hero Twins, Xbalanque and Hunaphu, overcame many of the perils of Xibalba when they journeyed to see the gods of the underworld.

Xilonen *Central America*
An Aztec maize goddess. Xilonen was the protector of the young ears of corn

The Aztec god Xipe Totec (see entry on next page). The illustration is based on a pottery statuette of the 8th–11th centuries AD.

Xibalba: *see*
UNDERWORLDS;
Xbalanque and Hunahpu

Xilonen: *see*
Centeotl; Chalchiuhtlicue;
Chicomecoatl; Tlaloc

Xipe Totec: *see*
Five Suns, The

and was associated with the maize deities Centeotl and Chicomecoatl.

Xipe Totec *Central America*

"The Flayed Lord", an Aztec god (of pre-Aztec origin) presiding over plants and springtime fecundity. During his festival, sacrificial victims were flayed and their skins worn by his devotees. The skin would rot and fall away, revealing the living man. In the Aztec creation myth, Xipe Totec was also identified with the aspect of the god Tezcatlipoca who ruled the first of the five "Suns" or world eras, thereby launching a cosmic sequence in which the destruction of each world was followed by its recreation. (*See illustration on page 225.*)

Xochipilli, *from* Codex Borgia *of the Late Post-classic period.*

Xochipilli and Xochiquetzal
Central America

The male and female deities of flowers found in the mythology of the Aztecs. Xochipilli (which means "Prince of Flowers") was a summer god who also presided over dancing, games, feasting and painting. However, he also had a more sinister side as the god who sent boils, piles and sexually transmitted diseases to those who had illicit intercourse during periods of fast.

Xochiquetzal (which means "Flower Quetzal") presided over pregnancy, childbirth and other aspects of female fecundity. She was the patron of women's crafts and was also venerated by the skilled craftsmen who served the wealthy.

The patron of women's crafts,
Xochiquetzal, from the 16th-century Codex Borbonicus.

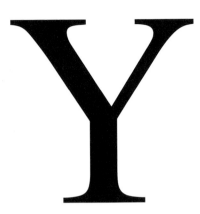

Yam *Middle East*

The Ugaritic (Canaanite) god of the sea. Yam, like his Babylonian counterpart Tiamat, embodied the forces of chaos and disorder, and was envisaged as a monstrous creature. According to Ugaritic myth, Yam challenged the storm god Baal for sovereignty on earth. Baal killed Yam, scattering his remains, demonstrating that he, the lord of storms, controlled the divine waters that fell as fertilizing rain.

Yama (1) *India*

The god of the dead and ruler of hell. According to Vedic myth, Yama was the eldest son of Vivasvat, the sun, and the first mortal man (in later Hinduism the first man was, however, said to be Manu). Vivasvat later appointed Yama to be the king of the dead.

Yama (2) *China*

A king of hell and judge of the dead, a figure derived from the Hindu Yama. The chief Yama (rendered Yan in Chinese) was Yanluo, the king of Hell, and was answerable to the Jade Emperor, ruler of Heaven. Yanluo oversaw ten law courts. In all of these courts except the last, the dead found themselves being judged and sentenced. Yanluo presided over the first court, while each of the nine other courts was also headed by a Yama. After

Yama, the Chinese ruler of hell, from a 14th-century AD painting.

*Yao, from a Sung
dynasty painting.*

*Yi, from an early 20th-
century painting.*

sentencing, sinners were assigned to any one of eighteen punishment regions. In the tenth court the dead souls were fitted into their new bodies before they could be reincarnated.

Yamato-takeru *Japan*

Meaning "The Brave One of the Yamato region", Yamato-takeru is the greatest hero of Japanese mythology. Originally called O-usu-no-mikoto, Yamato-takeru was the son of the legendary emperor Keiko. He first revealed his ferocity when he killed his elder brother for showing disrespect for their father. Keiko was impressed and sent his young son to kill two of his enemies, a pair of fearsome warrior brothers. O-usu-no-mikoto completed the task successfully and was dubbed "Yamato-takeru" by one of his victims.

The young hero then subdued the land of Izumo and killed its chief, Izumo-takeru. Then, on his next mission, he journeyed a long way and defeated the Emishi or Eastern Barbarians. During this mission a chieftain tried to kill Yamato-takeru by tricking him into entering a grassy plain and then setting fire to it. Yamato-takeru's sword, which the god Susano had originally found in the tail of the dragon called Yamato-no-orochi, magically wielded itself and cut down the blazing grass. After this the sword became known as Kusanagi (which means "Grass-Mower").

On his return journey the hero killed a deer which was really a god, and later declared that he would kill a boar that was in fact another deity. The gods caused him to fall mortally ill. Knowing that his end was near, Yamato-takeru travelled to the plain of Nobo. It was here that he died. On his death his body turned into a white bird and flew off toward Yamato.

Yao *China*

A mythical early ruler of China renowned for his humility and modest way of life. During his reign, Yi the Archer came to earth to tackle the problem of the ten suns which had appeared in the sky all at once. With Yu and Shun, Yao came to be regarded as one of the Sage Rulers of Antiquity.

Yarikh *Middle East*

The Ugaritic (Canaanite) god of the moon. One particular myth recounts the arrangements for Yarikh's marriage to Nikkal, the moon goddess, and the subsequent birth of his son.

Yei *North America*

A group of Navajo creator deities who are invoked during curing ceremonies by masked impersonators. The chief of the Yei is known as Talking God.

Yggdrasil *Germanic regions*

The World Ash, a great tree which links the upper and lower regions of the cosmos, in ancient Scandinavian cosmology. The name means "Horse of Ygg", another name for the god Odin, who is said to have hanged himself from the tree in an act of self-sacrifice that enabled him to acquire the power of the magical runes used in divination. The tree's roots lie in the underworld above a spring that is a fount of wisdom. Dew was said to be moisture which fell from its branches high above Midgard (earth), the middle region of the cosmos.

Yi the Archer *China*

A divine hero who figures in a myth dating from at least the 6th century BC. In the beginning there were ten suns, the sons of the rulers of heaven. Each day only one of them would appear in the sky, but one day, in the time of the wise emperor Yao, they disobeyed their parents and all appeared at once. At first the people on earth were delighted, but the heat soon withered their crops and calamity threatened.

Di Jun, the lord of heaven, sent one of his mightiest aides, the archer Yi, to tackle the problem. He only intended Yi to order nine of the suns home, but Yi became so angry when he saw the suffering they had caused that he shot all but one of them dead with his bow.

Yi was acclaimed a hero by the people but Di Jun angrily banished him with his wife, who was called Chang E, to live as mortals on earth.

Chang E, who was upset at losing her immortality, acquired some elixir of immortality from Xi Wang Mu, the Queen Mother of the West. Although half the elixir was meant for Yi, Chang E took it all in the hope of returning to heaven, but instead she went to the moon. Yi realized what had happened and became reconciled to his mortality. In some accounts he was later forgiven by Di Jun and went back to heaven.

Yin and Yang *China*
The two opposing but interacting and mutually dependent forces of creation. Yin (which had the original meaning "Darkness") and Yang (originally: "Light") came to be seen as cosmic powers which interacted to produce all the phenomena in the universe.

Yin represented qualities such as passivity, femininity, moisture and cold, while Yang, meanwhile, stood for activity, masculinity, dryness and heat. Yin and Yang may be seen in contrasting pairs such as female and male, life and death, good and evil, and so on. The Yin and Yang are represented by the circular emblem which is known as the *tai-chi.*

Yinlugen Bud *Southeast Asia*
A tree-spirit who taught humans to share their food after hunting and how to bear and raise children, according to the Chewong people of Malaya.

Ymir *Germanic regions*
A cosmic giant who arose from Ginnungagap, the abyss of chaos, at the beginning of creation, according to Scandinavian mythology. In one account, Ymir, an androgynous being of fire and ice, spawned the first man and woman and then three creator gods called the Sons of Bor. The three gods slew Ymir and formed the earth from his body, the ocean from his blood and the sky from his skull.

Yu the Great *China*
A mythical emperor of China, was traditionally said to have ruled between 2205BC and 2197BC. In the days of the ruler Shun there was a great flood. Shun appointed Yu to tackle the deluge, so he laboured for thirteen years to build canals which drained the floodwaters into the sea. Shun rewarded him by abdicating in his favour. Yu founded the mythical first imperial dynasty, the Xia.

Yurlunggur *Australia*
A great serpent which figures in the origin myth of the Yolngu people of Arnhem Land. Yurlunggur is believed to be manifested in the rainbow.

Yurupary *South America*
A culture hero who stole fire for humanity, to the Barasana people of Colombia. Yurupary, the "Manioc Stick Anaconda", took fire from the underworld and used it to kill his brother Macaw. Yurupary was also burned to death and his bones became the charred logs of the first manioc garden.

Yi the Archer: *see*
Di Jun; Xi Wang Mu

Ymir: *see*
CREATION; HUMANITY, THE ORIGIN OF

Yu the Great: *see*
FLOOD MYTHS; Yao

Yurlunggur: *see*
Wawilak Sisters, The

Yurupary: *see*
CULTURE HERO

The Emperor Yu, from a painting of the Sung dynasty.

Zagreus *Greece*

An alternative name for the god known as Dionysos.

Zeus *Greece*

The head of the Greek pantheon, the chief of the Olympian gods and goddesses and ruler of the skies. Zeus was the youngest son of the Titans Kronos and Rhea and the brother of the Olympians Demeter, Hades, Hera, Hestia and Poseidon. He ousted his

An image based on a bronze statue, dating from c.450BC, which almost certainly depicts the god Zeus.

father as ruler of the gods through a combination of deceit and cunning. After defeating the Titans in a great battle, Zeus took the heavens as his particular domain and allotted the rule of the seas and the underworld to his brothers Poseidon and Hades, respectively. He chose Mount Olympus, the highest mountain in the world (that is, Greece) as a home for the new ruling deities, who were from then onwards known as the Olympians.

Zeus was the supreme authority in all matters human and divine. He underwrote the power of kings and of the law and upheld the social order. Among his titles were Zeus Horkios (the guarantor of oaths), Zeus Hisekios (the guardian of sanctuary seekers) and Zeus Xenios (the maintainer of friendship between cities and families). As befitted a supreme god and ruler of the heavens, Zeus was symbolized by thunder and lightning and the eagle, the king of birds. His chief weapons were thunderbolts, which were made for him by the Cyclopes in their subterranean forges under the supervision of the smith god Hephaistos.

ZEUS, THE CONSORTS OF

The following are the most notable of Zeus' sexual partners and offspring.

Name	Status	Offspring
Wives:		
1 Metis	Oceanid	Athene
2 Themis	Titan	The Fates The Seasons Dike ("Justice') Eunomia ("Order") Eirene ("Peace")
3 Hera	Olympian; sister of Zeus	Ares Hephaistos Eileithyia Hebe
Other consorts:		
Alkmene	Queen of Sparta	Herakles
Antiope	Princess of Thebes	Amphion and Zetheus
Danaë	Princess of Argos	Perseus
Demeter	Olympian; sister of Zeus	Persephone
Europa	Princess of Phoenicia	Minos, Rhadamanthys, Sarpedon
Eurynome	Oceanid	The three Graces
Ganymede	Prince of Troy	
Io	Princess of Argos	Epaphos
Leda	Princess of Sparta	Castor and Polydeuces Clytemnestra Helen of Troy
Leto	Titan	Apollo Artemis
Maia	Pleiad	Hermes
Mnemosyne	Titan	The nine Muses
Semele	Princess of Thebes	Dionysos
Thetis	Nereid	

Zeus had three wives in succession, Metis, Themis and finally his sister Hera. The union of Zeus and Hera was called the Sacred Marriage and symbolized the important place of wedlock in Greek society. Even so, Zeus was a notorious adulterer and had a host of divine and human extramarital consorts. Hera was renowned for persecuting these consorts and their children by her errant husband.

ZEUS, THE CONSORTS OF *Greece*
See panel on previous page

Zhang Guo *China*
The sixth of the Eight Immortals of Taoist (Daoist) myth. Zhang Guo, or Zhang Guoli ("Old Man Zhang Guo"), was said to have lived at the time of the empress Wu of the Tang dynasty (AD618–AD907). He was renowned for his magical skills and possessed a mule that could walk for thousands of miles and be folded up when not in use. He bestowed babies on couples and his portrait would often be hung in the marital bedroom.

Zhu Rong *China*
The god of fire and benevolent ruler of the universe, according to early Chinese myth. He is said to have defeated the malevolent water god Gong Gong in a battle for cosmic control.

Ziusudra *Middle East*
A king who was the sole survivor of a great flood sent by the gods in an attempt to destroy the human race, according to Sumerian mythology. The full story of Ziusudra – which is the earliest known account of the Mesopotamian flood myth – is not extant, but it apparently begins with the gods An and Enlil, having been angered by humanity, deciding to destroy it. The wise god Enki, however, is said to have forewarned Ziusudra, who built a great vessel and rode out the floodwaters. After seven days of darkness and deluge the waters receded and the sun god Utu reappeared. Ziusudra emerged to make a thanks-offering which appeased An and Enlil, who repopulated the earth and granted Ziusudra eternal life.

Zu *Middle East*
The Babylonian storm god, who was usually depicted as a great bird. According to the Akkadian version of a Sumerian myth, Zu stole the Tablet of Destiny (the divine decrees which bestowed supreme power on their possessor) from the god Enlil. The tablet was wrestled back by the champion of the gods, Marduk (who was called Lugulbanda in Sumerian accounts). Zu was then apparently brought before the god Ea (who was known as Enki to the Sumerians) for punishment.

Acknowledgments

The publishers wish to thank the following contributors for material supplied for this book:

Professor John Baines (Egypt)
Dr Mary Beard (Rome)
Dr Martin Boord (Tibet)
Dr John Brockington (India)
Dr John Chinnery (China)
Dr Guy Cooper (North America)
Dr Hilda Ellis Davidson (Northern Europe)
Dr Simon Goldhill (Greece)
Professor Robert Layton (Australia)

Dr C. Scott Littleton (Japan)
Dr John MacInnes (Celtic World)
Dr Geraldine Pinch (Egypt)
Professor the Reverend Canon J.R. Porter (Middle East)
Dr David Riches (Arctic regions)
Dr Nicholas J. Saunders (Central and South America)
Dr Ing-Britt Trankell (Southeast Asia)
Dr Piers Vitebsky (Arctic regions)

Dr James Weiner (Oceania)
Dr Faith Wigzell (Eastern and Central Europe)
Dr Roy Willis (Africa and Southeast Asia)

Bibliography

General

Campbell, Joseph, *The Masks of God* (Penguin, Harmondsworth, 1982)
The Inner Reaches of Outer Space (Harper and Row, New York, 1988)
The Way of the Animal Powers: Historical Atlas of World Mythology, Vol. 1 (Times, London, 1983)
Dundes, Alan (ed.), *The Sacred Narrative: readings in the theory of myth* (University of California Press, Berkeley, 1984)
Eliade, Mircea, *Cosmos and History: the Myth of the Eternal Return* (Harper and Row, New York, 1959, rep. 1985)
Kramer, Samuel N., *Mythologies of the Ancient World* (Doubleday, New York, 1961)
Lévi-Strauss, Claude, *Myth and Meaning* (Routledge, London, 1978)
Maranda, Pierre, *Mythology: selected readings* (Penguin, Harmondsworth, 1972)
Propp, Vladimir, *Morphology of the Folktale* (University of Texas, Austin, 1968)

Africa

Davidson, Basil, *Old Africa Rediscovered* (Gollancz, London, 1959)
Finnegan, Ruth, *Oral Literature in Africa* (Clarendon Press, Oxford, 1970, rep. 1976)
Mbiti, John S., *African Religions and Philosophy* (Heinemann, London, 1969)
Willis, Roy, *There Was A Certain Man: spoken art of the Fipa* (Clarendon Press, Oxford, 1978)

Arctic Regions

Damar, D., *Handbook of North American Indians: Arctic* (Smithsonian Institution, Washington, 1984)
Ray, Dorothy Jean, *Eskimo Masks: Art and Ceremony* (University of Washington Press, Seattle, 1967)
Weyer, Edward, *The Eskimos* (Yale University Press, New Haven, 1932)

Australia

Layton, R., *Uluru: an Aboriginal history of Ayers Rock* (Aboriginal Studies Press, Canberra, 1986)
O'Brien, M., *The Legend of the Seven Sisters* (Aboriginal Studies Press, Canberra, 1990)
Warlukurlangu Artists, *Kuruwarri: Yuendumu Doors* (Aboriginal Studies Press, Canberra, 1987)
Western Region Aboriginal Land Council, *The story of the falling star* (Aboriginal Studies Press, Canberra, 1989)

Celtic Regions

Green, Miranda J., *Dictionary of Celtic Myth and Legend* (Thames and Hudson, London, 1992)
Loomis, R.S. (ed.), *Arthurian Literature in the Middle Ages. A Collective History* (Oxford University Press, 1959)
MacCana, Proinsias, *Celtic Mythology* (Hamlyn, London/New York/Sydney/Toronto, 1970; 3rd impression 1975)
McCone, Kim, *Pagan Past and Christian Present in Early Irish Literature* (Maynooth Monographs 3, 1990, rep. 1991)

Central America

Carrasco, David, *Ancient Mesoamerican Religions* (Holt, Rinehart and Winston, New York, 1990)
Coe, Michael D., *The Maya* (Thames and Hudson, London, 1987)
Fagan, Brian, *Kingdoms of Jade, Kingdoms of Gold* (Thames and Hudson, London, 1991)
Townsend, Richard, *The Aztecs* (Thames and Hudson, London, 1992)

China

Chang, K.C., *Art, Myth and Ritual* (Harvard University Press, Cambridge, Mass./London, 1983)
Christie, A.H., *Chinese Mythology*, (Hamlyn, 1968)
Werner, E.T.C., *Myths and Legends of China* (Harrap, London, 1922)

Egypt

Faulkner, R.O. (ed. C. Andrews), *The Ancient Egyptian Book of the Dead* (British Museum, London, 1985)
Hart, G., *Egyptian Myths* (British Museum, London, 1990)
Lurker, M., *The Gods and Symbols of Ancient Egypt* (Thames and Hudson, London, 1980)
Quirke, S., *Ancient Egyptian Religion* (British Museum, London, 1992)
Shafer, B. (ed.), *Religion in Ancient Egypt: gods, myths and personal practice*

Bibliography

(Routledge, London, 1991)

Thomas, A.P., *Egyptian Gods and Myths* (Shire, 1986)

Germanic regions

Davidson, H.R.Ellis, *Pagan Scandinavia* (Hamlyn, London, 1984)

Owen, G.R., *Rites and Religions of the Anglo-Saxons* (David and Charles, Newton Abbot, 1981)

Todd, M., *The Early Germans* (Blackwell, Oxford, 1992)

Greece

Carpenter, T.H., *Art and Myth in Ancient Greece* (Thames and Hudson, London, 1991)

Easterling, P.E. and J.V. Muir (eds.) *Greek Religion and Society* (Cambridge University Press, 1985)

Kerenyi, C., *The Heroes of the Greeks* (Thames and Hudson, London, 1974)

Morford, Mark, and Robert Lenardon, *Classical Mythology* (Longman, New York, 1991)

Vernant, J-P., *Myth and Society in Ancient Greece* (trans. Janet Lloyd) (Zone Books, New York, 1990)

India

Dimmitt, Cornelia, and J.A.B. van Buitenen, *Classical Hindu Mythology: A Reader in the Sanskrit Puranas* (Temple University Press, Philadelphia, 1978)

Ions, Veronica, *Indian Mythology* (Hamlyn, London, 1967)

Kinsley, David, *Hindu Goddesses: Visions of the Divine Feminine in the Hindu Religious Tradition* (University of California Press, Berkeley 1986)

Kuiper, F.B.J., *Ancient Indian Cosmogony* (Vikas Publications, New Delhi, 1983)

Mahabharata, trans. and ed. J.A.B. van Buitenen, vols 1-3 (University of Chicago Press, Chicago, 1973-78)

O'Flaherty, Wendy Doniger (trans.), *Hindu Myths, A Sourcebook* (Penguin, Harmondsworth, 1975)

Japan

Aston, W.G. (trans.) *Nihongi* (= *Nihonshoki*) (Charles E.Tuttle Co., Tokyo, 1972)

Philippi, Donald L. (trans.), *Kojiki* (University of Tokyo Press,1968)

Middle East

Dalley, S., *Myths from Mesopotamia: Creation, The Flood, Gilgamesh and Others* (Oxford University Press, Oxford/New York, 1989)

Gray, J., *Near Eastern Mythology* (Hamlyn, London, 1969)

Hinnells, J.R., *Persian Mythology* (Hamlyn, London, 1973)

Kramer, S.N., *Sumerian Mythology* (revised edn) (Harper and Brothers, New York, 1961)

Ringgren, H., *Religions of the Ancient Near East* (S.P.C.K., London/Westminster Press, Philadelphia, 1973)

North America

Burland, C.A. and M. Wood, *North American Indian Mythology* (Newnes, London, 1985)

Erdoes R. and A. Ortiz (eds.), *American Indian Myths and Legends* (Pantheon, New York, 1988)

Mariott A. and C.K. Rachlin, *American Indian Mythology* (Mentor, New York, 1968)

Plains Indian Mythology (Thomas Crowell, New York, 1975)

Radin, P., *The Trickster* (Philosophical Library, New York, 1956)

Turner, F.W., III, (ed.), *Portable North American Indian Reader* (Penguin, Harmondsworth, 1977)

Walker, J.R., *Lakota Myth* (University of Nebraska, Lincoln, 1983)

Oceania

Grey, Sir George, *Polynesian Mythology* (Whitcombe and Tombs, London and Christchurch, 1965)

Lawrence, P., *Road Belong Cargo* (Manchester University Press, Manchester, 1964)

Malinowski, B., *Magic, Science and Religion* (Anchor Books, 1954)

Rome

Dowden, K., *Religion and the Romans* (Bristol Classical Press, London, 1992)

Gransden, K.W., *Virgil, the Aeneid* (Cambridge University Press, 1990)

Perowne, S., *Roman Mythology* (Newnes, Twickenham, 1983)

Scullard, H.H., *Festivals and Ceremonies of the Roman Republic* (Thames and Hudson, London, 1981)

Slav regions

Ivanits, Linda J., *Russian Folk Belief* (M.E. Sharpe Inc., Armonk, New York/London, 1989)

Jakobson, Roman, "Slavic Mythology", *Funk and Wagnalls Standard Dictionary of Folklore, Mythology and Legend*, vol. II pp. 1025-28, ed. M. Leach and J. Fried (Funk and Wagnalls, New York, 1949-50)

Warner, Elizabeth, Heroes, *Monsters and Other Worlds from Russian Mythology* (Peter Lowe, London, 1985)

South America

Bray, Warwick, *The Gold of El Dorado* (Times, London, 1978)

British Museum, *The Hidden Peoples of the Amazon* (British Museum Publications, London, 1985)

Fagan, Brian, *Kingdoms of Jade, Kingdoms of Gold* (Thames and Hudson, London, 1991)

Moseley, Michael E., *The Incas and Their Ancestors* (Thames and Hudson, London, 1992)

Saunders, Nicholas J., *People of the Jaguar* (Souvenir Press, London, 1989)

Southeast Asia

Davis, R.B., *Muang Metaphysics. A Study of Northern Thai Myth and Ritual* (Pandora, Bangkok, 1984)

Izikowitz, K.-G., *Fastening the Soul. Some Religious Traits among the Lamet* (Göteborgs Högskolas Arsskrift, 47, 1941)

Tibet and Mongolia

Norbu, Namkhai, *The Necklace of Gzi, a Cultural History of Tibet* (Information Office of H.H. Dalai Lama, Dharamsala, 1981)

Tucci, Giuseppe, *The Religions of Tibet* (Routledge, London, 1980)

Yeshe De Project, *Ancient Tibet* (Dharma Publishing, Berkeley, 1986)

Index of themes

KEY:

Apollo *standard entry in dictionary*
Hares and rabbits *feature entry in dictionary*
Cross-references below refer to this index only, not the main dictionary

Index of Themes

Index of Supplementary Names, Pseudonyms, Titles and Places without main entries

Cross-references below refer to the main dictionary

Index of Supplementary Names